HIS WILDERNESS

Discovering the Splendors of God in the Wild Places He Has Made

Thanks for coming. I hope you enjoy the book and see Him in its pages. Ps. 9:1,2
Bill

WILLIAM C. LARSON

Cameron
Publications

CameronPublications@gmail.com

Acknowledgements

My sincere appreciation is extended to the following friends for thoughtful reading, helpful suggestions, and kind encouragement:

Karl Lachler, John Lerdal, Norman Lubberden, Dennis Larson, Tami Larson, Virginia Beach, Mary Fulton, Twyla Belk, Jan and Beverly Kotzian.

Picture on page xii, by Shirley Larson.
Picture on page 44, by Crandall Gustafson.
Sketch on page 60, by Beverly Dean McLinden.
Picture on page 90, from NASA images.
All others pictures by the author.

Preface

In her book, *The Writing Life*, author Annie Dillard pens an incredible sentence: "You were made and set here to give voice to this, your own astonishment."

Wow! What an amazing view of life and of writing. It rivets my attention each time I read it. It is a bold, compelling conception, one that strains my attempt to follow its daunting challenge. But that is what I have undertaken in the pages of this book.

Perhaps the word "astonishment" may seem a bit strong, for my experiences were hardly earth-shaking. Yet as they unfolded, and as I have recalled them in later years, that is precisely what they were to me, astonishing in their own right, and in their spiritual application as well.

Readers who enjoy the beauty and charm of nature, will hopefully find a modest sense of wonderment as they follow my footsteps. For those without religious inclinations, I hope the Bible passages and reflections will not detract from the experience. For those with spiritual sensitivity, my sincere wish is that they may see in the awesome world He has made, a greater God than they have previously known.

A Note to my Grandchildren:

Jenna, Christie, Brittney, Cameron, Jamison, Jordan, Alyssa, and Danielle

For three reasons this book is especially for you.

First, in years to come, you may want to know me a bit better. In my adulthood, I now wish that I knew more about my grandparents (and parents, too). I went off to college as a teenager and never really got to know them before they died shortly thereafter. I wish I had been able to know them as people and friends on an adult level. Perhaps you will someday want to know more of my "story." This book will be one way for you to discover some of it.

Second, I hope to encourage in you an appreciation and love for the fabulous world in which we live. While nearly everyone will "ooh" and "ah" over sunsets, oceans, and mountains, it is often a shallow and fleeting regard. Even more troublesome, most people are buried in an urban, mechanical civilization. It has its own proper value that should be enjoyed and esteemed, but it usually overwhelms the more subtle and remote natural realm.

Thirdly, and most important by far, I hope in these pages to give you a glimpse of the God who created the universe. I would like you to see beyond the natural world to behold the supernatural Creator who made it. My wish is for you to discover His glory through the beauties and wonders of all that He has made.

Actually, it is more than a wish. It is a command of God Himself. In Deuteronomy 4:9, it says that fathers are to teach God's truth to their children "and to their children after them." So I hope to teach you. While the Bible is the essential means of knowing God, the creation around us is also an important teacher (see Psalm 19). My desire is to be a guide for you, helping you see through my eyes, the author of the book of nature.

So here is my gift to you. I hope to have the great satisfaction of knowing each of you as an adult, but if not, at least by means of this book, you can know me a bit better.

With all my love,
G pa Bill

Contents

"The whole world is full of his glory."

Isaiah 6:3

Chapter One

THE CANOE

Others went out on the sea in ships...
They saw the works of the Lord,
His wonderful deeds in the deep.
Psalm 107:23

In my early years, I loved water. Neighborhood creeks and ponds were compelling, irresistibly drawing me to float sticks, splash, and wade. An occasional family trip to a nearby lake was a special treat, and so was a drive along Lake Superior's beautiful North Shore.

Like most Duluthians, I never tired of visiting our city's famous lift bridge, where huge freighters entered the harbor from distant ports, or departed down lake carrying grain or iron ore. These mammoth boats, hundreds of feet long, were the modern successors of the 40-foot birch bark freighter canoes of the bygone fur traders.

The great lake itself was endlessly fascinating and magnetically attractive, a stupendous inland sea stretching out of view beyond the mysterious horizon at the merger of water and sky, where huge ships simply vanished from sight, sailing into the unknown over the curve of the earth.

To the mind of a small boy, it was a mystery beyond comprehension, to a thoughtful adult, nearly as much so.

The largest fresh water lake in the world, Superior abounds in superlatives. Three hundred fifty miles in length and one hundred sixty miles at its broadest width, the lake covers nearly 32,000 square miles, exceeding in size ten separate states of our nation. Two hundred rivers pour water into its more than one thousand foot depths. Its shoreline measures an incredible three thousand miles!

How awesome must this huge body of water have appeared to its first visitors, forest-dwelling Indians? Even European fur traders, who had crossed the vastly larger Atlantic Ocean, must have thought it impressive when paddling over the lake's heaving surface in frail bark canoes.

In my teen years, the vast expanse of Superior continued to provoke wonder and awe whenever I gazed across the water. Whether tranquil in placid calm or stirred in ferocious agitation, it compelled my attention, the restless water a living presence of vast dimension and power. In its hidden depths were intriguing mysteries: multitudes of fish, living creatures of many kinds, sunken ships from bygone years, and who knows what else? Though I knew of its origin in ice age glaciers, my mind still sought a more adequate understanding of the enormous body of water. Visits to the lakefront were never tiring or commonplace, but provoked haunting questions.

Lakes, streams, and seas have always been alluring to people. On driftwood, hollowed-out logs, papyrus bundles, birch-bark shells, and other floatables, people from earliest times have launched out on the salt and fresh waters that cover the greater portion of the earth. Traversing the waterways was an economical and convenient method of transport, yet beyond its mere utility, there has been an attraction to the water itself.

Centuries ago, the great teacher, Jesus, seemed to find a special congeniality at the lakeside, for he moved from his hometown of Nazareth to dwell in Capernaum on the shore of Lake Galilee. He spent hours in prayer and meditation on the heights above its blue surface, and used its sloping shores as a schoolyard to teach the multitudes, sometimes speaking from the deck of a boat floating on the lake itself. And frequently, in the fishing craft of his closest companions, he crossed from one side to the other, or withdrew to a secluded place to instruct His disciples. A boat gave Him mobility over the otherwise impassable water.

That was my childhood problem! Though I lived near the shore of Lake Superior, in a state renowned for 10,000 lakes, I was handicapped since we had no boat in our family. Only on rare occasions did opportunity arise to get out on the water with someone who had a boat.

Imagine my excitement, then, of one day finding in a boys' magazine, plans for building a *canoe,* out of orange crates! Why, a canoe was the boat of all boats, the vessel of the Indians and early explorers, able to go anywhere, silently and swiftly, with only the power of the paddler's arms. And made of orange crates - in the days when fruit was shipped in wooden boxes - it would cost virtually nothing, for crates could be had for the asking at any grocery store. But, as they often do, this youthful dream came to nothing, though precisely why I cannot now recall. Yet one thing remained through the years. The image of a sleek canoe, gliding through the shallows in a setting sun or flashing down white water in a foaming blur, was never erased by the mundane realities of advancing adulthood.

I had moved away and twenty years had passed, when at last, the vision began to materialize. In a visit to my hometown, a friend had shown me the most beautiful canoe I had ever seen - and he had built it himself! Made of thin cedar strips overlaid with nearly invisible fiberglass cloth, it was a lustrous golden brown, gracefully shaped from bow to stern, and gunwale to gunwale. He had made it from "scratch" following a set of plans purchased from a man in the Twin Cities. I was envious to the core. How I wanted a craft like that!

Over our annual New Year's Day dinner of wild game, my friend John and I agreed to send for a set of plans. We decided to ask Jim to join us since he liked woodworking and a three-man team seemed better for our project. We would locate the "Boatworks" in the basement of John's store. In a couple of weeks, we were under way.

Following the instructions, we made templates of plywood and mounted them crosswise on an inverted "T" shaped spine. This temporary construction form would give the proper shape to the canoe. Sawing eighteen-foot lengths of 1"x 4" boards into thin strips, we nailed them along the length of the templates, gluing them edge to edge as we went. Eventually the hull was complete. Then, pulling the nails so it could later be removed from the form, we draped fiberglass cloth over the entire surface, and coated it with varnish-like resin. When cured, it bonded the cloth and wood into an incredibly strong and watertight shell. Next, we lifted the hull from the form, turned it over, and fiber-glassed the inside. Adding mahogany gunwales, decks, thwart, and seats, it was finished. Of course, it did not go as easily as it sounds. We spent many hours in loving labor, including "committee work," as we called our frequent discussions over how to proceed.

Finally, it was launch day. After church on a lovely spring Sunday, our three families gathered at a local park for a special picnic. This was one occasion when the food had to wait. Gently carrying our prize from the car top, we placed it on the quiet lake where it floated with elegant grace. As our wives and children watched in suspense, all three of us got in. To their amazement, it didn't sink or even leak. It paddled with easy agility, responding with eagerness to the most subtle shift of the paddles. In due time, each one of the group had their turn in the new canoe, skepticism turning to confidence and bemusement to admiration. We had built a beautiful ship, though to be fair, the real credit belonged to the designer whose plans we had simply followed.

Of course, one canoe for three families was hardly adequate, and eventually we made three more. Like the first, each was a marvel of mastery over the waters. Yet, the placid, dull waters of the Iowa farmlands seemed hardly worthy of such craft, for they were designed for the wilds, for the pristine lakes and rivers of the North. So, to the North we went, barely before the last canoe was finished. In fact, we completed the rawhide webbing of the seats only after our arrival in Minnesota's Boundary Waters Canoe Area Wilderness (BWCAW). With my son Scott, and several other men and their boys, we ventured into the great expanse of the Superior - Quetico canoe country.

Now our boats were in their rightful element, the fabled land of the fur-trading voyageurs, who like the Indians before them, had plied the myriad lakes and countless streams in canoes made of birch bark. Unlike them, we had no demanding schedule to keep, no driving necessity to paddle hundreds of miles between spring thaw and winter freeze, to earn a meager salary transporting pelts for European gentry. We could travel at ease, luxuriating in the splendor of the wilderness, and enjoying the challenge of river and lake. It was a marvelous trip, the beginning of many to come. The canoes fulfilled every expectation, providing a means of access to the wild and remote places, and allowing us to enjoy at first hand the marvels of the deep.

Sometimes, however, a boat can be a precarious conveyance when the winds howl, the waves rage, and the rivers roar. Even Jesus found it so. Once while crossing Lake Galilee in a boat with his disciples, a furious storm arose, causing even the professional fishermen among them to fear for their lives. Luke’s factual report states it bluntly, “they were in great danger” (8:23). Asleep in the stern, Jesus was awakened by his terrified friends. “Master, master,” they cried, “We are going to drown!” Miraculously stilling the storm, He then rebuked them, saying, “Where is your faith?” He expected them, and all of His followers since, to have full confidence in His caring presence regardless of external circumstances. He may not always rescue us from peril, but He is always present with us to accomplish His will for our lives. I came to treasure that truth on a canoe trip in the West.

Idaho's St. Joe River is one of America's most beautiful streams. Originating in the Bitterroot Mountains on the continental divide between Idaho and Montana, it tumbles through a remote valley, swelling with tributary streams to a mid-size river. In its upper reaches, especially in the high waters of spring run-off, the most skillful white-water enthusiasts can find all the challenge they can handle. In mid-section, intermediate paddlers discover brisk rapids that delight rather than threaten. At its lowest stretch, running through a valley dotted by small ranches, the river is tamed to docility by its juncture with Lake Coeur d'Alene, providing even novice canoeists with quiet but lovely water. Except for the lower portion, the river wends its way through uninhabited wilderness, civilized only by a twisting gravel road traveled by occasional logging trucks. A handful of Forest Service campgrounds are scattered along the river's course.

Scott was home from college for a week of vacation. We planned an easy two-day paddle down the river's middle course with time enough for fishing, loafing, and casual engagement with the wilderness. Stopping to buy fishing licenses at the tiny hamlet of Calder, we drove upstream beside the river. How it danced and leaped in its rush downstream, glittering in crystal transparency. Ponderosa pine and Douglas fir covered the steep hillsides, crowding to the very edges of the road and river.

As we continued along, drinking in the quiet splendor of the scenery, we were astounded to hear strange music through the open windows of the car. In the depths of the forest the skirling of *bagpipes* was unmistakable though inexplicable - but how, where, who? Rounding a bend in the road, we saw a tiny cabin perched on the far bank of the river with the mysterious piper seated before it, squeezing the bag and chanting out highland melodies. Unexpected as it was, it seemed not amiss, for the ancient instrument has been at home in the rugged crags of distant lands for centuries. We smiled and waved as we passed, the solitary piper simply nodding as he kept on with his haunting Celtic tunes.

Eager to reach our put-in point and get under way, I made a dreadful blunder, my one serious mishap in a lifetime of wilderness jaunts. I somehow misread or inaccurately recalled the Forest Service brochure. Intending to begin much further upstream, we *put in* at Tin Can Flat campground, rather than *taking out*. Instead of many miles of easy water, we were unaware that a mere five miles separated us from dangerous Skookum Canyon. The warnings in the brochure were emphatic: under no circumstances should the rapids be attempted! Boats and boaters alike had been lost in its furious rush through high rocky walls that squeezed the pounding water into a raging torrent a bare ten yards wide. We had no intentions to challenge its fury but would either end our trip just above it or portage around it as the pace of our journey determined. Impending disaster was far from our minds as we launched our canoe in innocent but perilous ignorance, with our lifejackets lying on the bottom of the craft.

Down the warbling stream we went, the water so clear that every rock and pebble could be seen with utter clarity. Transparent though it was, it seemed to impart a faint silver-green cast to the stones on the bottom as it splashed and surged along. In quiet sections, the depth was perhaps three to four feet, occasionally six to eight in deeper holes. Where the bottom sloped downhill, the water stretched out, thinning to mere inches as it flowed swiftly downstream.

Our canoe matched the mood of the water, floating calmly in silence as we paddled quieter portions, then darting this way and that as we pursued its more boisterous reaches, tumbling downward in mild rapids. We sang and laughed with its buoyant exhilaration. This was the way to live, free and strong, energetic and in tune with creation itself. The river was alive with voice, motion, and personality. We rode its surface as if on horseback, now calmly as an aged pet, and then briskly as a frolicky young colt. Our exertions were sheer delight, undaunted by the hazard toward which we raced.

The impression of flowing downhill was unmistakable and tantalizing, the rocky floor of the stream continually falling away as we advanced. Though our speed on average could not have exceeded a very few miles an hour, there was a distinct sense of brisk motion as the water slipped ever downward in slightly canted races or boiled over stair step ledges marked by bands of turbulence.

Then at a hard bend, the waters spurted in a fierce rush, much faster than before. With little time to respond, we dug our blades in fury to turn sharply right as the plunging waters surged over a deeper ledge into a rocky cliff. Pushed so suddenly by the crush of water, we were not quite quick enough, for though I stroked with all my strength, the stern swung too far, grazing the rocks with a rasping glance. In the calm water below, Scott and I looked at each other in astonishment. The short but savage section had been totally unexpected, completely out of character with the gurgling chuckles through which we had been paddling. Still unaware of the looming nearness of Skookum Canyon, we shrugged off our brief encounter as of little significance, failing to give it the thought it deserved.

We continued onward, enjoying our buoyant ride and treasuring the familiar beauty of the wilds. The water was now a trifle faster and the rapids more turbulent as the decline of the river increased. It only added more zest to our adventure, though requiring somewhat greater care in navigation and paddling.

As we approached a strait chute of a hundred yards or so, only inches in depth but flowing with surprising swiftness, an unexpected apprehension pierced my consciousness. The far end of the run churned in white froth before angling out of sight beyond the rocky cliffs lining the banks. The rapids ahead of us were not supposed to be bad but I was uneasy. Time was running out. We drew closer with each second and I had to decide. I spoke to Scott. "I don't like the looks of that water, let's head for shore."

Yet, indecision roiled my mind. The Forest Service brochure had described only class one and two rapids on the section we were traveling. Skookum Canyon had to be many miles downstream. We had taken only a few strokes toward shore when I told Scott, "Never mind. It should be o.k.; we can make it. Let's go for it."

Scott dug his paddle deep on the right and I put in a hard rudder to swing the bow back toward mid-stream, as the water now bore us briskly along. A few more strokes drew us to the point of no return - and sudden full awareness as well! Beyond the narrow gates of rock, we could now see the river in full view. As the floor of the stream sharply declined, the width of the river was constricted to a few scant yards by high canyon walls. Squeezed and falling, the water churned in fury, trying to force its way through the rocky channel. With more wishful hope than conviction, I shouted to Scott over the roaring waves, "Hit it hard and we can get through."

A narrow slot between two mid-stream boulders seemed to offer a slim chance. Two strokes further and I knew the chance was next to nothing. A five-foot high standing wave, created by tons of waters spurting upward against a submerged ledge, rose higher than Scott's head. One second more and we slammed into the liquid wall, hurtled forward by the torrent pushing us from behind. As our bow climbed upward against the face of the wave, it slipped sideways along its length. The stern broaching to the cascade racing down from behind completed our broadside exposure to the crushing waters. Shoved sideways up the wave our upstream gunwale now pitched sharply toward the water. In an instant, water surged over the side, filling the canoe and overturning it, flinging us into the melee.

Swept downstream in the torrent, I looked for Scott. With profound relief, I saw him swimming as the current carried him down the rapids behind me. "Are you O.K.?" I yelled. He nodded and waved to reassure me as he swam toward the rocky shore. Giving attention to my own rescue, I realized that I still clutched my paddle. Letting it go to float downstream, I swam for shore. In a few minutes we were reunited on the rocks, safe and sound except for a few bruises where we had been hurled against the boulders.

We were deeply thankful to have come through without injury. Though the danger of drowning in the relatively shallow waters of mid-summer was small, it was still a possibility. We could have been snagged under water or knocked unconscious in a blow against a rock.

How meaningful now are the Psalm writer's words,

Save me, O God,
for the waters have come
up to my neck.
I sink in the miry depths
where there is no foothold.
I have come into the deep waters;
the floods engulf me.
I am worn out calling for help.
Ps. 69:1-3

Our accident had been so sudden, violent, and brief that we had no time or thought to call for help, and no one was around to hear or give assistance had we done so. Our lives, however, were surrendered to God at all times. He had observed our crash, and indeed, in divine omniscience, knowing it beforehand, had allowed it to happen. His love for us and our trust in Him were in no way diminished because He chose not to intervene in warning or miraculous rescue. While the abruptness of our plunge into the river kept anxiety from gripping my mind, I was also calmed by the certainty of God's continual presence and care. My only real concern had been for Scott. Even in the midst of careening down the rapids, the question had formed in my mind, "how could I ever go home to Shirley without our son?" Happily, I didn't have to attempt such a dreadful experience. Yet, even if such had been the case, the Lord would have been our strength.

Now that we were safe, we had to salvage our gear. A quarter mile downstream, we found the canoe, lodged upside down in the middle of the river, with torrents of water pouring over it. Eventually we were able to wade out and pry it loose, letting it float into shore. Our once lovely craft was now a battered hulk, decks and seats torn loose, and both bow and stern split at mid line. We were even able to recover some of our other equipment.

Our anticipated adventure came to sorry conclusion as we drove home with our canoe crippled and our egos shattered. Never before had I more than scratched myself in the wilds. My confidence as a prudent and competent outdoorsman was rudely broken. Tragic injuries and deaths occur each year by just such careless miscalculation. Truly, we were grateful to have escaped relatively unscathed. Even the canoe would later be repaired and patched to roam the waters again, though not as sea worthy as it had once been. Our pride, too, would heal in time. The accident itself would serve as a useful lesson in greater caution, reminding us that the forces of nature deserve utmost respect and careful attention.

In retrospect, beyond putting in at the wrong place, I realize I had made two other critical errors. The first was to rely on the brochure. Accurate in the main as it was, no generalized description can ever cover the continually changing variables of wilderness locale and weather. A normally sedate stream can be changed into a snarling deathtrap by a heavy thunderstorm, a falling tree can suddenly block a watercourse, warm summer in the mountains can become life-threatening winter in a few hours time. The outdoorsman can never totally rely on anything but up-to-the-minute information, gathered by his own careful observation. I had let the brochure overrule my own sense perceptions.

The other error was my reluctance to respond adequately when my awareness was aroused. Whenever the safety of a route or proposed action is in doubt, prompt and careful investigation is required before proceeding further. When first viewing the rapids, I should have paddled to shore and gone downstream on foot for a close-up inspection. A single glimpse would have determined the right decision with finality. To be safe in the wilds, one must know accurately his own abilities, and just as significantly, his true *limitations*. Allowing for a reasonable margin of error, these must not be crossed. At least we survived to learn from my gross miscalculation.

What, then, about the future? Did the lakes and rivers seem too threatening, and the canoe too dangerous, things to be avoided as treacherous and harmful? Not at all. Even as we stood above the scene of our wreck, our gear broken or missing altogether, and ourselves bruised and bedraggled, the spectacle of the rushing torrent was entrancing. The surge of the water as it poured through the canyon in cascades, boils, spouts, and swirls was as fascinating as ever. The inherent danger could not dispel the awesome wonder. How to explain its attraction is beyond my understanding and ability to tell.

Yes, there is an inescapable element of hazard when we encounter the lakes, rivers, and seas, but so it is with many of the things in life. However, the rewards are worth the prudent risk. There is a compelling beauty about the water that can scarcely be resisted, and only a boat provides adequate access. As for Scott and me, we would build other canoes and would venture out again, hopefully more aware of possible dangers, and mindful always that the Master was in the boat with us.

Chapter Two

WILD WINDS

He sends lightning with the rain
and brings out the wind from his storehouses.
Jer. 10:13

Sandy was getting sick. We were on our way back from a week in the wilds but the elements had triumphed. We had miles to go to reach civilization but the contrary winds that had plagued our journey were now blowing their strongest, not creating impossible conditions, but turning a modest day's travel into a grueling endurance event. Nasty waves slashed at our bows, now from one side, then the other, requiring continual counter measures with the stern paddles to maintain our course and minimize the slosh of water into the canoes. The constant rise and fall upon the waves, and the sliding left and right adjustments needed to challenge the whitecaps, were making Sandy nauseous. To provide some relief for her and a useful breather for the rest of us, we landed at an island for a break from our toil. The elements had gotten the best of us, multiplying our labors, shortening our trip, and now afflicting us with the indignity of seasickness as well.

We had promised our wives a glorious week of carefree adventure in the canoe country. "You'll love it," we said. "The scenery will be gorgeous and the fishing great. You'll have a ball. Come on. What do you say?"

Sensing a wary hesitation, we sweetened the proposal, adding, "and we'll do all the cooking, and do the dishes, too!"

It was a bold and costly bid, but it worked. How could they refuse? The three women said “yes,” and the trip was on. Hoping to find the best balance of good fishing and nice weather, we decided on the third week of June. Soon we were busy planning menus, gathering equipment, checking the maps, and reminding Sandy and the two Shirleys how wonderful it was going to be.

At last, the day arrived. The warm and sunny weather was perfect, a fitting start for our jaunt to the North. The women rode with Jim in the station wagon, and John and I followed in my old sedan. As we traveled, talking, joking, and laughing in high spirits, the miles rolled by in a blur. Whenever we stopped to stretch our legs or to get a bite to eat, the graceful, hand-made canoes perched on top of our cars, attracted attention from fellow travelers. Our wilderness journey seemed to stir a wistful envy in the hearts of the less fortunate.

The cornfields of Iowa and southern Minnesota gave way to the urban sprawl of the Twin Cities, followed further north by the mixed hardwoods of the central region of the state. Finally, some twenty miles south of Duluth, the real north began; a country of bold rock outcrops, iron-red soil, and dense stands of aspen and birch, interspersed with spruce, balsam, and pine. Further still, where tiny villages eke out a precarious existence on the fringe of the vast forest, civilization gave way to the overpowering wilderness. We ended our long day's travel in the town of Babbit.

The next morning, a short drive brought us to our departure point where we loaded the canoes and set out under gray skies and light sprinkles of rain. At lunchtime, hunched under headgear and ponchos, we ate our sandwiches upon a speck of rock in a vast watery world. The gray drizzle was too feeble to wet our bodies or dampen our spirits. We paddled eagerly on, arriving at our campsite in the late afternoon. As we had promised, we men cooked dinner under a nylon tarp stretched over the fire. Perhaps feeling sorry for us, the women helped with the dishes. Because of the soggy weather, we did not linger around the fire but turned in early.

On the next day, we paddled in a cold rain. The third day was more of the same. Compounding our efforts, a surly east wind had been blowing in our faces, making progress laborious and slow.

On the fourth day, the sun finally came out, giving us a chance to dry wet clothes and enjoy more fully the beauty of our surroundings. We relaxed over breakfast as our gear dried in the sun. Whiskey jacks (Canada Jays) came to search for leftovers. We even caught a few small fish. What a pleasure it was to linger over our simple chores, enjoying each other's company, and relishing the majesty around us. This was what we had promised the women. Late in the morning, we launched into a warm south wind. Despite the opposing breeze, we treasured the magnificent day, marveling at the ever-present beauty. Sunlight danced on the chuckling waves, brilliant white gulls sailed overhead, yellow lilies adorned the surface of shallow water, and countless green spires fringed a flawless sky. This was the North Country pictured on the outfitters' brochures, a land unspoiled and little changed since the retreat of the glaciers twelve thousand years before.

Reveling in the sun, we paddled with zest, glad to be alive, and for a change, warm and dry. But change is often brief. Shortly after we had finished our evening meal, the unstable weather brought clouds and rain again. This latest alteration came with a shift in the wind, gusting now from the northwest, which meant that the next day's travel would be in the teeth of a rising storm. Yielding to the adverse elements, we decided to cut our trip short by a day. With the rain, cold, and wind, we had been largely deprived of the usual pleasures of camp life, especially sitting around a late evening fire. We were alert to the glories of the country but had not been fully able to enjoy their splendor. We would try again another year.

As I lay in my tent that night the wind gave me some concern. It would be tough paddling the next day, perhaps even impossible if the winds and waves were too high. Listening to the lashing of the trees, I was not only thinking of the morning. A sharp crack and crashing thud, not far distant, revealed the fierce power of the surging wind. Though I said nothing to Shirley, I thought much of the sixty-foot pines under which we were camped. Their sturdy trunks and spreading limbs groaned and shuddered as they bent before the rushing currents of unseen air. It was not likely they would fall, yet a short walk in any direction revealed vanquished monarchs overcome by past storms. I silently prayed that God would keep us safely through the night.

The wind continued to blow, furious currents of air streaming over the water and thrashing the trees. Their perverse fluctuations had frustrated and disappointed us, and now raised a host of questions in my mind as I listened to the tumult overhead. From where did the wind really come, what caused its often sudden and violent shifts in direction, how can virtually weightless air cause such enormous destruction in its frequent rampages? Yes, everyone is familiar with the weather reporter's explanation of high and low pressure areas, jet streams, cold and warm fronts, but for all of our scientific understanding, the wind remains a baffling mystery. Like invisible electricity, it lurks beyond the fringe of genuine understanding. Jesus' remark is as appropriate today as it was centuries ago, "the wind blows wherever it pleases. You hear its sound, but you cannot tell where it comes from or where it is going." (John 3:8).

After our rest on the island, we got into the canoes again. Sandy felt a bit better, which was fortunate, since we still had far to go. At least it was not raining and our strenuous exertions kept us from being chilled. The fierce wind and high waves required constant, powerful strokes to make headway. I felt sorry for our wives, for this exhausting labor was not exactly the easy joy ride we had promised. Still, despite the poor weather and laborious paddling, I had enjoyed the trip. Even our defiant combat with the waves was satisfying. John seemed to feel the same way. Pulling deeply with our paddles, our canoes were abreast and only a few yards apart. I caught his bright smile, indicating zestful fun despite the effort. I returned a knowing glance, and broke into an exaggerated, silent singing, to which he responded in kind. Not wishing to mock our wives' genuine weariness, we did not audibly express our delight, but it was real, nonetheless.

Nasty weather is usually just that, ugly and unpleasant. Yet fierce weather has been intriguing to me from my teen years on. As I got older, I occasionally went for short walks in some of the fiercest storms, testing the winds and groping to understand the furies of nature. They were often dangerous, and sometimes deadly, but were compelling nonetheless.

On and on we paddled, making grudging but real progress. At least we were able to travel, not forced to land somewhere to sit out the storm, waiting for the winds to drop. Although an occasional wave broke over the bows and dumped a lapful of water on the women, their ponchos kept them somewhat dry. Heading into the waves helped to keep us on course, reducing the threat of a broadside exposure that could cause us to capsize. With life jackets on and our packs tied to the canoes, we were prepared even for that. If we flipped, we would get wet, but would still be safe.

Spurred on by the thought of a comfortable motel, hot shower, and someone else's cooking (other than the men’s!), my Shirley paddled with determined purpose, setting the pace for the other canoes. Reaching the landing at last, we quickly loaded the cars and drove to Ely where we found a nice motel. In a short time, showers and clean clothes made a huge difference in our outlook. How quickly our spirits and energy revived when we were clean, dry, and warm. Enjoying a fine meal at a restaurant in Ely, we laughed and made light of our battle with the weather. Though we had not experienced the wilderness as we had expected, we had encountered a no-less real view that had its own unique worth. Even a gray, windblown landscape has a unique appeal to the perceptive eye. In time, the wind, cold, rain, and extra labor, would lose their edge of disappointment. And, if we had spent little time lingering over evening fires, we had still drawn closer together, for as John's Shirley said with a laugh, "misery loves company."

Misery, pain, or fear. These powerful afflictions often blind us to deeper considerations. In the immediate encounter with the elements, emotions and personal circumstances may stifle observation and reflection. Repeated experience with dangerous storms convinces most people of the reality of forces beyond their control. So they take prudent precautions when unprotected outdoors, build sturdy shelters to live in, and buy insurance for overwhelming disasters. Yet, open encounter with the rushing wind often raises amazement, awe, and wonder.

Years after the windy canoe trip, friends George and Gus joined me in a climb of Mt. Adams in Washington State. It was the last week of June and the weather had been especially pleasant - warm and dry, though somewhat breezy. Approaching the mountain from Interstate 80, we followed rural highways until they gave way to graveled roads in the surrounding forest. As often happens, flexibility was required to meet changed circumstances. Intending to begin our hike at an elevation of 7,000 feet, we had to modify our plan when we discovered impassible snow blocking the road at a much lower level. This made our effort significantly longer and more strenuous than we intended. But that's the way it is in the out-country. The wilderness wanderer must expect the unexpected.

Shouldering our packs, we trudged beneath a canopy of lofty hemlock, fir, and pine. Though we had seen the mountain from a distance, it was invisible now in the dense woods of the lower slope. Several hours later, the trees thinned considerably. Through scattered openings in the forest, we could again glimpse the peak to confirm our bearings.

Typical of Cascade Range volcanoes, Mt. Adams has a conical summit of moderately inclined slopes. Starkly white against the bold blue of clear skies, I was never quite prepared for its stunning beauty. Knowing the mountain was there, and even expecting at any moment to see it through the trees, there was still an acute jolt to my senses each time I beheld its majestic splendor, arresting me in mid-stride, with its riveting presence.

As vistas opened, we were compelled to look, again and again. A mind-picture was simply unsatisfactory. Each new view, of course, was essentially the same, since our upward progress changed its perspective with dragging slowness. Still, we had to see, physically and often, frequently stopping in our tracks in fruitless effort to absorb the mountain's magnificence. As we did so, we confronted a change in conditions. Our heated and sweat-drenched bodies were chilling quickly. A brisk wind, unnoticed in the trees below, was now evident at our altitude over 8,000 feet. Further, against the blue sky at the summit, a flat ribbon of white streaked eastward. Since no clouds were then visible, it indicated a snow plume, a stream of fine snow blown from the highest slopes by powerful winds. It would bear watching.

Later, as we labored ever higher, clouds did begin to form, wisps of vapor, shifting in fluid configurations. Lying on my back while waiting for my lagging companions, I noticed that when they sometimes covered the sun, a rainbow spectrum would often appear. Attempting to catch the display on film, I was aware of the speed at which the clouds were moving across the sky. They were advancing very swiftly.

At last, we called it quits for the day in the shelter of a low ridge of rock and ice at over 10,000 feet. Setting up camp, we were now fully aware of the wind. Fierce gusts buffeted and chilled our weary bodies. We pounded our tent stakes into the hard snow as well as we could, and piled large rocks against them as extra security. After dinner, as daylight drained from the sky, the wind increased, rather than diminished in intensity. When we lay down in our bags, sleep did not come quickly. Just two feet above our faces, the slanted tent roof shuddered and shook, snapping and jerking in the onslaught. The shrieking wind whistled and howled. Like two sheets of sandpaper rubbing together, the tent and rain fly rustled in ceaseless agitation. Fearing the wind would tear the anchoring clips from the fly, I went out and removed it. It would be colder inside without the fly but, hopefully, a quieter tent would help us sleep.

Finally, we dozed off. Several times, however, the raging wind woke me up with its incredible agitation. At times, stronger gusts battered the tent so fiercely that the sloping fabric above me flattened to just a few inches from my face. How strong the winds were, we could not tell. It is easy to overestimate, but my best estimate is from forty to sixty miles an hour. I wondered if the lightweight nylon could withstand the battering. If a seam failed, we would be in serious trouble. The rip-stop fabric had withstood many previous storms but this was by far the strongest wind in which I had ever camped.

Yet, its force, while impressive to us at the time, was of relatively modest proportion. On Mt. Washington, in New Hampshire, where the fiercest weather in the world occurs, a wind speed of 231 miles an hour occurred on April 12, 1934, the highest surface wind velocity ever recorded on earth. On this awesome peak, hurricane force winds occur in every month, and in winter do so an average of *four days a week.* The January *average* wind speed, is fifty-five miles an hour.

When fully unleashed, the power of the wind is truly beyond comprehension. Even people who survive devastating hurricanes and tornados have difficulty in sensing their reality, though the aftermath of death and destruction is inescapable. Sturdy buildings torn apart, trains blown off bridges, oceangoing ships hurled on shore, are undeniable evidence of the stunning impact of "weightless" air streaming at high velocity.

In the morning, George unhappily discovered evidence of such vigorous power. He had put his glasses in a nylon mesh pocket, sewed to the side of the tent. The constant shaking of the tent had severely abraded the plastic lenses as they shook in their "scouring" pouch.

As the morning advanced, the winds abated somewhat, but then rain and snow moved in. After a brief attempt to gain more elevation, we gave it up, turning downhill to await a better day. We would long remember this beautiful mountain and would not soon forget its powerful winds, both realities of an incredible creation.

While properly awed, and sometimes rightfully fearful of the forceful elements of nature, there is more to be considered. The physical effects of ordinary winds, gales, tornados, and hurricanes, impressive as they are, are suggestive of even greater, ultimate power. Throughout the centuries, people have seen beyond the brute force of nature to its Primal Source. In the magnificent nature poem, Psalm 104, the inspired writer sees the rushing winds as messengers sent to do God's biding.

He makes the clouds His chariot
and rides on the wings of the wind,
He makes the winds His messengers,
flames of fire His servants.
(verses 3, 4).

He means us to see, as one commentator remarks, that the forces of nature are "charged with his energy and alive with his presence." Our scientifically oriented minds may have trouble with such a pictorial view, for we tend to see the weather mechanistically, as the inevitable effects of prior causes. The Bible, instead, focuses on the First Cause. It portrays the invisible God through the visible presence of the natural elements. In doing so, it describes all secondary causes as His personal agents, inviting us to see more than wind and hail, lightning and flood.

In 1999, granddaughter Jenna and I joined Scott's family on a short trip to the BWCA, one week after an awesome catastrophe. Jenna was my bow "man," as were Cameron and Brittney for their parents, Scott and Tami.

Somewhat understaffed for portaging, we merely paddled to a convenient site on the west end of Lake One. It was not a great location but in view of conditions elsewhere, we cheerfully accepted its limitations. It displayed hard evidence of the previous week's mammoth storm.

Several trees around our camp were missing their tops. At the edge of the water, a twelve-inch diameter tree was sheared off, eight feet from the ground. Most intriguing was a trunk further along the shore, the upper portion bent at a 45-degree angle, the wood fibers splintered into long fragments.

We were on the fringe of a massive area of destruction. A week earlier, on the Fourth of July, a huge storm broke out, covering an enormous territory more than 1,300 miles long, from North Dakota to Maine, and a hundred miles wide, the most severe storm recorded in the area over the past two hundred years. Straight-line winds in excess of 100 miles an hour rushed through the area over a period of 22 hours. In the BWCA, one person was killed and 60 were injured. Damage to the forests and private property exceeded one hundred million dollars in Minnesota alone. Estimates of downed trees were as high as *20 million.* In the area around Ogishkemuncie and Seagull Lakes, virtually every mature tree was destroyed. Because of blocked roads and trails, it took more than two weeks for some people to return to civilization.

To see the power of God in the mighty winds is a not unreasonable, for He is power incarnate. He is more, however, than brute force. While we need not see the tragic results of destructive storms as God's direct intervention in human affairs, they should surely arrest our attention, remind us of our frail mortality, and confront us with the issues of life, death, and beyond. The invisible, unpredictable, uncontrollable winds, keep us off balance in this world, preventing our total security and comfort, arresting a deadly and deceiving complacency. To seek the reality behind the elements is the course of wisdom.

Observing only the more violent effort of the wind, however, fails to do justice to the whole picture of nature and its spiritual counterpart. While power is certainly demonstrated in the wind's destructive force, reminding us, if not actually exercising it, of judgment to come, there is another important perspective. We should also consider the warm spring breezes that melt winter snow, the moisture laden currents bearing rain from distant seas, and the cooling winds of a summer thunderstorm. These gentle and good effects are the usual weather conditions, the *norm*. Tragic injury and death from wind-sheer, blizzard, and hurricane are the rare, infrequent event. Could we sense, as the Psalm writer does, that these lifesaving expressions are the gracious gifts of a loving God, perhaps we would be more thankful and worshipful. Our focus dwells overmuch on the damaging impact. We are often too dense, giving inadequate consideration to the life giving winds. Like Elijah long ago (I King 19), we would do well to develop the capacity to hear the voice of God, not only in the furious wind, earthquake, and fire, but in the stillness of His quiet whisper.

Chapter Three

STANDING ON HIGH PLACES

He makes my feet like the feet of a deer;
he enables me to stand upon the heights.
Psalm18:33

Minnesota has some very nice hills but no real mountains. Duluth, where I grew up, is built on an impressive hillside, rising from Lake Superior at 600 feet above sea level, to about 800 feet above the water. The elevation differential provides some wonderful views of the city and lake, and some heart-stopping driving in the winter. For most residents, a tour of the Skyline Drive traversing the hillside is a continuing pleasure, and 80-foot tall, Enger Tower, is a popular destination because of its commanding view of the cityscape below.

As a youngster, I delighted in exploring and hiking the western end of the hill, particularly around an abandoned quarry and in the territory around the Duluth Zoo. But images of true mountains, formed by pictures, films, and maps, were powerfully attractive to my mind.

It was not until I was married and had children, that I saw a real mountain. We were living in Iowa, a state even flatter than Minnesota, when we finally took a trip out west. With dense forestation, the Black Hills of South Dakota were dark, indeed, but were genuine mountains nonetheless. Driving south into Wyoming, we saw the snow-capped peaks of the Rockies on the western horizon. Traveling up Big Thompson Canyon, from Loveland to Estes Park, we were immersed in them. Twelve thousand foot peaks were everywhere, and some soared over 14,000. What a feast for the eyes! And what a place to worship and discuss the work of God!

The church conference was a week of activities for all of us, including outdoor events for Scott, Leigh, and Karen. Swimming and riding horses were their favorites. Shirley and I were busy inside, but whenever we went from building to building, the mountains loomed above, their presence inescapable. Fortunately, there was a small window of free time one afternoon, just enough for a jaunt up a nearby trail. Scott and his friend, Karl, came with me on a hike to Gem Lake.

Driving up Devils Gulch Road, we came to the trailhead, at elevation 7,700 feet. The route was not severely steep but did take serious energy. I wondered how long the enthusiasm of the 11-year-old boys would last. A two-mile walk is trivial, but 1,100 feet *uphill* is another matter. The way led through sparse aspen and pine trees, which became more thickly clustered as we went along. Great boulder formations appeared in profusion. The bold cliffs of Lumpy Ridge came into view as we neared the lake.

At last we arrived, all of us breathing heavily. The tiny but lovely lake nestles in a granite bowl, a literal wall on the north side, and jumbles of boulders on the west and east. At the edge of the water on the south, a broad opening in the rocks revealed the awesome panorama of

Estes Park, spread across the valley below. Both the lake and the vista were spectacular.

We were not the only visitors at the lake. Four young men and women, with the long hair and scraggly clothes of the hippie era, were having a meal along the narrow beach on the western shore. We were soon chattering about the great scenery and other topics. One of the men, preparing a hot dog, dipped his finger in a jar of mustard, and spread it along the wiener. Since we had dinner planned for our return, we politely declined the offer to share their food. Retracing our route, I treasured this first encounter with a mountain.

When we moved to Washington State, mountains were close at hand. I frequently spent a day hiking the slopes of Mica Peak, Mount Spokane, Boyer Mountain, and others. These forested mountains were 5,000 to 7,000 feet in height, had gentle slopes, and many roads and trails. They were wonderful places to gain healthful exercise, discover old mining and logging activity, and enjoy peaceful solitude. Unfortunately, because of the extensive trees, most of them had limited views from their summits. Still, their pervasive beauty was delightful, and there was always something new to discover.

Some of this mountain rambling was with Scott. We had often talked, however, about a backpacking trip in the mountains, and now was the time. Soon he would be leaving for college in the Midwest and our jaunts in the outdoors would be significantly limited. He could spare just three days from his job but we would enjoy them to the utmost. Checking some maps and other resources, we decided on the North Cascades National Park, an awesome region of peaks and forest. Our specific destination was Easy Pass Trail, considered by many people to be one of the most superb areas in the park, suitable for a day hike or a multi-day trip. I also had thoughts about climbing 9,000-foot Mt. Logan, a short distance to the west. It did not sound overly demanding, but as I discovered, Easy Pass was hardly easy.

With Scott driving his car, we set out early in the morning. Traveling west and north, we passed Grand Coulee Dam, then on to the North Cascades Highway. A few miles past the crossing of the Pacific Crest Trail, we pulled into a small parking area at the trailhead for Easy Pass. Since only one other car was present, the trail would not be crowded. Lacing up our boots and shouldering our packs, we began our hike from elevation 3,700 feet.

A short walk brought us to Granite Creek, about 40 feet wide and fairly shallow, but cold and fast. There was no bridge, but a sturdy tree spanning the stream provided access to the trail beyond. I volunteered to go first. The bulk of my 35-pound pack made getting up on the trunk a modest challenge. The rough bark helped as I stepped sideways a few inches at a time. Only about ten inches in diameter, it provided adequate but less than secure support for my feet. Projecting stubs of branches complicated the footing and the pack made balance a bit dicey as well. Eventually I got across and Scott followed without difficulty.

The trail ascended for a couple of miles at a moderate pitch through Hemlock and Fir trees. The greenery was thick but the path was well cleared. At about 5,000 feet, the trail left the trees and entered a broad and steep avalanche field of stones and boulders, sloping from Ragged Ridge, 1,500 feet above. How trivial that differential sounds, but our labors increased dramatically. Soon we came to Easy Pass Creek, a silvery brook tumbling down the slope, small enough for us to easily step over. Numerous switchbacks made the incline more manageable, but it was laborious nonetheless. After awhile, the trail re-crossed the creek.

From above I heard the crunch of boots on rock. Looking up, I saw another hiker coming down, a woman dressed in the uniform of a Park ranger. We chatted with her about the trail and the valley beyond. As she continued down, she seemed to move a lot easier than I did.

I was working hard, sweating bullets, and getting tired. My hips were hurting - a lot! I stopped a couple of times, not just to rest and enjoy the scenery, but to let my hips "unfreeze." Like rusty hinges needing lubrication, the sockets seemed to be grating under the burden of weight and incline. At the third pause, I noticed Scott looking back at me with some apprehension, but he said nothing. I was quietly more alarmed than he was. What was wrong with me? Was early arthritis coming on or was middle age truly setting in? Perhaps I was simply out of shape. I didn't know but kept struggling on.

We crossed the creek yet again, and a few hundred feet from the summit, found its source in a gushing crystal spring. Arriving at the top several minutes later, we put down our packs with sighs of relief. Ragged Ridge is a narrow saddle overlooking Fisher Creek Basin far below, where we had to go since camping is not allowed on the ridge. For a few moments, however, we would rest, rehydrate, and drink in the splendor heaped around us; Red Mountain, Fisher Peak, Eldorado Peak, Forbidden Peak, Boston Peak, Buckner Mountain, and most glorious of all, Mt Logan, robed in glistening glaciers and snow fields. It was incredible, awesome, and breathtaking!

After twenty minutes or so, we continued, coming to a wooden sign that read, "Entering North Cascades National Park." Between two piles of rock further on, a tangle of bushes was smothered in purple-red flowers. While my gaze was mainly focused on the cliffs and summits, something closer at hand and near the ground caught my attention. A bird was crossing the path in front of us. About the size of a small chicken, it was obviously a member of the grouse family. Its mottled dark back, reddish-head, and white belly identified it as a ptarmigan, a bird I had only seen in pictures. Like snowshoe hares, it would turn white when the snow fell in a couple of months. Without alarm, it pottered off into the underbrush.

The weather had been sunny when we had begun our hike, but had turned partly cloudy as the day progressed. Now, as we made our way to the valley below, the clouds settled lower and lower, hiding the surrounding peaks, and hanging like drapes along the side of Fisher Basin. Light sprinkles of rain fell and a few snowflakes swirled about. I hoped it would not get worse before we reached the bottom and set up camp. I was more than tired but at least my hips gave me less discomfort as we trudged downward.

Late in the afternoon we reached the valley floor and pitched our tent. After a brief rest, we cooked a freeze-dried supper over a small camp stove. After cleaning up, we looked around a little, but the fog obliterated everything beyond a hundred yards. We checked out the bank of nearby Fisher Creek but decided to postpone major exploration until morning. Turning in early sounded like good strategy.

As I lay in my sleeping bag reviewing the day, I was grateful for the hike but concerned about the discomfort in my hips. Attempting to climb Mt. Logan seemed highly questionable, especially if the weather did not improve. There was much for us to discover and enjoy with far less effort. Tomorrow we could leave the heavy packs in the tent and explore the nearby areas without encumbrance.

It rained off and on through the night but at least it did not snow. We woke up about 6:30 to some whistling and snorting outside the tent. Mystified, we quietly opened the tent flaps. A thin mist filled the air and moisture covered everything in sight. At first we saw nothing and all was quiet. Then from some distance away, we heard a brief whistle. Looking further back in the basin, we saw a deer looking toward us, then another one a short distance further, reddish-brown does, perhaps one hundred pounds in weight. Soon there was a snort and one of the deer dashed off, quickly followed by the other one. Their dark tails identified them as black tail deer, common to the Pacific coast. They seemed to ignore our presence, but could undoubtedly smell us.

The first deer ran again, stopped, faced the other, then turned and ran in another direction, quickly chased by the other. Running, bounding, swiftly turning, halting, they charged around the open ground as we watched in intent silence. Were they dashing madly about in sheer fun, trying to drive each other out of the territory, or even putting on a show for us, the audience? We did not know. We only watched in amazed fascination as the performance went on for several minutes.

The agility of the deer was astounding - turning almost instantly, accelerating to awesome speed, stopping abruptly, bounding off in a new direction, leaping over a bush - all of this across slanting ground, since Fisher Basin is not a level bowl but merely the lower, less severe slopes of converging mountainsides. They were masters of the terrain, however, at home in the mountain heights, creatures well able to live off the land. Eventually the deer disappeared in a dense stand of trees at the western side of the bowl.

After breakfast, we started our day of investigation, following the creek to the west. Since there was no easy way to cross the stream, we explored the slopes on the north flank of the valley. The day continued in damp, heavy overcast, but the weather was only a minor nuisance. While the distant vistas were often obliterated, the closer walls and cliffs were awesome. We were fully pleased to clamber from place to place, happy for the ability to do so. Like David in Psalm 18, we acknowledged God as the giver of our strength to stand upon the heights, or to do anything else for that matter.

Mindful of the previous day's trouble with my hips, I couldn't quite say, "he makes my feet like the deer," that had so easily scampered about that morning, but I was grateful for the stamina and strength to reach this majestic arena.

In the morning we hiked back out, up and then down Easy Pass Trail. Fog and sunshine alternated. Our feet were so wet from saturated vegetation, that at the summit of the pass, we stopped to wring out our socks before descending. Perhaps it was there that Scott left his nice leather hat, for when we got back to the car it was nowhere to be found. Driving home in a swift, comfortable car was a significant pleasure after the labors of the trail.

It was about three years later that the mountain rambles took an upward turn. I was talking with my friend Gus, who had recently climbed Mt. Hood with his daughter, Sonja. During the conversation, he said that he wouldn't mind doing it again. It was not long before we set a date to do it together. This would be a major escalation for me, since at over 11,000 feet, it would be much higher than I had ever hiked before. Furthermore, its upper elevations, containing twelve glaciers, were snow and ice covered year around. Some of the more difficult routes had dangerous crevasses and cliffs, though the easiest and most common one had only one serious crack to bypass.

Many people consider it a beginner's mountain, and indeed, about 10,000 people climb it each year, many for the first time, even by youngsters hiking in tennis shoes. Hood is the most visited and climbed mountain in the country, and in the entire world, is exceeded only by Japan's Mt. Fujiyama. Its popularity is explained by several factors: it is close to the major population center of Portland, Oregon, it is a beautiful landmark, visible from as far as 100 miles away, and it can be climbed in a single day. In addition, Timberline Ski Resort on the lower slopes is the country's only lift-serviced mountain open for year round skiing. Skiers sometimes zip down the hill in swimwear.

I was eager for the attempt, but thought prudence would be advisable, since well over 100 people have died on Mt. Hood. I did some reading about climbing, ice axe self-arrest, rope technique, etc. We would be prepared with adequate clothes, even for severe weather, wear sturdy boots, carry emergency gear, and wear crampons and utilize a rope for safety on the steeper upper slopes. This may sound like "overkill" for a warm sunny day, but such weather can change quickly, bringing danger and worse.

Finally, it was time. Driving in Gus's camper, we arrived at the campground in the early evening. Probably too keyed up with anticipation, neither of us was able to sleep well. At 4:30 a.m. we decided we might as well get ready, and by 6:00 we set out.

The sky was black but filled with familiar stars, promising a clear day, which was especially encouraging, since the previous few days had been nasty with rain and snow. There was little wind but the early May temperature was biting at 5,800 feet. Already the eastern sky was brightening. We quickly found a comfortable pace and settled into our silent walk. A few other hikers were underway as well. Our way paralleled the ski lift for the lower half of the route. One thousand feet above Timberline Lodge, we came to Silcox Hut, originally a part of the chair lift installation, but now used by some skiers and climbers as a shelter from the weather.

The sun now broke the horizon above a shoulder of the mountain. Its bright presence added a lift to our spirits and even perhaps to our bodies. Without the need for sleeping bags and a tent, our packs carried little weight, but a long uphill slog is still demanding, especially for someone like me, who spent most days at a desk or in a car.

With continual advance upward, the views became more and more spectacular. We were now well above tree line with nothing to hinder the view. Fifty miles to the south the spire of Mt. Jefferson stood above the horizon, as did the Oregon Twin Sisters, another fifty miles further. Westward, the blurred outline of the Coast Range Mountains formed the horizon. At least in this section of Hood, mountaineering required only determination and dogged tenacity. Ahead of us, a dozen others were engaged in their upward efforts. A few others followed behind, and further below, skiers were now out on the slopes.

Approaching the upper portion of the hill, rock sentinels stood out above the general profile of the mountain. Now we could see the effects of the recent storms. Crater Rock and the summit headwall were coated in hard ice, even on vertical surfaces, the result of freezing rain. Conditions just two days earlier would have been extremely difficult if not impossible. Our choice of date for the climb was fortunate, indeed.

With steeper terrain and icy surface, we stopped to put on our crampons, metal plates with inch long teeth that fastened to the bottom of our boots. We also harnessed ourselves to the rope for added protection. As we did so, I noticed that Gus was moving quite slowly. Asking if anything was wrong, he said he had a severe headache and his stomach was unsettled. His face seemed drawn and pale.

"Maybe we should go down," I said, but he dismissed the idea, wanting to continue.

Soon we approached the modest crevasse that blocked the way to the summit, which we bypassed by walking around its closed end. Now we were only a few hundred yards from our goal. Immediately above us were the Pearly Gates, a marvelous label for two scalloped and fluted walls of rock, on each side of a thirty-foot passage leading to the top of the mountain. As we passed through and took a short breather, I urged Gus not to go on. Since he was not well, I thought we should turn back, but he wouldn't consider it. He was determined to get me to the top, and we were nearly there.

In a few more minutes we were. Feeling miserable, probably altitude sickness brought on by a quick ascent and little sleep the night before, Gus was not overly excited about looking at the scenery. But I was. It was fantastic. The sky at this height was more black than blue. The snow and ice were brilliant white and the suns glare almost blinding. Several hundred feet below, a knot of climbers looked like ants as they rested before their push to the summit. In every direction, nothing obstructed our view for a hundred miles.

It was a wonderful experience to stand on Oregon's highest place, a site unreachable by customary transportation. We had achieved our objective, reaching the summit as we had planned and hoped. It had required hours of continual effort, muscular exertion, and mental purpose, but it was worth it. Our deep satisfaction seemed proportional to the labor expended. But there was more than simply reaching the goal.

There were the exalted views, spectacular and unique. In every direction from Hood's summit, a magnificent landscape stretched to the blue horizon, beautiful and immense, not remote and unreal as seen from an airliner, but intimate and familiar. Now we could see the great peaks to the north in Washington State, Rainier, St. Helens, and Adams. Beholding the mountains produces admiration, awe, even worship. To believers they make the unseen God nearly visible. With the eye of faith, they see Him in the face of His creation, as did a discerning prophet:

He who forms the mountains
creates the wind,
and reveals His thoughts to man,
He who turns dawn to darkness,
and treads the high places of the earth,
the Lord God Almighty is His name.
(Amos 4:13)

If seeing His handiwork from afar reveals His greatness, what might be discovered by actually climbing the high places, where He himself "walks?"

In gaining any height, the greatest thrill for me, is the change in perspective. I love looking down, and out, as most people seem to do. The elevated view allows the immediate apprehension of far more territory, a single glance encompassing vastly larger scale and distance. Could this high view provide a hint of God when we see vastly more than usual, allowing us a glimpse of near omniscience, like the all-seeing deity? Are the great hills a realm of special affinity, or at least receptivity, to the near presence of the Creator? Moses received the Law and saw the glory of God on a mountain and Abraham was tested on a peak. Jesus taught, prayed, and met the Father on a mountain. The omnipresent God is equally available in every locale, but perhaps his human creatures are more aware in the high places.

For several minutes Gus and I drank in the views but there was much still to be done. We had reached the summit, but our climb was not complete; now we had to hike down. While not requiring quite as much energy, it took significant care.

Passing climbers on their way up, we made our way back through the Pearly Gates, down to a level ridge below, a customary resting place where we stopped for a bit of food. Nearby, a thin veil of sulfurous steam arose from an open gash in the snow, reminding us that inner forces were still at work. Although classified as a dormant volcano by some experts, seismic tremors frequently disturb Hood's bowels.

In due time, we started down again, step after step. Going down was certainly easier than going up. With great satisfaction, and less discomfort for Gus, we reached the end of our climb.

Leaving Mt. Hood National Forest, Gus suddenly slowed the truck because of a mother deer and fawn standing in the middle of the road. In panic, the doe dashed into the woods on the east side of the road and the fawn ran to the west. Hopefully, they would find each other after we passed.

We returned home with pictures, rich memories, and a deep appreciation for the splendor of creation. Those who see the mountain from afar find its beauty to be extraordinary, but for the fortunate who walk its slopes and reach its crown, there is an intimacy of acquaintance surpassing the distant perspective.

Over the years I have had the joy and privilege of climbing a few other high places, "steep hiking," as I call it. Each encounter has been richly rewarding; physically, mentally, and spiritually, stocking my memory with experiences that remain alive across the progression of years. Now, once again, I live in the mid-western flatlands, mindful of their beauties and treasures, yet grateful beyond words, for the delight of standing upon His high places.

Chapter Four

THE MOUNTAIN

The mountain peaks belong to Him.
Ps. 95:4

When we had first moved out West, we enjoyed several experiences of driving and hiking among the nearby hills, modest heights of five to seven thousand feet, and of course, Mt. Spokane, our own "community" peak, was a frequent destination. Yet, always in the back of my mind, was an eager anticipation of visiting the west side of the state, where the peaks rose twice as high. In particular, I wanted to see Mt. Rainier.

Opportunity finally arrived during the early days of summer. With Shirley and the children, we made the long drive, only to be disappointed by dense fog. Of the great bulk of the mountain, we could see nothing beyond two hundred feet. As is often true of fishing, we should have been there the day before. This day the weighty fog obscured even the tops of nearby trees. Our discoveries of Rainier would have to wait for another time.

During the next couple of years, I had to travel to Seattle several times. On each trip, I greatly enjoyed the drive across the irrigated bowl of central Washington, then up and over the Cascade Mountains, down to the shores of

Puget Sound. Whatever the season, the mountains produced a deep fascination in the depths of my being. Their ageless presence displayed the continual changes of the year; white of winter, summer green, and the palettes of fall and spring. But Rainier remained elusive, hidden in the clouds.

Then one day I needed to be in Seattle for a mid-morning meeting. Rather than going the day before and spending a night away from home, I decided to leave Spokane early enough in the morning to make the drive in time for my appointment. Starting out in the 4:00 a.m. darkness, I reached the Columbia River by the time the sun had been up for about thirty minutes. Across the bridge, a ten-mile incline rose from the river gorge to the height of land at Rye Grass Summit on Interstate 90. At 3,000 feet, it is not a high pass, but it does give an impressive view to east and west.

As I crested the ridge, an incredible phantom appeared on the western horizon, 80 miles away. Rising high above the surrounding terrain was a mammoth cone of pink dominating all other features of the skyline. With a gasp, I burst aloud, "My God!" The involuntary exclamation was not profanity, but an expression of startled wonder. The mountain would have been awesome enough in the light of full day. Now, in the early light of morning, the snow clad slopes were tinted an astounding hue of pale rose. Never in my life had I seen such an apparition, for so it seemed to be. Its sudden appearance was a distinct jolt to my unsuspecting consciousness. Majestic, beautiful, marvelous, awesome, but words were hopeless to express the sensations that stirred me. Mingled with the emotions and thoughts of the mountain itself, were praise and worship of the One who caused it to be. "How great You are, Lord, to make such a magnificent wonder, and how marvelous of You to let us behold such beauty."

Following this introduction to the mountain, I had several other occasions to see it from a distance. A few times, it was visible from Rye Grass, though never in such clarity as in my first sighting. From various vantage points in the city of Seattle, I was able to see it when the skies were clear, and a view from Tacoma was the closest of all.

Beyond these "normal" perspectives, I treasured a couple of special views to see the lofty peak. When the weather is clear, flying to Seattle provides a spectacular panorama. The whole Cascade Range is visible, stretching for hundreds of miles north and south. The great volcanoes stand out prominently as silent sentinels guarding the vast wilderness. Baker, Glacier, Adams, Hood, and Jefferson tower above 10,000 feet. Yet, Rainier surpasses them all, thrusting more than 14,000 feet into the sky. Covered by ice and snow, its brilliant whiteness etched upon the blue background, it is a never to be forgotten wonder, visible in an airplane from more than 300 miles away.

The other special view is from the waters of Puget Sound. An inexpensive ride on one of the ferries that cross the Sound can provide an exhilarating prospect of the mountain, especially in the late afternoon when the western face catches the full light of a lower sun. From a vantage point less than 50 miles distant, Rainier displays its awesome height, for its full scale is apparent from sea level to summit.

Though Mt. Whitney in California is higher than Rainier by a mere eighty-four feet, and several Colorado peaks are nearly identical in height, no other peak in America, and few in all the world, reveals such a differential between base and summit elevation. Most other mountains are inland, upon high plateaus. From the height of the surrounding terrain to their tops may be only a few thousand feet, exposing only a modest summit to the observer. Even lofty Everest, though higher than *two*

Rainiers piled one upon the other, displays not much greater vertical scale since the base terrain itself stands higher than 12,000 feet.

Rainier is a truly magnificent mountain, not only for its height, but for its mammoth bulk as well. To the visitor at Paradise on the mountain's south flank, or at Sunrise on the north slopes, the mountain not only rises to the heights but also spreads expansively to the sides. Thirty-five square miles of glaciers crown the mountain, spilling down the valleys from the crest above. Beholding these rivers of ice stirs the imagination. To truly experience Rainier's vast scale, however, would require a circuit of the mountain on the Wonderland Trail, a journey on foot of nearly one hundred miles!

To most people, even modest hills are appealing. Whether looking up to the summits or down from the heights, the visual impact is deeply moving. Mountains convey strength, power, and permanence, dwarfing the greatest constructions of mankind. Not surprisingly, they have conveyed an awesome grandeur to people of every age.

The day came at last when I would attempt to know this great mountain, *The* Mountain to me, on more intimate, personal terms. Gus and I began our ascent early in the afternoon on a beautiful sunny day in September. At first my mind and body were aghast at the effort. Though the incline is not overly steep, the routes to the summit pitch upward without relent, rising nearly two miles in elevation, over a distance of nine miles. Under the burden of food, tent, sleeping bag, clothes, rope, and ice ax, each step requires incredible energy. To let the mind dwell upon the endless footfalls to the summit is a certain prescription for failure. Two alternatives, strangely effective since so opposite, make the task manageable. Avoiding all thought of the future, even of the next minute, exerting total concentration on the next step, then the next, then the next again, and so on, reduces an awesome labor to only the next single stride. It does work, for a while at least. A second alternative is essential.

While the eyes continue to scan the ground for secure footing, the conscious mind largely bypasses the process, engaged instead with the breathtaking panorama in every direction, or as you may choose, occupied with countless mental tasks, problems, reveries, memories, projections, reflections, etc. The trick is to be so involved mentally that the external labors are lost in the background. It, too, works, for a while.

Alternating between the techniques of mental diversion and focused attention, we made our way upward. Following the Skyline Trail to Panorama Point, then along the ridge overlooking Nisqually Glacier, we crossed Pebble Creek, leaving the gravel trail for the winter world of the Muir Snowfield. Firmly consolidated by warm summer sunshine, it was little different from other hiking except for being a bit more slippery.

Advancing steadily higher, a distant "boom," suddenly alerted our attention. Looking up, we saw a white plume rising. A slab of ice had avalanched off the Nisqually Ice Cliff. It was a forceful reminder that the "solid" snow and ice upon which we walked was actually a frozen river, flowing downward to the sea. Usually the motion is imperceptible. Occasionally, however, there are violent spasms to prove otherwise. In fact, we observed a second icefall about an hour later.

Up and up we continued. Preoccupied with the task of each step, I gave little notice to a small group of climbers coming down. As they drew near, however, I was startled to hear one of them speak up, saying, “Hi, Bill.” That got my attention! It took me a moment to identify my acquaintance, Dave, a colleague from another part of the state. Neither of us knew of our common interest in climbing the hills. We exchanged a few words about the experience and then continued our opposite direction. What are the odds of such an encounter on a lofty mountain slope?

Eagerly we watched for landmarks to note our progress. With dismaying slowness, we reached McClure Rock, then Sugar Loaf. When we neared Anvil Rock, we could still not see Camp Muir, our objective for the day. At last, in the fading daylight, we drew near enough to see Muir's stone huts situated on a low ridge between two glacial systems.

Gus had forged ahead of me. We were almost at our resting place, but I was wasted as I struggled on. I wondered if I could even make the last thousand yards, but with wearied effort I kept plodding until at last, I was there.

After a brief respite for regaining our breath and surveying the facilities, we cooked a bit of supper. With a dozen other climbers, a few on their way up and some going down, we sacked out on bunks in the shelter hut. Falling asleep was difficult. Though my breathing had returned to normal, the rush of blood striving to re-oxygenate my depleted muscles pounded fiercely in my ears. Thin air and the anticipation of our 2:00 a.m. departure added stress to my mental state. Small furry creatures (mice at 10,000 feet among the glaciers!) rustling among our packs - and across our bodies - did not help either.

At 1:00 a.m., others began to stir, putting on gear and cooking breakfast. We, too, began to get ready. An engaged couple, and the man's brother, were also setting out. Chatting together and sharing expectations of the climb made us instant companions, so we decided to join forces. Outside in the icy night we strapped crampons on our boots and tied ourselves to the climbing ropes. Our flashlights stabbed feebly into the black, but did manage to light up footprints of previous climbers crossing the

Cowlitz Glacier. As we walked beside, or occasionally stepped over cracks in the ice, the darkness obscured their frozen depths.

A half-mile along, we came to the barrier of Cathedral Rocks, a stony spine separating the Cowlitz from the Ingraham Glacier, where a steep section of loose rubble caused us to sweat despite the frigid night air. Crossing the crest, we followed the base of the rocks as we worked upward. Disconcerting "clatters" in the darkness alerted us to the presence of loosened boulders falling from the cliff. The mountain seemed dangerously alive. Fortunately, our route soon swung away from the rocks, wending its serpentine way among the crevasses, around gigantic ice "boulders," always upward, and now, much more steeply. Our pace slowed considerably. When we stopped for a brief rest, we hacked out level platforms with our ice axes to form secure sitting places, which was immensely helpful.

During the passing hours of darkness, we had seen faint flickers of aurora to the north. Now in the east, the sun broke the horizon. Below us, was a breathtaking sea of white, its gleaming surface cracked and splintered. We could clearly see our trail stretching behind us, scuffed into the surface of snow-covered ice. In every direction mountains receded into the blue distance. At our left, the dome of Rainier stood high above us, though we had now reached more than 12,000 feet.

At this point, the woman and her fiancée decided to go back, but the man's brother joined Gus and me on our rope. As we started upward once more, I was uneasy about the weather. Although blue sky and sunlight surrounded us, in the valleys below churning black clouds were visible and seemed to be rising higher.

Another surprising sight was visible thousands of feet below. We looked *down* on an airplane in flight! It circled laboriously, striving like us to gain elevation, until at last after many minutes of furious buzzing, it finally reached our height and passed beyond to the summit. Even to the mechanical genius of technology, the great mountain presents a formidable obstacle.

We continued our wooden shuffle as hours of effort and little oxygen had slowed our steps dramatically. We had passed 13,000 feet. The summit was perhaps two hours away but the sky was now dark and a rising wind spat stinging grains of snow through the air. The mountain is notorious for its treacherous weather, claiming several lives from the unwary and ill prepared. Should we press on or return? We were well equipped but did not want to challenge severe weather. Choosing discretion over valor, we turned around. Hopefully, we would try again another time. For now, we savored the experience of the climb if not the achievement of the summit.

Our return was anticlimactic except for the painful discovery that going down is incredibly hard on the knees. Next time I would be in better condition. As we descended, our gaze continually turned back to the mighty peak. To come to terms with its magnificent beauty, its monumental size, its sheer "presence," proved impossible. The scale was too vast. To internalize this object, or even our brief experience on its slopes, was not possible. Instead of millions of tons of inert rock and ice, the mountain seemed to convey a living force, a magnetic, dynamic personality. And beyond the mountain itself, imponderable as it was, was a still more powerful Reality, made greater to our perceptions by our encounter with the overwhelming mountain. As we drove home, we marveled over the mountain and its Maker.

One year later, we were again on the slopes of Rainier. Earlier in the summer, we had tried a second time, but had failed again because of bad weather. Now we hoped the third attempt would succeed. Starting early in the day, we reached camp Muir in the late afternoon. After a welcome rest, we traversed the Cowlitz Glacier, crossed Cathedral Rocks, and started up Ingraham Glacier. At a place called "the flats," (only relatively so!), we pitched our tent after leveling out an area with our axes. Though camped on the ice itself, we were far enough from Cathedral's cliffs to be safe from falling rocks. Foam pads kept us insulated from the frigid temperature of the snow. A supper of Chicken Tetrazzini cooked over a white gas stove, prepared us for a night of rest, zipped in our warm sleeping bags. Before blowing out the candle, we read a selection from the Psalms. How meaningful was the statement, "The mountain peaks belong to Him." (Psalm 95:4). We thanked Him for the strength to participate in such a venture and for the opportunity to see the marvels of the hills, especially the splendor of Rainier.

Like the starry skies, the high peaks often stimulate a powerful impression of awe, reverence, and a sense of the Creator who brought them into being. The Bible declares their formation to be the active, personal agency of God himself. "You...formed the mountains by your power," (Psalm 65:5, 6). Of course, the inspired writers do not discuss plate tectonics, volcanism, faulting, folding, and other geo-mechanical processes that are the immediate causes of mountain building. The Scriptures are concerned, rather, to identify the ultimate source of reality. The infinite Creator is the cause of everything, including the lofty mountains.

In a most suggestive image, God asks the prophet Isaiah (40:12), "who has weighed the mountains on a scale and the hills in a balance?" No one, obviously. They are too gigantic. But to God, they are only a wisp of dust on the pan of the balance, too insignificant to even measure. How great is the God who considers such monumental objects of trifling notice? If His human creatures gaze with awe, wonder, and even reverence, on mere piles of rock, should they not rightly kneel in worship before Him who made them? As one of the most popular hymns of the twentieth century puts it,

When through the woods and forest glades I wander,
and hear the birds sing sweetly in the trees,
When I look down from lofty mountain grandeur
and hear the brook and feel the gentle breeze.
Then sings my soul, My Savior God to Thee;
How great Thou art, how great Thou art.

Tonight we would sleep much better than the previous year. We were settled in earlier, were undisturbed by other campers, not bothered by rodents, and were in better physical condition. Best of all, we would sleep later. With our higher campsite, we would not begin our start for the summit until daylight. Though early season climbers are hampered by deep snow, and thus want to reach the top and start down before the surface is softened by afternoon sun, the fall climbs are made on much firmer, compacted snow. The trade-off is a greater difficulty with crevassed and jumbled ice.

The next morning, we were underway by 6:30, a short trek upward bringing us to the foot of a mammoth icefall. The contour of the glacier was vastly altered from that of the year earlier. The year before, we had climbed a steep but relatively smooth incline up the Ingraham Glacier. This year, a huge, chaotic pile of ice blocked the way. Chunks of every size, some larger than a car, were piled upon one another. Under ever-heavier accumulations of snow falling from the heights above, the vast sheet of ice had slipped over the uneven contours of the rock beneath, breaking and crumbling as it moved.

It had happened just weeks before, a tragic event on Father's Day, when sudden catastrophe engulfed eleven people. Without warning, the ice broke loose, crashing down and burying the climbers in a frigid grave. In a ghastly coincidence on that same day, four other climbers fell to their death on Mt. Hood in Oregon. It was the worst day ever in American mountain climbing history.

Wasting no time to pass this grim spot, we reached the relative safety of Disappointment Cleaver, another of the rocky up-thrusts that pierce the mantle of Rainier's ice. Here we had to pick our way through boulders and stony rubble, up and around the icefall. At its upper end, we went back out on the unbroken upper glacier. Except for the increasing labor of gaining elevation, our only problem was skirting or crossing crevasses. These cracks in the ice may be only a few inches or many feet wide, their length varying as well. The sheer sides may descend for a few feet or may plunge to forty feet or more. When we could, we skirted their apparent ends. When they were too long, or merged with others, we stepped or jumped across.

Following standard safety techniques, we traveled on the ice roped together but seventy-five feet apart. If one of us lost his footing or fell in a crevasse, the others would have a few seconds to react, attempting to arrest the fall by dropping to the slope, jamming the ice ax into the surface, and anchoring it with his body. When crossing a crack we were especially alert to prevent or minimize such a mishap.

Threatening obstacles though they were, the crevasses were also beautiful. In infinite gradations of white, silver, gray, and blue, they gleamed in brilliance as the sun penetrated the layers of ice. Their mysterious depths captured the imagination. How far did they extend? Most seemed only a few feet deep, but others were twenty feet or more. But were the bottoms solid, or only thin roofs over still deeper caverns, reaching far into the bowels of the ice cap? Though we were equipped for extricating ourselves from such places, we hoped we would not find out, for a fall into even a relatively shallow crack can be disastrous.

Nearing the high point of our previous year's climb, we came to the huge uppermost crevasse that often blocks a climber's route. The bergschrund, as it is called, is where the slope of the terrain below finally overcomes the tensile strength of the ice cap, causing it to fracture into a yawning split that may be hundreds of yards long, dozens of feet wide, and very deep. Such a moat frequently offers no easy means of access. On this occasion, the route was not difficult for a tilted slab of ice had fallen into the hole, filling it to within a few feet of the top. Steps chopped into the side of the crevasse enabled climbers, assisted by a piece of rope anchored to the near wall, to reach the slab about ten feet below. Sloping to the far side, it formed a natural ramp out of the crevasse.

Pausing only long enough to take a picture of this awesome place, where one portion of the chasm's upper wall slanted outward seventy feet over our heads, we trudged ever upward. This time we would make it. Two tenacious hours later, we reached the lip of the great summit crater nearly three miles high in the thin air. The highest point was on the other side of the bowl, a half-mile away. Slipping off our packs, we enjoyed a welcome rest while we melted some snow for a much-needed drink. Then, blissfully unencumbered, we walked across. With deep satisfaction, we signed the logbook kept in an aluminum box at the base of the rim on the other side, then walked to Rainier's highest point, 14,410 feet above Puget Sound. To the west, we could see the heights of the Olympic Mountains. Northward, Glacier Peak and Mount Baker revealed their splendor, as did St. Helens, Adams, and Hood to the south. All, however, knelt with lowered heads to Sovereign Rainier. We stood at the top of our world. It was a thrilling experience, shared each year by three or four thousand others, who complete the climb.

We had achieved our objective. We had *not* conquered the mountain. It had only been our privilege to tread its flanks and walk briefly on its crown. Under unusually fine conditions, we had enjoyed one of its benevolent moods. Pride did not accompany our "success," rather, humility filled our hearts. No discovery in our wilderness travels or urban excursions could compare with the magnificence of this mammoth rock. Incredibly, geological evidence indicates that in ages past, Rainier was even higher and larger than at present!

To our satiated senses, it was big enough. Whatever its ancient past, its present is one of superlatives. Consider, for instance, the snowfall at Paradise Visitor Center. During the past few years, it has exceeded *1,000 inches,* each year! True, mightier mountains are found elsewhere: Logan in Canada, McKinley in Alaska, Aconcagua in Argentina, Kilimanjaro in Tanzania, and of course, Everest, and its peers, in the Asian Himalaya and Karakoram ranges. Nonetheless, Rainier stands erect among them, deserving full recognition and honor. Many who have scaled the higher peaks, have acknowledged its noble status.

Descending as rapidly as our weary legs would allow, we retraced our earlier route. Though going down was much easier, care was still needed, for a misstep could be disastrous. How good it was to feel the bite of our crampons on the icy crust underfoot. In only half the time spent going uphill, we made our way down to Camp Muir. We could have gone all the way down to Paradise, but to do so would have meant a cold, exhausting walk in the dark. Our savaged bodies were weary enough. We deserved a rest.

Disdaining the hut, we pitched our tent on a narrow ledge nearby. Perspiration and respiration had severely dehydrated us, producing a raging thirst that snowmelt seemed not to quench. My offer of five dollars for a cola went unmet by the handful of Muir's visitors. I would have to wait until morning. Though a fierce wind, shaking and flapping our tent through the night, made sleep elusive, it was something else that kept us awake. While our bodies were grateful for the rest, our minds could not shut out the powerful, overwhelming image of the mountain. First in our conscious thought, and when sleep finally came, in our dreams, we continued to scale the mighty giant.

In the morning, we returned to Paradise, a terrific name for an entrancing place! Paradise River and Paradise Park, so named surely for the incredible beauty of its summer landscape - a wild extravagance of flowers gracing alpine meadows, backed by the immensity of the mountain. Was its naming only a casual choice, or might there have been some notion that here, indeed, was a garden made by God?

To us, The Mountain was indeed His handiwork. Language failed then, and does now in the re-telling, to express its splendors. Words are often too feeble to articulate the natural, the human, the finite. How, then, shall we express the greater majesty of God Himself? The mountain itself, however, speaks in wordless eloquence, addressing the supernatural and infinite, awaiting a final day to “burst into song,” in praise of its Creator (Is. 55:12).

Chapter Five

WHERE MOUNTAIN GOATS ARE BORN

"Do you know when the mountain goats give birth?" *Job 39:1*

At 6:00 a.m. on a bright September day, we started our trip to the mountain, a long drive from Gus's home in Post Falls, Idaho. Our hope was to reach the top of Granite Peak, Montana's highest mountain. Rising 12,799 feet above sea level, it is located roughly fifty miles northeast of Yellowstone Park. The surrounding terrain is a high plateau inaccessible except by foot or horseback.

After twelve hours on the Interstate, we turned south, traveling over increasingly poorer roads, until we stopped at a Forest Service campsite where we spent the night. After breakfast the next morning, a short drive took us to the trailhead.

"Well, Lars, only six thousand feet to go," said Gus with a laugh.

"Sure, Gus," I replied. "Six thousand feet up, plus whatever we might have to recover from downhill sections. Too bad it takes about a dozen miles of hiking to gain that elevation. We've got our work cut out for us."

Hitching up our packs, we begin. Each new trip brings dismaying uncertainty, raising doubt that strength and stamina will be sufficient. Forty-five pound loads are heavy enough on the level. On a climb they seem overwhelming, especially during the first mile as the body rebels at the unaccustomed labor. Straps bite into shoulders and hips. The inescapable weight threatens to overcome the effort of each upward step. "If the first hour is so daunting, how is it possible to keep going for hours on end?" is a question that haunts my mind. Yet, somehow, breathing and heartbeat adjust to the enormous demand.

We were barely under way when Gus suddenly stopped. Looking in the direction of his gaze, I saw two mule deer just off the trail, eyes, ears, and nostrils testing the intruders. After a brief standoff, they turned and vanished into the trees as silently as they had appeared. Their presence at the beginning of our trip was a promising omen, investing the quiet forest with an anticipation of life and surprise.

Our way rose gently through small aspens to the base of a cliff. Here the incline increased as we traversed the bordering talus slope. An hour of relatively easy going brought us to a dam, forming lovely Mystic Lake at 7700 feet. Half a mile along its southern shore the trail turned upward again, upward with a vengeance! Switchbacks contoured a broad peninsula leading ever higher to a plateau three thousand feet above. Step by step we trudged upward, gaining elevation slowly but steadily.

Though most backpackers and climbers would claim they pursue their activities because of the awesome beauty of the mountain views, it is astounding how much of their time is spent staring intently at the ground a mere three feet ahead. The incline of the hillside, the uneven ground, and the twisting trail demand a constant surveillance of the immediate vicinity. Where to place the next foot is a continual preoccupation. Somehow, the procedure becomes nearly automatic, and while the eye processes the relevant information, the mind seems often to be almost detached, exploring and pondering a multitude of concerns and interests. Eventually, of course, the need to survey the more distant surroundings becomes compelling, justifying a brief halt, and giving the body a momentary respite as well.

As we gained each additional hundred feet, the lake below shrank in size, though appallingly, the rim above seemed as distant as ever. The beauty of the surrounding wilderness defied description. Near at hand wild flowers grew in incredible profusion and soaring pine trees studded the steep slopes. Across the valley, the mountainside rose to a broad tableland, backed in the distance by receding tiers of nameless peaks. To the west far below, several lakes formed lustrous pearls on the silver thread of Rosebud Creek. Southward, a deep gash in the mountain was partly visible, showing bold cliffs plunging abruptly to hidden depths. It was a panorama of overwhelming magnificence.

Occasionally we stopped for longer rests. What a relief it was to be free for a while from the burden of our packs. A refreshing drink from a water bottle helped to replace moisture lost through sweat and respiration, and peanut M&Ms provided a tasty snack. Knowing that pictures can capture neither the panoramic breadth nor the awesome elevations, we blazed away with our cameras, nonetheless. In distant times and places, they would provide a feeble reminder of what we now beheld. Our eyes and minds grappled with immensity, attempting to comprehend and absorb the splendor before us.

No description can possibly recreate such staggering impressions; indeed, personal experience, even if frequently repeated, cannot retain such stirring of consciousness. Only the living present, the immediate encounter with the grandeur of God's creative majesty, is sufficient. To experience again the wonder, the mystery, the reverence of such momentous confrontations, requires a fresh, firsthand engagement with His wilderness. It is not surprising that the lure of wild places is addictive to those who appreciate its enchanting glory. To know its fullness of thrill and delight one is compelled again and again, to venture into the wilds. Like vitamin C, it cannot be stored in the body. A new supply is continually needed.

Refreshing as our rest stops were, the trail mounted inexorably above our view, so shrugging into our packs, we started upward again. Separated in single file by the narrow track and with little extra breath for conversation, we were joined in heart, mind, and experience, yet wrapped in private worlds. We plodded upward in quiet contemplation, the silence broken only by the crunch of our boots upon the rocky soil, the creak of our pack frames, and the deep rasp of our breathing. All else was still, the light breeze barely ruffling leaves and needles. Occasionally a small bird would flit from bush to bush without singing. Up an up, we hiked, with occasional downward steps where the path crossed shallow watercourses. At noon we called a halt, an hour's rest more treasured than the food. Gus's altimeter read 9500 feet.

"It must be reading low," I protested. "We've been climbing for hours. Are you reading it right? Maybe you didn't set it when we started?"

"Of course I did," Gus replied. "Check it yourself. If you look at the topographic map you can see that it's about right."

Reluctantly I agreed. At the rate we were going, our campsite was still a long way off. Oh, well, backpacking is basically picking them (feet) up and putting them down, one step at a time. We would get there eventually. What was important now was to munch a cheese and sausage sandwich and savor the vistas. Both could best be done while reclining on a soft rock, helped immeasurably by prying heavy boots off of weary feet.

How good it felt to rest, letting the pulse return to normal. We were not hungry, for strenuous exertion tends to depress the appetite. Our conversation was limited, since words were feeble means to express our impressions. In any case, they were scarcely needed, because we react so much alike to the wilderness. What surprised us was the silence of so much space. We were aware of no other creatures, human or otherwise, in all the vast surroundings. There were many nearby, of course, but their presence was hidden to our senses. Deer, squirrels, mice, birds, and many other animals inhabited the mountains, but the only sound we heard, now that our breathing had calmed, was the buzzing of an occasional fly, incongruously loud in the quiet wilderness. It was as if no other life existed, as if the multitudes of earth had ceased to be.

All too soon, our interlude was over. Reluctantly we put on our boots, stowed lunch leftovers in the pack, and took a final drink. The packs seemed heavier than before, our shoulders ached from the morning's labors, and knees and hips, too, complained of the strain. The first quarter mile of our ever-upward hike was not pleasant, but to our satisfaction, the systems adjusted once again to our strenuous exertions. The human body is truly a marvel, able to accomplish incredible feats, beyond both normal experience and routine imagination. Demanding as our efforts were to us, they were nothing extraordinary, for serious climbers sometimes carry packs of double the weight, at twice the altitude. French-Canadian voyageurs in the fur trade two hundred years ago, carried 180 pounds at a time as their regular load, though most of their portages were relatively short and on fairly level terrain.

As we toiled continually higher, the trees had been thinning out. We were now above ten thousand feet and stunted pines, mere shrubs at this height, appeared only in sheltered south-facing hollows; a bit further, we were above them all. To our pleasant relief the slope of the mountain had flattened considerably. We were making our way across a broad plateau, tilting upward to a low ridge of rock across the southern horizon, beyond which Granite Peak was hidden several miles to the southwest. The well-defined trail we had followed throughout the day now disappeared as we walked across open grassland. As we neared the ridge, more frequent and ever larger fields of boulders appeared in the grass, until the rocks began to predominate and the grassy areas became mere islands among the stones. In every direction, distant peaks surrounded our slanted tabletop, sharply etched in the angled light of a now declining sun.

Though the trail had vanished, we had a reasonable knowledge of our direction since we were following a Forest Service route description. Unfortunately, we would not get as far as we had planned for our first day, our weary bones telling us we had gone far enough. As we surveyed the near surroundings for a suitable area of grass, I suddenly noticed an animal about two hundred yards away.

"Look, Gus," I whispered, "it's a mountain goat!"

The stocky animal stood about thirty inches high at the shoulders and weighed perhaps 150 pounds. Long, shaggy white hair completely covered its body, except for the hooves, sharp curving horns, nose, and eyes, all of which were ebony black. Since males and females differ only slightly in size, we did not know if it was a billy or a nanny.

Of course the goat had seen us long before. It stood unafraid, staring intently at us, then walked slowly away, keeping its distance, wary but unalarmed. As we continued onward, we discovered three more goats further away. Eventually they all disappeared among the broken contours of the hillside. For us the wilderness was now truly wild, a place of magic inhabited by the white creatures of the crags. The visible presence of life made the harsh and lonely landscape more exciting and enticing.

At last, our day's journey came to an end, an acre of grass in a jumble of rock serving as our homestead for the night. With great relief, we dropped our packs and simply rested for several minutes, then set to work pitching the tent, unrolling sleeping bags, and beginning dinner. Tonight we would eat beef stroganoff cooked on a one-burner backpacker's stove. While our meal simmered, I experienced the exquisite pleasure of exchanging my two-pound (each!) hiking boots for the nearly weightless caress of down booties. What joy! In the fading light of a lengthy day we ate our dinner, not really hungry, but needing to replace over five thousand calories of energy consumed by laborious hours of uphill hiking. After our simple meal, cleanup was quickly finished and we turned in.

While early by urban standards, nine o'clock, or so, we gladly stretched out in our sleeping bags. We joked about our aching bodies and wondered about tomorrow's unknown, but mostly we talked of the day's experience. With no manmade distractions or complex problems, there had been opportunity for us to think, to feel, to be aware. Surrounded by mighty mountains, overwhelmed by the vastness of earth and sky, surprised by wild creatures, the presence of a great God had been palpably real. As was our custom, by the light of a candle we read a few chapters from the Bible. The Psalms were especially appropriate in the setting of such nature. "When I consider the heavens," the author wrote, "what is man that you are mindful of him?" (Psalm 8:3, 4). We, too, felt as he had. Even in daylight, Montana's big skies are impressive. Now at night, in the thin air of the mountain heights, the stars blazed in incredible brilliance, beyond computation in number. How could such things be accounted for?

In all history, only two explanations have been proposed: either a great Creator made all the glories of earth and sky, or else they came into being by themselves. True, we cannot fathom how a God could always exist, but that the material universe could simply "happen," matter somehow create and organize itself, is a more incredible notion by far. Though beyond proof, the Biblical statement, "By faith we understand that the universe was formed at God's command, so that what is seen was not made out of what was visible." (Hebrews 11:3), is a satisfying, and so I believe, an accurate explanation.

Warm and relaxed as we were, we reluctantly thought it best to venture out for a final task, one that is easier to take care of ahead of time than in the middle of the night. As I pushed my head through the netting of the tent flap, I saw another goat, much closer this time, but barely visible as a silhouette against the background. Gus joined me and we watched for several minutes. Whether it was feeding or had merely stopped in its travels, we did not know. It simply stood, looking away from us toward the distant north, as if contemplating the fierce beauty as we had. Then it vanished in the dark.

When we returned to the tent, we agreed that the goats were an unexpected bonus to our trip. We knew they lived in these mountains but had never thought of them as we contemplated our trip. Before falling asleep, we prayed, thanking God for safety, asking His protection for our families, and praising Him for His greatness.

Then we tried to sleep. Exhaustion, excitement, thin air, and barely adequate foam pads can keep a tired person awake for a long time. As usual, Gus resolutely burrowed in his bag, attempting to induce sleep by determined stillness, and as usual, I thrashed about for quite some time until I, too, fell asleep, long after Gus had begun to snore.

We awoke the next morning to a brightening eastern sky, our stiff bodies reluctant to move, and not overly excited by a breakfast of instant hot cereal and granola bars. Since we planned to scale the peak and return to the site by nightfall, we left most of our gear in the tent. Taking only the essentials for our climb in a single pack, we set out following the base of the ridge. One miscalculation was mildly disconcerting. Breakfast had used up most of our limited water supply and the snowmelt ponds that dotted the plateau were now frozen after a sharply cold night. In due time, however, the rising sun would unseal their icy covers.

Our planned route was west about two miles to the end of the ridge where we would turn south, going uphill again, to reach Granite three miles beyond. Traveling nearly on the level we made rapid progress at first, expecting to skirt the ridge in well under an hour. As often happens in the wilderness, reality overwhelmed expectations.

The further we hiked, the more piles of precarious boulders covered the terrain. At times we could find short stretches of sandy pebbles to follow, but increasingly we had to pick our way from rock to rock, stepping carefully since many were balanced upon others like teeter-totters. A misstep could easily result in a fall, sprained ankle, or worse. To make matters still more difficult, the rocks were not spread evenly over the ground, but were often piled like long windrows of mown grain, requiring an exhausting clamber up one side and then down the other. Nearly every step required constant vigilance. Finding the least difficult route was a largely useless exercise. How we missed the luxury of yesterday's clearly defined and unobstructed trail. Two hours of arduous "stepping" were needed to finally reach the end of the ridge. To our dismay, the boulders continued on, and now we would have to walk on them, uphill.

Beyond the ridge, we discovered more of our companions from the previous day. Three goats were crossing the hillside in front of us, and to the west, several more grazed the scattered clumps of grass at the edge of a great chasm. They seemed completely untroubled by the rocks that so badly hindered our travel.

Rocky Mountain goats are incredible animals, not really goats at all, but relatives of the antelopes. Endowed with special hooves that contain a spongy inner portion, which acts almost as a suction cup, they can perform incredible feats. Watching them leaping from rock to rock, especially *downhill*, balancing on the narrowest of ledges, scrambling up nearly vertical slopes, they seem to defy gravity. Where a single misstep would result in a fall of hundreds of feet and sure death, even the young kids dash and cavort with abandon. In comparison to their mastery of the high cliffs, the most expert human climber is a clumsy incompetent.

After watching and picture taking, we continued our slow, grueling journey. Our meager water supply was now gone but at least we could finally see our objective. Granite Peak loomed before us as the summit of a nearly sheer cliff soaring upward from the gorge just to the west. We were near enough that despite our snail's pace, our spirits quickened.

Eventually we came to the edge of a canyon separating us from Granite Peak itself, just a brief mile away. Then our hearts sank. Where we stood, our elevation was over 12,000 feet and the summit was less than 800 feet higher. To reach it, however, we would first have to descend over the same kind of rubble we had been crossing, 1500 feet down to a narrow saddle connecting the two slopes. On flat city pavement, it would be a piece of cake. For us, however, working cautiously down the treacherous rocks took nearly an hour! Our entire morning's labor, which would have taken us one hour to accomplish on smooth, level ground, had taken *five* hours. Since it was nearly noon, we ate lunch before starting up the opposite incline. We were very thirsty but happy that water would soon be available from melting patches of snow on the steep hillside in front of us. At last, the real climb was at hand, and to our joy, the loose boulders were finally left behind.

Despite its name, Granite Peak proper, on the first part of the ascent, is not all rock. At least in some spots, soil and grass managed to cling to the slope. In other places, slabs and faces of continuous rock protruded, and in still others, boulders made irregular stair steps. The angle of incline was not severe enough to cause great danger but made the climbing slow and strenuous. Reaching the melting snow, we could at last fill our water bottles.

Several hundred feet higher, and another hour later, we topped a small ridge. Working our way along the other side, we came to another separation from the summit, this one filled by a snow bridge. The descent on either side was awesomely steep and long, dropping without obstruction for more than a thousand feet. A fall would be deadly. The bridge, perhaps thirty feet across, was a wedge of compacted snow tapering at the top to a narrow crest, only inches wide. After respectful contemplation, we prepared to cross. I found a secure stance among the rocks to belay Gus with the rope. Straddling the bridge with a leg dangling down each side, Gus hunched along on his seat and hands. This was no place for elegance. Safely across, he secured the rope for my crossing.

The next tricky part was to step around a jutting corner at the end of the bridge. The hand and foot holds were generous and more than adequate, yet, as we shifted our bodies around to more secure footing on the other side, we were briefly suspended over empty space plummeting straight down. At such times, it is best to concentrate on the careful placement of the next hand or foot.

We were almost there. Scaling another steep but short section, we crossed yet another ridge. Descending a bit on the opposite side and working west along a short ledge, the summit was a mere two hundred feet above us, so close, but to our dismay, so far. Before us was a nearly vertical rock face thirty feet high, with no projections or fissures. At the far left, the ledge on which we stood petered out to nothing, at the right a narrow crack slanted upward for about twenty feet. Above the face, it was clear sailing to the top, but how could we manage the blank wall?

"Maybe I can get up here, Gus," I said, pointing to the crack. "What do you think?"

“I think it's too tough, Bill. The exposure is terrific. If we slipped, nothing would stop our fall for hundreds of feet. It won't work. I don't think we should risk it."

We glumly surveyed the scene. It was a bad situation. Though we had a short rope, we had not brought other equipment, believing that technical climbing was not necessary on Granite Peak. By climbing down a couple of hundred feet and working beyond the face further to the west, an alternate route seemed possible, though we could not be sure. But, we were running out of time. It was well past mid-afternoon. Getting back to camp would require hours of strenuous effort and we were tired now. If we had brought more gear, especially our sleeping bags, we could have bivouacked for the night and tried a different approach in the morning. But, we didn't have the equipment with us.

Sadly, two hundred feet short of the summit, we turned around for the long hike back. More skillful, more determined climbers, would perhaps have triumphed. For us, however, prudence was in order. We had come to the wilderness for enjoyment, refreshment, and spiritual renewal; the mountaintop was only a secondary objective. To press beyond the boundaries of our personal limits was to risk too much, there was a stewardship involved. Our decision was conditioned by family obligations and by our sense of responsibility to God Himself. We were His servants. To hazard our lives by venturing beyond the margin of reasonable safety was to gamble with property that belonged to Someone else.

So, we descended. It was not the first time we had failed to achieve a summit. Perhaps it was just as well. We might try again another time as we had done with other mountains. For now, we had done our best. Though minor miscalculations prevented our full accomplishment, ninety-nine percent was not to be despised.

Our return to camp was relatively uneventful. If the laborious footwork of the morning was demanding and tiresome, it can easily be imagined how much more so it was going back. Only the modest benefit of going downhill made it bearable at all. The sun had set long before we finally arrived at the tent, which we could barely find in the failing light.

By the time we completed our late meal it was utterly dark. We were too tired to be much interested in goats or stars. With great relief, we laid our worn-out bodies in our sleeping bags. Our Scripture passage and prayers were brief this night, but sincerely filled with praise and thanksgiving.

We slept later than usual the next morning after the exertions of the previous two days. That meant our arrival home would not be until the early hours of the next day, but it was a choice we happily made. After breakfast, we reversed our previous route down the mountain.

Walking in quiet contemplation our thoughts were a mixture of contradictions: disappointment over not making the summit, satisfaction in the trip itself, eagerness to see our families again, and genuine sadness that the adventure was ending. As usual, we both agreed that this was it, our last climb; we were getting too old for such demanding toil. Yet I knew, and I knew that Gus knew, too, that we didn't mean it. Two days of our normal daily routine and we would again be dreaming of the next jaunt, scanning the maps for another challenge.

As we hiked down the trail, following the zigzag switchbacks, we were each absorbed in our own inner world. I pondered the marvel of the mountain goats that had provided such a pleasant addition to our trip, and recalled an incident from the Bible. After an incredible ordeal of suffering, the wise man Job, had a conversation with God. Protesting his innocence, he challenged the Lord that he did not deserve to be so severely afflicted, for he had served Him faithfully. God did not answer his charge, but instead reviewed with Job some of the wonders of his creation, revealing thereby His overwhelming greatness. One of the questions He asked Job was, "Do you know when the mountain goats give birth?" Like the other questions, it was designed to reveal Job's limited understanding of the world, and by contrast, God's omniscient greatness. God who created the goats knows all about them: when the young are conceived, how long is their gestation, when and where they are born, how they develop and grow to maturity. Though they dwell among the lofty crags, far removed from the normal habitations of men, they are clearly visible to the all-seeing eye of God.

To men they are a mystery. Born in the spring when the snow lies deep upon the remote high passes, only a handful of the most curious and energetic people will spend the time and effort to discover the newborn kids. The great multitude of mankind will never see a wild goat except in a zoo or national park. Though the animal about which God questioned Job is not the same species as the

North American mountain goat, all wild goats inhabit remote areas of rough, steep cliffs.

It had been our great privilege to observe them in their natural home. Though not present at the time of birth, it had been our good fortune to experience a brief encounter with the goats in their own habitat, perhaps something that Job himself had not been able to do. It was as if we had entered the secret chambers of God Himself, for like the goats, He inhabits even the inaccessible heights. Seeing His creatures and traversing their remote homeland, we could almost say, "Yes," to God's question. If we had not been present *when* they gave birth, we had at least seen *where* they were born. Our reaction was like Job's, producing humble praise. To encounter the wonders of the world is to reveal its Creator as more wondrous still.

So we left the heights to return home to civilization. The mountains, indeed, belong to the wild goats (Psalm 104:18), their permanent inhabitants. But the goats, the mountains, the whole universe, including ourselves, belong to Him who made them all.

Chapter Six

STREAMS IN THE WILDERNESS

Then will the lame leap like a deer,
and the mute tongue shout for joy.
Water will gush forth in the wilderness
and streams in the desert. Isaiah 35:6

I have lived most of my life in cities located on the shores of large rivers. In Duluth, the St. Louis River formed the headwater of vast Lake Superior. The great Mississippi wended through the Twin Cities of Minneapolis and St. Paul on its journey to the Gulf of Mexico. In Washington State, Spokane was named for its river, as was Des Moines in Iowa. While rivers are important for transport and drinking water, it is unfortunate that the aesthetic appeal of many urban streams, hemmed in by buildings, constricted by banks, levees, and dams, and often burdened with soil from surrounding farmlands, is often severely marred.

It was the unconfined and undomesticated rivers that stirred my youthful pulse, wild streams of the countryside, forests, and mountains. Along the North shore of Lake Superior were small, but unrestrained rivers that tumbled down the hills into the vast lake; the Lester, French, Knife,

Gooseberry, and Baptism Rivers. In the spring, they roared with melting snow, and fishermen flocked to them when trout season opened. The lively waters were magnetic, powerfully drawing people to watch their swirling, turbulent discharge. Whatever the size or character of the water, I too, was entranced.

Away from the lake, on Highway 53 leading to the Iron Range, the Cloquet River, Helwig Creek, and the Whiteface River, flowing smooth and dark through bogs, prairies, and woodlands, intrigued me. How I wished to fish in them, follow their twists and turns, and discover their hidden secrets. Yet, when I was able to drive and could inspect them if I wished, I bypassed them all for the unknown country further north.

With my brothers Tom, Kenny, and Denny, we drove and walked the dirt roads and trails of the Superior National Forest. Sparsely inhabited except by wild creatures, including the ruffed grouse we were hunting, it was ours to explore and enjoy, federal land open to all for recreation. Lumbering and mining were nearly over, settled communities were few and small. More than the hunting, there was a magic about the land itself that lodged deep within me. The streams had special fascination.

Little Isabella River was the first that I can recall by name. Just north of Highway One, along the Little Isabella Road, was a favorite place for us to hunt. Where the river gurgled under a wooden bridge, I stood and watched the water sliding by. It was only a tiny stream in a vast land of swamps, brooks, rivers, and lakes, melt waters from a bygone ice age. It was dark and mysterious, different from home-area streams. Most of those ran to the east, into Lake Superior and the Great Lakes. Not far to the west of Duluth, rivers flowed southward, on a long journey to the Gulf of Mexico. The Little Isabella, however, was northern water. The small swirls, eddies, and bubbles that

I watched from the bridge were on their way to Rainy Lake, Lake Winnipeg, the Nelson River, and distant Hudson Bay.

The Stony River was another early discovery. Meandering for forty miles through swamps, lakes, and streambeds, I first found it where it passes under a bridge at the edge of Slate Lake. It seemed irresistibly "fishy," as the water swirled over and around the numerous rocks. I was greatly intrigued each time I crossed its dark, bouldery water, but I was always headed somewhere else. Then one day, on our way to Birch Lake, Shirley's dad, Erv, and I, finally stopped to discover what lurked beneath its surface. Half an hour of fruitless casts was disappointing. Just as we had decided to give it up, I had a vicious strike, the rod bent in huge bow, and the line peeled off, but not for long. With a sharp "zing," the line broke, and my eager excitement with it. It was almost certainly a large northern pike with a mouth full of razor-edged teeth.

Another time the Stony was more rewarding. Shirley's brothers and I were fishing where it enters Birch Lake. Gary hooked something on the bottom and to our surprise, he did not reel in a fish, but a perfectly good fishing rod and reel that he used for several years. A while later, Phil had a strike. Steadfast cranking finally brought it in, a ten-pound walleye, too big for the net, but he finally managed to get into the boat.

It was the Kawishiwi River, however, more than any other stream in the canoe country that symbolized for me the enchantment of the wilds and the fascination of flowing water. I first crossed it driving east from Ely on the Fernberg Road, where the river enters the north end of Birch Lake. At a nearby Forest Service campground, I walked along the river's bank and watched its sinuous flow, voicing the syllables of its name, letting them glide across my tongue and lips. They whispered of mystery and beauty, the past and unknown. On this occasion I was unable to explore the river and its lands, but I would return in years to come.

Back home, a little map work and reading, expanded my awareness. The Kawishiwi's alluring waters flow through an area of beautiful lakes and hundreds of square miles of forest, abounding in deer, moose, bear, wolves, and smaller animals. Walleyes and northern pike swam in its depths. In former years, Indians lived along its banks, at some places leaving their mysterious pictographs, visible still today. The name they gave to the river is of uncertain meaning. A book on Minnesota geographical names explains it as "river full of beaver, or muskrat, houses." Sigurd Olson, however, in his book, *Singing Wilderness*, derives it from the Chippewa, "Kawashaway," for "land of no place between," meaning an enchanted land of the spirits, belonging to the departed dead of ancient generations, a region forbidden to the living.

After a handful of approaches to the Kawishiwi country, the time came at last to enter it fully, and to encounter the river itself. With a group of men and their sons, we set out on a canoe trip, embarking on Lake One, or more precisely, at Lake One Landing, where the Kawishiwi flows out of the lake in a broad spread of water. A short distance to the west, small rapids indicate the river's decline. We were traveling east, however, paddling upstream through the number lakes, One, Two, Three, and Four.

Scott, age 10, was my bowman. Leading the others, we traveled northeast through a narrow defile about 50 feet wide and a quarter mile long, then turned south as the lake broadened to a half mile in width. An hour later, the route turned to the east where the lake spread in all directions. With many islands and bays, we had to pay careful attention to the map and compass. No route marker appeared on the flashing water and no beacon signaled from the distant shore. Only an invisible force deflecting a tiny sliver of metal gave clue to our direction on the trackless water.

Though seldom-used muscles were severely tried by our exertions, our pleasure in paddling was delightful. Engaged in the repetitive swing of the paddles, our minds were unencumbered, set free to absorb the powerful wilderness, to ponder the issues of life and existence, or to simply appreciate the joy of being. This pronounced contrast to our normal daily routines was a deep satisfaction, engaging us in a pattern of living at the most basic level.

The great forest around us, though unknown and uninhabited, was solid, secure, and familiar land. The river and lakes were another matter, spreading everywhere and allowing us easy passage, but were tenuous, fragile liquid, an alien medium for creatures of another environment, yet alluring and powerfully attractive.

How can one account for the mystique of water? I do not know. Perhaps it is the challenge of the visual barrier. Except for the narrow shoreline shallows, the eye cannot penetrate the deeper regions, hindering the scrutiny of wondering watchers. It may be that the tantalizing glimpses at the water's margin, is what sets up our intrigue over the unseen depths. The opaque earth, which also teems with unobservable life, offers no ready window to its hidden secrets. We seldom think of what lies beneath our feet since it remains out of sight. But stimulated by its shoreline transparency, we continually try to peer beneath the waves.

Or could its unsubstantial surface be the magnet that draws us, provoking our efforts to overcome the thin, elusive material? Even if there is no need to cross a body of water, there is still an overwhelming compulsion to be out upon it. So with rafts, canoes, and boats, we venture out in indirect mastery, suggesting to me that the unconscious attraction may be an inner wish to actually *walk* on it! Who has not felt an exhilarating delight in walking on the frozen surface of a lake in winter? Unfortunately, to saunter over the waves is beyond human capacity.

Little wonder, then, that the first followers of Jesus, were astonished and terrified, when out in a boat on Lake Galilee, they saw Him actually walking upon the water. Fulfilling an Old Testament statement about God who "stretched out the skies and treads upon the waves of the sea," (Job 9:8), Jesus displayed His undeniable deity. To walk on water is child's play for a God who can create it from nothing. In all likelihood, Jesus did this astounding feat to demonstrate that He truly was and is God! If He was only a man, like us, He could do no such thing.

Since we could not hike across the water, we did the next best thing, paddling our slim canoes across the tantalizing surface, reveling in its mystery and charm. The river's course through the lake was not discernable until we reached the far shore, where we found it tumbling down a boulder field from a small pond a short distance way. Unloading our canoes, we carried everything across the 30 rod (165 yard) portage. Loading everything back in the boats, we paddled across in ten minutes, and then portaged again, this time for 45 rods, into Lake Two. The rapids were not powerful or dangerous, simply too shallow and filled with boulders for the canoes to navigate.

As we walked each portage, it was readily apparent that these were well-used trails. Only scant vegetation survived the tread of thousands of passing feet. For decades, recreational canoers skirted the Kawishiwi rapids at these passageways. Before them in bygone centuries, fur traders and Indians used the same routes. And for millennia before that, the Kawishiwi fell downhill under the force of gravity, on its way to Hudson Bay and the Atlantic Ocean.

Somewhere on Lake Three, we camped for the night. It had been a full day of paddling, portaging, setting up camp, and making dinner. But no one had enough of the water. In the evening, everyone was out fishing or exploring the shore until it was time to head for the tents.

Next morning, we paddled to the end of Lake Four where three narrow bays intersected, at a portage around another Kawishiwi rapids, followed in quick succession by two more, leading into Hudson Lake. Another hour of paddling brought us to one more portage, this one longer at 105 rods. Then at last, we were in Lake Insula, a superb lake of substantial size, filled with numerous islands and many bays. It, too, was part of the Kawishiwi watershed.

In late afternoon we found a campsite on a ragged peninsula on the west shore. As before, once finished with dinner, we were back to the water, swimming, paddling, and fishing. We decided to stay for two nights, allowing for a "day off" from normal travel the following day.

When morning came, some of the crew went off to fish for the day, while the rest of us wanted to see some Indian pictographs a few miles away. Paddling to the northeast end of Insula, we followed the Kawishiwi to the south end of Lake Alice, then over a couple of portages further east. The clear, dark water was a liquid roadway through the trees: jack pine, balsam fir, birch, and alder, along with occasional white and red pines. Turning south toward Fishdance Lake, we came to some cliffs extending forty feet above the water. Paddling close to the rocks, we found the red images left by Indians long ago. They were a bit indistinct; one seemed to me like a Japanese torii, and another like a weeping sun.

What did they mean and how old were they? No one now knows. They are scattered all over the North Country, and were there when first Europeans entered the land. Made by mixing iron oxide with animal fat, they are nearly all located on a sheer rock face, about as high up as a person could reach from a canoe on the water. Were they simply random doodles, like the hand prints and wavy lines found in some places? Or merely sketches of animals (moose, deer) and abstract designs. Or did they have magical or religious meanings? The mystery remains.

After taking pictures, we made our way to shore where we beached the canoes, and hiked to the top of the cliff. The view was marvelous. At our feet blueberries grew in profusion, which we cheerfully ate. Cal thought a fallen twenty-foot long tree trunk would make a big splash. It did indeed, piercing the lake like huge spear, then rocketing back out of the water, and then falling flat on the surface, surrounded by expanding rings of ripples.

Eventually we headed back to camp, paddling back downstream on the Kawishiwi. The helping current was hardly noticeable since the river drainage is nearly flat. Only at the few portages was there a modest gradient, where the water flowed from one level to a lower one. The blueberries we had enjoyed, the tree trunk we had launched into the lake, the surrounding greenery, and of course, the lakes and streams themselves, were continually dependent on the constant fall of precipitation and the natural irrigation system that laced it together.

That very morning it had rained, causing mild inconvenience in preparing breakfast, but reminding us of its necessity in sustaining life. Urban dwellers that we were, and though living in the most intensely agricultural state in the nation, we often thought merely of rain's hindrance to an afternoon of golf, or when it came too precipitously, of its expense and damage as a flood.

But farmers in all places and times know otherwise. The waters from above and those pooled on the earth below are critically necessary for life itself. A bygone sage expressed it well, and gave credit to its source.

He makes springs pour water into the ravines;
it flows between the mountains.
They give water to all the beasts of the field;
the wild donkeys quench their thirst.
The birds of the air nest by the waters;
they sing among the branches.
He waters the mountains from his upper chambers,
the earth is satisfied by the fruit of his work.
He makes grass grow for the cattle,
and plants for man to cultivate,
bringing forth food from the earth:
wine that gladdens the heart of man,
oil to make his face shine,
and bread that sustains his heart.
The trees of the LORD are well watered,
the cedars of Lebanon that he planted.
Ps. 104:10-16

As we retraced our course on the Kawishiwi, it was no longer full of beaver houses; they were far scarcer than in the days of the earliest settlers. The notion of a spirit land seemed far more attractive. For me, it was a land of fascination, filled with the memories of bygone peoples: the original Indian dwellers, the fur-trading voyageurs, the lumberjacks and miners who followed them, and the recreational canoers who came still later. Above all, the river and its surrounding territory, extending across the U.S.-Canadian border into the far North, as much water as land, seemed to reveal the world as it was, a primeval creation unspoiled by the intrusion of men and machines. The Kawishiwi captured all - past and present, substance and spirit.

In later years I paddled several other rivers in the BWCA, and in other states, too; the Spokane in Washington, the St. Joe in Idaho, the Cedar,

Wapsipinicon, Boone, Iowa, and Des Moines in Iowa. They each had their particular pleasures and charms, but the more remote and wild they were, the more enchanting their waters seemed. Still, water anywhere, is an irresistible attraction.

The short rivers of western Florida offered a measure of special interest, because of their spring-fed clarity and the novelty of their wildlife. On the final day of one of our visits to the state, Shirley and I paddled down the Weeki Wachee in a rented canoe. The winding route was through a protected natural habitat, until the final mile where it joined the Gulf of Mexico. The startling clarity of the water was absorbing. Fish swam in perfect view from above. Along the tree-lined banks, egrets, anhingas, herons, and blue jays preened and calmly watched our quiet passing. The current was relatively easy, causing little difficulty except at some sharp bends in the channel.

Then at a deeper section, in an off-set pool at a turn in the stream, we saw our first wild manatee, "wild," meaning non-captive, for they are the most docile of animals. There were two of them, about ten feet long, weighing 800-1,000 pounds, and grayish-brown in color. They had a bulbous snout, large flippers, and a huge paddle-shaped tail. They made no effort to swim away, but simply remained in place as we floated by, just over their backs. It was a marvelous experience, seeing such an unusual creature in its own habitat, and at such close proximity. I thought of paddling back for another look but decided not to disturb them any further. With its unexpected surprise, it was a very pleasant paddle and a delightful way to end our visit. We were eager to explore southern water again in the future.

When we moved to Florida, we often went for a day of recreation at Rainbow Springs State Park. The Rainbow River, is only ten miles long, from its spring-fed source to its juncture with the Withlacootche River, but is the clearest water I have ever seen, bubbling up from limestone formations, so transparent that if the water was deep enough, the bottom would be visible at a depth of 225 feet! Since it is actually only ten to twenty feet deep, every stone, plant, and fish could be seen. Though houses line the west bank, the east side parkland is natural vegetation. Despite the attraction of its crystalline water, its popularity and only semi-natural setting diminished its wild character.

Rivers that ran directly into the Gulf of Mexico were more attractive in their wilderness appeal. The Chassahowitzka, Homossassa, and the Weeki Wachee carried daunting names but lovely water. Like the Rainbow, their source was not just rainfall, but pressurized water surging from the underlying rock. Completely fresh at the start of their flow, they soon mingled with the salt water of the Gulf, offering a habitat for both freshwater and marine wildlife.

One of our best trips on these streams was a pontoon boat ride down the Homossassa with family members, Dick and Judi, and Phil and Berta. With no paddling, plenty of food, and Dick at the wheel, it was easy going. Beside countless birds, we spent several minutes watching manatees calmly resting in the water. In strong contrast to their repose, we were thrilled to see dolphins dashing through the water, *and out of it*, as they engaged in aerial displays for our entertainment. The Florida rivers and their novel creatures are delightful.

Whether in the north or the south, east or west, flat water and slanting streams sustain life and give especial pleasure to humankind. I cannot really say that I like rivers and streams more than lakes or oceans. I treasure them all. They are inseparable segments of a fabric of necessity and delight. Warm air evaporates moisture that rises until it condenses as rain, flowing again to the great basins of water, where it begins once more in a ceaseless process that at least two sacred writers mention (Job 36:27, Ecclesiastes 1:7). I find great satisfaction, that God, who planned and created the water cycle, designed His human creatures to enjoy water for pleasure, as much as utilizing it for life-necessity. With eager anticipation, I await the next discovery of rushing water, wherever I may find it.

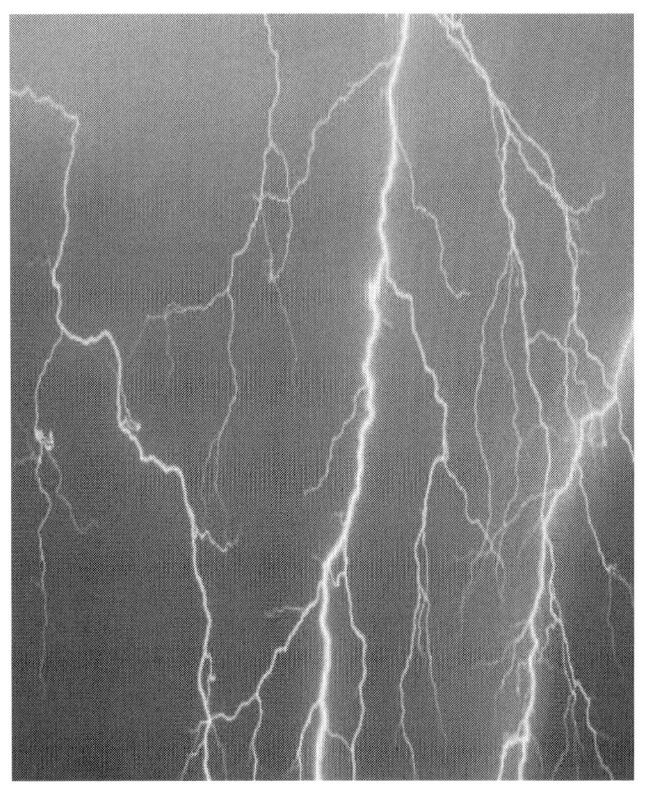

Chapter Seven

SUMMER STORM

He spoke and stirred up a tempest.
He stilled the storm to a whisper.
Psalm 107:25, 29

We were camping on Lake One. I was "home" again, after living for several years in Washington State. Now Scott and I were together once more in the Minnesota wilderness. Though he had joined me for a few outings in the West, we had not been together in the canoe country for more than ten years. Then he had been just an early teen-ager, now he was a grown man. Our pleasure at being together again was the richer for sharing as adults; now he was a peer, a comrade in wilderness adventure, an adult friend, as well as my son. What a treasure it is when parents and children share bonds of affection and interest, as well as ties of blood.

In my early years, I had explored and hunted on the southern fringe of Minnesota's Boundary Waters Canoe Area. The region from Two Harbors on the shore of Lake Superior northward to the Isabella Lake territory had been a happy hunting ground for my brothers Tom, Denny,

Kenny, and me. After marriage and moving to the Twin Cities, only occasional visits provided opportunities to fish with Shirley's dad and her brothers. When Scott was about five years old, however, he became a frequent companion in my jaunts. When he was ten, we paddled the Isabella-Island River area together, and at thirteen, he was with me when I led a group of fathers and sons on a canoe trip along the Kawishiwi River system.

Now we were back again in the Kawishiwi country, where the river ran through Lake One, Two, Three, and Four. Did some early geographer or explorer grow tired of finding names for the countless lakes, resorting to unimaginative numbering to ease his task? How much more satisfying are the names of four lakes a bit farther north in Canada – This Man's Lake, That Man's Lake, Other Man's Lake, and No Man's Lake! Happily, the American lakes are more beautiful than their colorless designations. Irregular as splatters of spilled blue paint, and studded by islands of every size, the lakes tip gently westward along the flow of the river from Lake Four in the east to Lake One in the west.

Because I had a recent kidney stone scare, we decided against making a normal circle route. Instead, we camped at the west end of Lake One and made day trips to various places, or simply stayed put as we chose. Our leisurely objective was merely to share together the fascination of the wild, unspoiled country. Without schedules to keep, predetermined miles to travel, or finding and setting up of nightly campsites, we enjoyed the luxury of unhurried relaxation. We fished but only casually. We explored the lakes, circling islands, inspecting unknown shorelines, and investigating tiny creeks in out-of-the-way bays. We swam in the cool amber water, soaked up the hot sunshine, and stared into evening fires for hours. It was a time of perfect communion with the wilderness, with each other, and with God as well.

One day we journeyed to the east. Without haste or fatigue, our strokes bit deep into the water, powerfully driving our cedar strip canoe, slicing through the water mile after mile, trailing a ribbon of foam behind. Portages took but a few minutes, with no wasted motion and little effort. It was a day of zest and pleasure, enjoyed to the utmost.

Adding special charm to this memorable day, we observed two "spectacles" as we paddled into Lake Three. Along the shore, we spotted a magnificent bald eagle perched in a tree. We drew closer for a better view but as we did so, we saw a still more intriguing sight. A dark form was moving in the water ahead of us. As we came nearer, we could see it was a large northern pike with its head completely out of the water. For at least a minute it swam before us with its huge jaws slowly opening and closing, then it sank out of sight. From the size of its head, it appeared to have been at least ten pounds in weight. Was it sick or simply being "playful"? We could not know. We had never before seen such a thing, but it is novelties like these that make wilderness experience so enjoyable.

The eagle in the tree allowed us a splendid view. A massive head of brilliant white crowned its huge dark brown body. Steady yellow eyes, down-hooked beak, and powerful talons gave it a look of ferocious strength and unruffled dignity. To behold our national emblem in living reality, free, strong, and like us, "at home" in the Kawishiwi country, was a deeply satisfying pleasure.

Another day we traveled west, into little Confusion Lake, then down the Kawishiwi. The fish were not biting - but we didn't care. What was important was to be alive, to take full enjoyment in just "being." The sun was bright and warm, gleaming upon the flashing waters. The sky was a vast ocean for great white galleons. A tangle of trees and shrubs blanketed the land in every direction.

What made it all so attractive, so riveting? Surely many would see it as desolate, foreboding, perhaps even frightening. To me, however, it was utterly absorbing, each new vista as the river twisted and turned, captivating and enchanting. I wanted to take it all in, to internalize it, not in any intellectual comprehension, but in a union of identity, a oneness of belonging. Beauty, solitude, silence, a presence of wild creatures - these and perhaps other subtle elements composed an inner yearning. I understand it no better now after many years than in my first encounters as a youth. I suspect, however, that what I really crave is more than flowers, birds, lakes, and islands. Rather, there is a hunger for communion, a burning desire to know and to share, to communicate with the marvels of creation, and even more, with the Creator.

I do not talk to plants or hug trees, but I do resonate with the Bible's poetic imagery of inanimate nature voicing praise to God. The rivers clap their hands and the mountains break forth in singing (Ps 98:8). The trees, too, sing and clap (I Chron. 16:33, Is 55:12). Jesus, at His triumphal entry into Jerusalem, said that if His disciples restrained their cries of praise, the very rocks would proclaim the honors of the King (Luke 19:40). Perhaps my wonder, awe, and longing in and for the wilderness, are really an attempt to pierce the veil of the physical and to engage the Spirit, to commune with Ultimate Reality.

Our day passed in pleasant enjoyment. We loafed, fished a little, pushed through a mucky swamp until stopped by a beaver dam, laughed a lot, nibbled smoked almonds, but mostly we feasted our souls on the majestic presence of (and the Presence in!) the wilderness. We saw only one other canoe throughout the day. Late in the afternoon, we returned to our camp, richer and fuller than when we left.

Years after this event I came across a statement that gave me encouragement to believe I was not some kind of wilderness wacko. C. S. Lewis, one of the most profound thinkers of the twentieth century, also had great emotional surges in wilderness encounters. In an essay entitled, *The Weight of Glory*, Lewis said we want to do far more than to simply behold beauty. Our real desire, he explained, is to be united with it, to enter into it and receive it internally, to be immersed in it until we are one with it.

I was not alone, then, in my deep, inarticulate longing! Someone smarter than I felt it, too. Surely, there are others as well, with whom these words will strike a chord of recognition.

Like the others, our last day was full of small satisfactions. We treasured our companionship and prized our shared activities through a day of singular beauty. After dinner, we gave the fish one last chance.

"Well, Dad," Scott said, "it's been a great week. Even the weather has been super. The sky tonight is fantastic."

Scott was right about the sunset. It was gorgeous, a magnificent kaleidoscope of changing hues, shifting from yellow to orange to crimson, with a multitude of shades between. Low in the northwest, however, was a broad band of cloud with a hard edge of purple.

"You said it, son. We've never had a better time or finer weather. I wonder about that cloud, though. It looks a bit suspicious. Maybe it won't amount to anything but a change could be coming. We're certainly overdue for rain, but we couldn't ask for a more beautiful evening, right now."

Indeed, our final evening could hardly be improved upon. Though there was a whiff of breeze in the highest treetops, the water of the small bay was like glass. With every shoreline doubled in mirror image, reality and reflection were difficult to separate. As lofty clouds floated upon the water, only the ripples of our lures disturbed the illusion of two skies. As before, the fish were not interested in our enticements, which was of small importance in the perfection of the evening. Fortunately, there is more to fishing than catching fish.

At length we returned to camp. Ignoring the irksome mosquitoes, we sat up late, before a glowing fire. We were reluctant to end a superb day and unenthusiastic about rejoining civilization on the day to come. Sipping hot chocolate and needlessly tending the fire, we attempted to restrain the passage of a golden time in our lives, a few days to be treasured to the utmost. Like water seeping through enclosed fingers, the most precious of life's events trickle away in an irreversible cascade of seconds and minutes. At best, they can be dimly preserved in memory, cherished anew, though with fading precision, in years to come.

Yielding to the inevitable, we headed for the tent. Giving thanks to the Lord was easy this night, for we had much for which we were truly grateful. For a long while I looked out across the dark water, filled with profound love for the gifts He had given me, especially for Scott sleeping beside me, and for Shirley, and the girls at home in the city. Eventually sleep closed my mind.

Sometime in the night, I woke up. I was not groggy and confused, struggling for consciousness, nor startled wide-awake in alarm. I was merely conscious of listening, piecing together vague hints of awareness. It was fully dark outside, darker than when we had lain down to sleep. I could see no stars or tinge of dawn in the east. Without bothering to look at my watch, I guessed it might be sometime after midnight.

A high murmur in the trees revealed a rising wind though no waves were stirring the lake. Except for Scott's quiet breathing, everything was still. Then from far to the west I heard a low rumble, not loud or long, but an almost certain sign of things to come; it would rain after all. No matter, we were snug for the night and a wet day would be of slight significance since we had only a few miles to paddle back to the car. With the puzzle solved, I fell asleep again.

I awoke a second time, this time checking my watch. It was nearly two. A muffled boom sounded, some distance to the west, followed by a brief flicker, a bare hint of lightning still far off. Other dull rumbles of thunder succeeded the first. I lay listening as the storm advanced, intrigued as always by the power of the elements.

Because we usually seek shelter during violent weather, people often miss unusual but fascinating phenomena. One of the strangest experiences of my life had occurred several years before, barely sixty miles from where we were now camped. Scott was with me then, along with Shirley's dad, Erv, and her brother Phil. We were fishing on Greenwood Lake when a fast-moving thunderstorm approached from the west.

Since the walleyes were biting, we stayed as long as possible, expecting lightning and high winds at any time. Just before we headed for shore, an incredible phenomenon occurred.

As we made our final casts, our monofilament lines actually floated in the air, forming symmetrical arcs from our rod tips to the bobbers resting on the water. They remained suspended in the air, defying the law of gravity. If we shook the rod tips vigorously, the lines would fall gently to the surface and sink as they normally did. Reeling in and casting out again, however, the aerial arches would form again. We had never seen such a thing before or since, nor have I heard of others reporting similar happenings. Yet, happen, it did. I suspect the nylon lines developed a static charge of electricity in the ionized air of the approaching thunderstorm. We did not prolong our "experiment," for before we reached the shore, the rain was pelting down.

Who knows what other mysteries might be discovered when the skies convulse and the earth shudders? To be sure, danger is undeniably real when the winds shriek and lightning sears the air. The curious and the bold, however, sometimes risk the odds to investigate. The story of John Muir climbing to the top of a tall tree in a storm, letting it whip him back and forth in the fury of the wind, has always captured my imagination, though I have not chosen to follow his example. While prudence dictates a need for reasonable caution, how much of reality do we miss because we are such fair-weather, daytime beings? The realm of night is largely unknown since we hide indoors surrounded by artificial daylight. The winter season remains unexplored except by a hardy few. Who has sought to discover what the birds do in heavy fog or how the deer take shelter from the hail? Of earth's continual wonders and surprises, we have perhaps barely scratched the surface.

As I continued to listen, the storm drew closer, thunderclaps becoming more distinct, louder, and longer. Brilliant lightning blazed nearer and more often, filling the tent with brightness. Thunder and flash were becoming simultaneous. Scott was now fully awake.

"We're in for a doozey," I said. "I hope we've got all our gear stowed away."

At that moment, a blinding bolt lit up the night. A sizzling crackle hissed through the air, ending in a thunderous explosion. The ground itself seemed to shake.

"Wow, that was close," Scott, said. "And loud! I like my fireworks a bit further away."

In the quiet between thunderclaps, we heard the first gentle drops of rain, a light "plop" on the tent fly, a "blip" on a leaf outside, a "splat" on the ground in front, quiet little sputters here and there. Then they stopped, but only for a few moments. They started again, with quicker pace and volume, though still merely a soft splatter sifting through the trees. Knowing what was to come, I unzipped my bag and stepped out of the tent to see that everything was secured. Stowing a few things under some rocks and gathering towels and swim trunks off our clothesline, I ducked back into the tent. We did not yet close the storm flap but watched in fascination as the elements came storming into action.

Now the rain began to come in earnest, beating down in liquid pellets, drumming a staccato rhythm on our nylon roof, roiling the lightning-illumined surface of the lake into spikes and pits. The driving rain intensified to a downpour, then a deluge, pounding with such force and frequency that splash from the ground forced us at last to zip the tent shut. We were not alarmed for we had been in storms before and our tent had weathered them all, though as the rain hammered down, we hoped no seams would leak. Of course, the rain was of little consequence, for being wet in summer is seldom a danger. Being hit by lightning was another matter, but the odds of a direct strike in a vast forest were minutely small. More likely, was the possibility of being struck by a falling object, for winds break limbs and may uproot trees completely. Mindful of remote possibilities I silently committed us to the safekeeping of our Heavenly Father.

The flashes and crashes continued to increase in number and magnitude. Repeatedly, electric charges split the sky in white-hot fury, shattering the darkness with incandescent radiance. The thunder was astounding, erupting in shuddering peals overhead, cannonading down the open reaches of water, and ricocheting among the islands. Separated from the elements by a mere wisp of nylon, we were in intimate contact with their violent energy, engulfed in turbulent chaos. Fortunately, the winds were not too severe and our sturdy tent kept us dry.

At length the fury of the storm began to subside as its center passed beyond us to the east. Dazzling flashes were replaced by more distant glimmers, deafening rolls by fading rumble, flailing limbs by limp, sodden branches.

The rain, too, had lessened to a light but steady throbbing, then to a muted drip, falling from open skies and slipping from every needle, leaf, and stalk. Spent of its violent power, the storm for us had faded in exhaustion.

In the Bible, such dynamic outbursts of natural forces are often described as displays of God's power and majesty. In bold metaphor the wind, thunder, and lightning are described as His breath, voice, and flaming darts. Psalm 29 is a magnificent example, a sublime poem exalting the glory of God, which uses not only the storm imagery, but even its literary structure to magnify the transcendent sovereignty of the all powerful Creator.

1 Ascribe to the Lord, O mighty ones,
ascribe to the Lord glory and strength.
2 Ascribe to the Lord the glory due His name.
worship the Lord in the splendor of His
holiness.

3 The voice of the Lord is over the waters;
the God of glory thunders,
the Lord thunders over the mighty waters.
4 The voice of the Lord is powerful;
the voice of the Lord is majestic.
5 The voice of the Lord breaks the cedars;
the Lord breaks in pieces the Cedars of
Lebanon.
6 He makes Lebanon skip like a calf,
Sirion like a young wild ox.
7 The voice of the Lord strikes
with flashes of lightning.
8 The voice of the Lord shakes the desert;
the Lord shakes the desert of Kadesh.
9 The voice of the Lord twists the oaks
and strips the forest bare.
And in his temple all cry, "Glory!"

10 The Lord sits enthroned over the flood;
and the Lord is enthroned as King forever.
11 The Lord gives strength to his people;
the Lord blesses his people with peace.

The storm is portrayed in forceful, moving imagery. Beginning over the offshore waters, the powerful winds rush inland, thundering over the mountains, breaking and uprooting even the giant cedars of Lebanon. So mighty is the storm that the Lebanon Mountains and lofty Mt. Hermon (Sirion), though grounded in the depths of the earth, are as wildly shaken as a leaping calf or ox. Lightning bolts flash, earthquakes convulse the distant desert, and the trees are stripped of leaves.

In reply, the fitting response of the heavenly beings is to utter a profoundly simple but eloquently expressive exclamation, "Glory!" They understand that the surging forces of nature are a material representation of the Sovereign's divine power, a conception given dramatic aliveness by the human author who seven times in as many verses, ascribes the natural phenomena to the "voice of the Lord."

The poet shows us still more, highlighted in modern translations, which separate verses one and two, and ten and eleven, from the storm section in verses three to nine. Rather than being identified *with* the storm as a mere extension of natural forces, the Lord is seen as distinct from the creation, calmly enthroned in heavenly glory. The storm occurs only by His permissive decree. Ruling as King over both nature and His human subjects, He rightly deserves worship, the acknowledgment of His greatness, glory, and splendor. To those caught up in the storms of life, physical or otherwise, He gives strength and peace to endure, for He is master of all. While not blind to earthly realities, the eye of the believer will behold in the fierce furies of nature, the awesome presence and power of almighty God.

The skeptic, of course, will reject the notion that a divine being is discernable in a storm or any natural event. Dismissing the sacred text as an ancient superstition, he will argue that wind, rain, and lightning are purely physical, ordinary occurrences, not the personal activity of a supernatural deity. To read such Biblical passages with wooden literalness, however, is to fail to give fair and intelligent judgment to its poetic character. The Psalmist no more imagines the thunder to be caused by the bellow of God's mighty voice than we do when with less beauty we describe it as the angels "bowling" in heaven. To say that it is raining cats and dogs, and coming down in buckets, is to go beyond literal precision in an attempt to express reality that often exceeds the limits of conventional language. Such figures of speech are a graphic device that all societies have found useful in communicating extraordinary, abstract, subtle, intimate, and ultimate truths.

The inspired writer, even if unaware of barometric pressure and cold fronts, is a keen observer and a masterful artist as he portrays the effect of the storm with impressive images. His real concern is not with the actual forces of nature but with their ultimate source, the mighty God who brought the world into being and arranged all its dynamic and powerful interactions. By describing a great storm, he draws our attention to the One who sets its forces in motion, thus commending our worshipful appreciation.

Modern awareness of the true magnitude of thunderstorms can only create yet more awe-stricken reverence for contemporary believers. Cumulonimbus cloud formations, rising to 40,000 feet and higher, are gigantic weather-makers, producing a variety of storm effects depending on conditions. Winds generated by the conflict of warm and cold air masses may easily reach fifty, occasionally upwards of one hundred, and when tornadoes are spawned, can surpass three hundred miles an hour. Explosive decompression occurs in the eye of the tornado, sucking up huge objects in its near vacuum, exhibiting astounding and capricious power, as in transporting entire buildings to other locations or shattering them to fragments.

Hail frequently accompanies the thunder and lightning, stones growing to golf ball and sometimes baseball size, at times covering the ground to a depth of several inches. Cloudbursts, devastating inundations of many inches of rain, are often triggered when certain conditions prevail. While thunderstorms are often very limited in size locally, storm systems of many associated cells can cover enormous areas of thousands of square miles.

The causes, development, and total effect of storms have become more fully understood during the past hundred years. With the invention of measuring and recording instruments, we can now properly appreciate a thunderstorm's incredible power. The statistics are truly astonishing. Lightning which generates the sound of thunder by heated compression of the air, can carry electrical charges of millions of volts and hundreds of thousands of amperes. At discharge, the temperature of surrounding air may exceed a million degrees! Bolts conducted horizontally between clouds may be as much as one hundred miles long. In recent years, newly discovered phenomena called red sprites, blue rays, and elves have added to the complexity of understanding a storm's visual display.

A single storm of ordinary size expends more energy than an atomic bomb and large storms may equal several hundred nuclear devices. Multiplying that force by the 1800 storms occurring *simultaneously* on the earth at any moment (more than 50,000 storms per day!), will provide some notion of the stupendous power of the weather.

Surrounded by the rage of the elements, His powerful majesty was vividly displayed to Scott and me. As the storm receded, we lapsed into fitful sleep, disturbed throughout the remaining night by the boom and crackle of more distant cells.

When morning arrived, the fireworks had vanished but the clouds continued to empty their vast reservoirs. The saturated air seemed like a barely thinner lake above ground. Wisps of fog shrouded the high trees. Incredibly, the downpour left no puddles. The thirsty ground, dry for several weeks, had swallowed it all, a voracious sponge absorbing the life-giving moisture, wicking every drop into billions of rootlets, filling the spaces between microscopic grains of earth, and raising the lakes and streams to more normal levels. Only in depressions in the rocks did the crystal liquid reveal its abundant, new presence.

As the rain continued, moderately now, yet unrelenting, we were not eager to be up and moving. We lay in our bags dozing off and on, waiting for clearing skies that did not come. Internal rumblings reminded us that it was well along toward breakfast time. To kindle and tend a fire in such weather would be a wet, messy chore, even with the dry wood that we had sheltered in anticipation of rain. As modern woodsmen, however, we were fortunate, not needing to depend on a wood fire for cooking. Opening the tent flap just beyond the end of my sleeping bag, I set up our little white-gas stove outside the tent but under the overhang of the roof. Putting on a kettle of water we had filled the night before, I began to prepare breakfast without getting up at all, still luxuriating in the soft cocoon of my warm bed!

In a few minutes, the water was boiling, ready for tea and instant cereal. However, a slight problem had to be solved. The food items were not at hand but dangled high in a tree out of reach of any bears. Since I was slaving over a hot stove, it was Scott's sad lot to make a hasty dash to bring home the groceries. With the chill rain as an incentive, he was soon back in his bag, waiting to be served at our recumbent table in the wilderness. Such are the privations in the far north at the tail end of a storm.

After stalling as long as we could, we gave in to necessity, striking our temporary home and paddling back to our car in the lingering rain. Until the last stroke of our paddles, we drank deeply of the surrounding glory, a Glory announced and displayed in a summer storm.

Chapter Eight

THE SKIES OF THOMAS

The heavens declare the glory of God,
the skies proclaim the work of His hands.
Psalm19:1

It was an afterthought that led us to Thomas Lake, and an error on a map that almost turned us away. We had been paddling the Kawishiwi River, territory familiar to me from previous journeys. At our midmorning "goody break," perhaps a quarter mile from the entrance into Alice Lake, we pulled our boats together, hooking our legs over the side of the next canoe to keep them clustered together. As our flotilla drifted slowly with the current, we passed a sack of nuts and candy from person to person. Everyone found something to enjoy as we engaged in friendly chitchat and drank deeply of the surrounding beauty. Idly scanning the maps during our pleasant lull, a new notion formed in my thoughts.

Scrutinizing the map more carefully, a new and not too demanding route seemed very inviting. From the narrow eastern arm of Alice Lake, a short portage into little Cacabic Lake, and another into Thomas Lake, would be an easy afternoon jaunt. It sounded good to the group, so we altered our plans, turning north, rather than further east. Resuming our paddling, we soon left the Kawishiwi to cross the sparkling waves of Alice, stopping for lunch a short distance from the portage to Cacabic.

During our lunch, as I looked again at the map, I noticed a discrepancy. The portage from Cacabic to Thomas was marked as a mere 32 rods, a trifling 175 yards. Yet, the orange line on the map was far too long. A mistake of some kind was apparent. Comparing the width of the land between the two lakes to the scale at the bottom of the map showed a true distance of 3/4ths of a mile! Checking a different map confirmed our unhappy discovery. An easy afternoon suddenly became a grueling chore for my rookie crew of three adults and four teen-agers.

"Well, gang, what do you want to do?" I asked. "We can go back across Alice and follow our original route, or we can tackle the long portage. I'll leave it up to you."

Groaning a bit over either alternative, they decided without much enthusiasm, to go ahead. Hoping to give encouragement for our formidable task, I gave them a brief pep talk.

"Thomas Lake is supposed to be beautiful. You'll be glad we went on. The portage will be tough but we can make it. When the trip is over you'll be proud of yourselves. In fact, it will be one of the highlights of the week."

I was not sure they believed me. There was uncertainty even in my own mind that Thomas Lake would be worth the effort, but we were committed.

Portaging into Cacabic and paddling its one-mile length was a breeze, highlighted by Shane's catch of a four-pound northern pike. Unloading at the trail to Thomas, I started out carrying the first canoe, Brent followed with another, and the rest of the crew carried packs and paddles. The portage climbed a hill for a short distance, and then stretched on, and on, and on. Actually, it was not too bad. The tormenting mosquitoes, however, were especially irksome when both hands were needed in balancing the canoe overhead. It was precarious to let go with one hand to take a wild swing at the vicious biters drilling on the other arm, but desperate measures are sometimes needed.

In one place, the trail descended to a swampy area where lengthwise poles had been laid down to give more secure footing. Rather than stumble off the slippery wood, I merely slogged between them in mud a few inches deep. A hundred yards later, the trail rose to solid ground again.

With each step, the seventy-pound burden of the canoe seemed to increase as muscles unaccustomed to strenuous demands sent hot, stabbing reminders down my arms and back. Eagerly I watched for canoe rests - sturdy poles secured horizontally between two trees - strategically located at half a dozen places along the trail. (These have since been removed due to changed regulations in the BWCA). At each one I leaned the forward end of the canoe on the bar located ten to twelve feet high, lowered the back end to the ground, and with delicious relief ducked out of the carrying yoke that formed the center thwart of the boat. A minute or two of rest did not really allow the weary body to recover, but it did provide a psychological boost. Stepping back under the canoe, lifting slightly and backing up a couple of feet to clear the bar, I continued onward.

At last, the glint of blue water was visible through the trees. Eager to escape my load, I increased my pace and soon reached a beautiful sand beach. With a surge of energy, I pushed the canoe upward, twisting my torso sideways and bending down at the same time. As the canoe arched down I flipped it over, just before catching it on my extended thigh, then slid it gently to the sand.

I was tired and beads of sweat trickled down my face and back. How inviting the glittering water looked, but it would have to wait. Since each of us had to make two carries across the portage to convey all our gear, there was much work still to be done. After the second trip a refreshing dip would be even more satisfying and needed, for we would all be wearier still after walking back for almost a mile, then bearing our final loads to Thomas. Thinking I should start back quickly and encourage the others, I retraced my steps.

Brent was almost at the lake. At irregular intervals Shane, Amy, and Doug came resolutely along. To each I gave cheerful approval, telling them it was not much further. Finally, Shirley, Bev, and Jules appeared, spattered with mud like the losers in a tug of war. What a sight they were! Bev especially, was daubed to the waist. Sputtering with mock indignation and hilarious laughter, they described how they tried, without success, to stay out of the swampy area by balancing on the slippery poles. Skidding off to the outside of the trail, Bev had been mired above her knees. Weighed down by a huge pack, she could not move. Helping comrades finally pulled her free but not without stumbling in the muck themselves. No real damage was done. Thomas Lake would clean most of the dirt from their grubby jeans. More thorough scrubbing could wait until our return home.

Eventually we all carried our loads across the long portage. Tired, sweaty, and muddy from our labors, we plunged into the warm waters of Thomas Lake for a well-earned swim - with our clothes on! Why not rinse bodies and clothes at the same time? After such hard work, our wet frolic was refreshing fun. In due time, we dripped back into the canoes and paddled a mile westward to camp on a lovely island. We would travel no further for the day. It was time to relax, to set up our simple housekeeping in the wilderness, and to marvel at yet another gem of the

Boundary Water's treasures. Thomas Lake was truly beautiful. It was the sky above the lake, however, that would reveal one spectacle after another, capturing our spellbound wonder.

After dinner chores were over, we broke up to follow individual pursuits - fishing, exploration, sketching, picture taking - whatever was of personal importance. Shirley and I went out again in the canoe, a voyager's holiday, perhaps, but this paddling was different from the focused effort of the earlier hours. Now was a time for easy finesse, for paddling with subtlety, extracting the last bit of motion before silently dipping the blade for another stroke. We circled the island, inspected gigantic boulders jutting from the water, and explored neighboring islets, easing the canoe through still water.

As we paddled, the sun sank slowly until it touched the trees on the western shore. Floating toward the radiant skyline, Shirley's silhouette was edged in lustrous gold. From the brilliant disk, a gleaming ribbon stretched across darkening water, gilding us with a Midas touch. For a brief moment, we had a hint of the golden streets of heaven. Then the gleaming aisle vanished, replaced overhead by a heavenly display, shifting slowly from pale yellow to pink, orange, and red. How feeble are words to describe a sunset, and how limited, for the human eye can accurately distinguish a thousand shades of color, which no language provides words enough to label. The kaleidoscope of color was entrancing, and our lake-level vantage point provided a superb gallery from which to view it.

As darkness came on, we returned to camp. A pleasant fire and hot drinks drew us together to review the day. We complained in feigned agony but modest pride as we talked of our long portage. After a while, some of the group turned in, but Jules wanted to go out in the canoe to see the stars, since even the light of a small campfire obscures their full brilliance. Doug and I joined him, paddling quietly into the soft blackness.

How unfortunate city dwellers are, seldom out at night except under the roof of a car, and barely able to see the stars in the surrounding glow of manmade light. Even in rural areas, nearby towns and villages contribute their visual pollution, as do the mercury vapor lamps now found on nearly every farm. Only in the uninhabited areas does the silent display reveal its true splendor.

The two dippers hung over our heads. The crooked "W" of Cassiopeia, Orion with his studded belt, and many other constellations spangled the dark vault. Throughout the centuries, nocturnal watchers have pondered the skies; reverent ones have seen and worshipped. In a sermon to the Israelites, the prophet Amos declared that God - Yahweh, the Sovereign - made the Pleiades and Orion (Amos 5:8). Even before Amos, Job also knew the constellations, mentioning the Bear (probably Leo, not the dippers, Ursa major and minor), seeing in it the surpassing greatness of the Creator.

Little wonder that we stared in silence as we floated in the dark, on a liquid star-field, reflecting light back into space. The high, piercing light bored through space, penetrating cornea, retina, and optic nerve, reaching brains and being. We gazed in awe, trying to absorb, to understand, to relate - but to little avail. It was too much, too vast for our mortal capacities, but the yearning for comprehension remained.

If the stars were wondrous to the ancients, how much more are they to modern people. To know, as the scientists now tell us, that 100 billion trillion stars fill the universe, simply “blows” the mind. If grappling with the distance of the nearest star beyond our sun, sixty-four trillion miles, overwhelms us, how can we cope with the astounding immensity of the universe, billions of times greater? At best we can say with the singer of old, "Oh, Lord, our

Lord, how excellent is thy name in all the earth." (Psalm 8:1).

Our senses, however, had more with which to deal. Across the high dome above, was a pale swath of white, a bare hint of actual substance. Smoke or luminous haze might describe it, though ancient people thought it looked like milk. Arching from east to west, in width perhaps covering a sixth of the sky, it streaked the dark sky with a soft wash of light, revealing little of its true nature. Through long centuries it has been a mystery, a visual puzzle beyond the power of pre-scientific ages to understand.

Yet this concentration of stars, now known to be our home galaxy, just one of billions of similar clusters, is itself too stupendous for comprehension. The scientists' device of using exponential numbers to discuss such enormous distances and quantities, may be a necessary technique to measure the heavens, but in no way can it convey genuine perception. How can anyone grasp an "object" stretching through space for 100,000 light years, ($2x10^{42}$ miles - the number 2, followed by 42 zeros!). This mass of billions upon billions of stars, rotates around its center at incredible speed. While we sat motionless in the canoe, our planet was actually hurtling through space at the ferocious speed of 475,000 miles an hour! We meekly accept the teaching of the experts, unable to dispute their unbelievable facts, but for us they remain essentially meaningless.

There was still more to see in the sky. Low on the North horizon was a faint glow, a dim flicker of color that seemed to flirt with the boundary of imagination and reality. The summer appearance of the northern lights is not like the neon display of winter, but is softer, muted, more transient, leading the watcher to wonder if he really saw what he thought he saw. As we strained to see, a shimmery green gauze draped the horizon. Like a curtain fluttering at an open window, it slowly altered in position, color, and intensity. The silent specter charmed us with its spell, hushing our words to whispers. After a few brief minutes, it faded to nothing, disappearing before our eyes. After waiting without success for a re-appearance, we headed for camp, stirred by all that we had seen, unable to grasp such mysteries. But the canopy over Thomas Lake was not finished with the display of its glories.

In the morning, Jules, our most dedicated photographer, went out alone for some early picture taking. When he returned to find us awake at last, his attempt to share his excited impressions met with total failure. A substantial breakfast was all that aroused the rest of us, more concerned about feeding our stomachs than aesthetic pleasures. But Jules had indeed seen splendor, though we treated his verbal re-creation with kindly apathy. Only weeks later did he finally break through our dim perceptions, showing us an entrancing spectacle on film, freezing a fleeting image of awesome beauty.

It hangs now on my wall, where my chance gaze is frequently immobilized, my inner being transported in an instant, to the northern skies of Thomas Lake. In the picture is a huge rock piercing the surface of the lake. Upon the rock is a gull, opaque in silhouette. Behind the rock and dominating the scene, is a newly risen sun, shining through the mist. Radiating from the white-gold disk is a succession of vivid halos, auras of yellow, orange, rose, and lilac. An outline of rocks, trees, and skyline is suffused in reds and magenta. The choppy surface of the lake shows no familiar blue but a deep wine, even maroon. The projecting rock is black except for its outermost profile, etched in dark reddish black. I have never seen such a sunrise. How fortunate I am (thanks to Jules and photography), that it is mine now to enjoy, as often as I wish, a continual reminder of a wondrous world, and its haunting, often fleeting beauty.

Several months later, Jules told me of his efforts to seize that magic moment, how he tried to place himself in just the right position, only to find something not yet right. Three times the wind pushed his canoe out of range as he endeavored to frame his composition. Paddling back a fourth time, the elusive instant was born at last, barely before the sun lifted from the horizon, but happily, not before the image was crystallized in time, captured for years to come in the glowing colors of his film. To see the splendors requires more than mere vision. Persistence is often needed, and timing, and even luck.

Another lucky timing revealed one final spectacle in Thomas' high dome. Exactly a year later, I was back on Lake Thomas again, with a mostly different crew though Jules was along again. This time we entered Thomas from the north, through the narrow channel from Fraser Lake. We had had a wonderful day, enjoyable paddling, a few easy portages, cheerful companionship, and an early campsite on the west side of the lake. We swam in the warm waters playing "Keep Away" with a Frisbee, sun bathed on the rocks of our new home, and did some fishing. In the darkening sky after sunset, a half-moon hung in the southeast, its pewter luster gleaming across the water.

Our brief excursion into the wilds had taken on a relatively ordered routine, our days and nights acquiring comfortable structure. Though vastly different from our urban lives, even living in the outdoors takes on a familiar pattern. While each day's locale was new, we knew in general what to expect - canoeing across lakes much like others we had traveled, making camp on a wooded shore, cooking over a simple stove, swatting annoying mosquitoes, enjoying purposeful activity rather than passively observing make-believe displayed on a glass tube. Yet, wherever we happen to be, life may offer the unexpected, sometimes even, the spectacular.

Sitting around the fire and enjoying the moonscape before us, we were abruptly startled by a blazing meteor, flashing across the sky. Appearing in utter suddenness from the southeast, it streaked across our vision to the northwest, astonishing for both its brightness and an incredible tail of sparks and smoke. It vanished in seconds, as suddenly as it appeared. Our incredulous exclamations were hardly adequate for such a display. "Wow!" "Fantastic!" "Did you see that?" We kept peering toward its point of extinction, vainly wishing it to re-materialize, but of course, it did not. It was gone forever from sight but never from memory. The skies of Thomas Lake had revealed one more fabulous wonder to our watching eyes.

Experiencing the visual phenomena of Thomas Lake was not unique to our time and place. Watchers anywhere may see similar objects and events if they will only go out in the dark, especially in the wilds, where manufactured light does not dim the sky. Even the meteor was commonplace, for astronomers estimate that an astounding *200,000,000* visible meteors enter the earth's atmosphere in a single 24-hour period! Of course, the number observable from any one spot is vastly smaller, and traveling at nearly 100,000 miles an hour, they are visible very briefly. Yet, we fail to see them, largely because we seldom look for them. Even the splendor of the stars, sun, and moon are taken for granted, observed but not really seen, largely obscured by the blizzard of trivialities that swirl before our eyes. To those who would *truly* see, however, they glow with profound significance.

For multitudes, they are evidence of a brilliant and powerful creator. Until just recent generations, common people and scholars alike, have acknowledged the sun and stars as evidence of the existence and power of a great God. In every culture and age, the celestial display has "spoken" in silent language of the Creator's majesty. The writer of Psalm 19 continues his poem:

Day after day they pour forth speech;
night after night they display knowledge.
There is no speech or language
where their voice is not heard.
There voice goes out into all the earth,
their words to the end of the world.
(verses 2-4)

The next morning we left beautiful Thomas Lake. Glorious sunlight filled the sky. Laughing water and whispering forest sang their subtle duet as we paddled along. We were positively attuned to the divine communication as we traveled, pausing for a time on the narrow "handle" of Hatchet Lake to meditate, to ponder the surrounding splendor, to appreciate His goodness. We were well aware of His majesty and thankful for a perception of personal intimacy. Each of us in silent, private conversation communed with Him as friend to friend, speaking without sound in the language of the heart.

As we paddled on, we came to the narrow defile of Jordan Lake, where high, overhanging cliffs jutted from the water, a daring prospect too challenging for Vince and Vickie to resist. With nervous boldness, they leaped outward, shrieking and plummeting feet first into the shocking depths, emerging in gasping victory to our resounding applause. Climbing back up, they jumped again as we cheered them on, an interlude of sheer fun captured in memory and film, temporarily overwhelming the impressive skies of Thomas.

As limited beings, we could not retain the splendor coming from the Infinite. Our capacities are too small, absorbed with necessary tasks, and often attracted by the superficial. Yet, the Glory is not far off, and a trip to Thomas Lake is not required. We can recall in the mind's eye, images of the past, and whenever we will, can find present marvels in the skies, for they are always overhead. As David wrote,

When I consider the heavens,
the moon and the stars,
what is man that you consider him...
how excellent is thy name in all the earth.
Psalm 8:3, 4, 9

Chapter Nine

THE BIRDS OF TOE LAKE

Look at the birds of the air; they do not sow
or reap or store away in barns, and yet your
heavenly Father feeds them.
Matthew 6:26

Small birds heralded the dawn of a new day. Their soft chittering in the bushes and treetops was a more pleasant wake-up than a harsh alarm clock. The rustle of wingtips just outside the tent walls signaled their busy search for food. It was time for us, too, to be up and about.

As we emerged from the tents, we encountered bright sunshine and a brisk breeze from the southwest. Since the day's route was longer than normal, the tail wind would give us helpful assistance, easing our efforts considerably. To make matters even better, we had only a single, short portage at the end of the day's paddle.

I had anticipated the wind in planning our route, hoping that on our longest stretch of open water, the prevailing breezes of summer would give a boost to our canoes. Yet, winds are often fickle; many canoeists convinced they are nearly always contrary. Today, however, would be a delightful run, racing with the crests of moderate waves. We were especially grateful for we were a bit weary from our interrupted sleep of the night before.

We had been warned that bears were a problem this year, particularly along the southwest shore of Knife Lake. Ensign and Vera Lakes, too, had trouble. On Vera, we met a solo paddler who had lost his food pack to a marauding bear. Knife Lake's one permanent resident, the legendary Dorothy Molter, had given him some replacement supplies. We added some from our packs as well.

Expecting trouble, we took extra care in hanging our packs high in a tree and far out on a limb. Even so, we were a bit apprehensive, for bears are incredibly smart and learn quickly how to get a free meal.

About 3:00 a.m., I was aroused from my sleep by excited commotion from the women’s tents. Apparently undisturbed by our scent, a bear was shuffling through our campsite headed toward the shore where our packs were suspended. Fortunately, he seemed to dislike the glare of flashlights and the clatter of metal cups and plates banging together. He quickly turned and disappeared into the woods along the shoreline to the west. Perhaps he was making his rounds, visiting other parties camped along the lake. We hoped he would not return and that our food was safe for the night.

Our day's journey proved as pleasant as we had hoped. Faster than we had ever traveled, our canoes rushed with the wind, surging ahead as the foaming crests outraced us to the east. Paddling seemed like child's play, our blades biting deeply into the curling waters, driving our slim hulls toward distant shores. How different this was from the grim toil of opposing winds. This was a day of laughter and song, of joyous revel and boisterous exhilaration.

Adding the spice of variety to our paddling routine, we stopped at mid-morning to climb Thunder Point, a 150-

foot hill overlooking miles of Canadian wilderness to the north and a similar American landscape to the south.

Even with this break, we were making faster progress than usual, so much so, that we delayed our lunch until arriving at our destination. Shortly after 1:00, we landed at the portage to Toe Lake. A question remained to be answered, however; was the single campsite on the lake occupied? To our joy, it was not. The lake would belong exclusively to us for the remainder of the day and the night to come.

Toe Lake is a small, undistinguished body of water in northern Minnesota's Boundary Waters Canoe Area. Located just a few miles south of the Canadian border, it is separated from sprawling Knife Lake by brief portages at its north and south ends. Roughly horseshoe-shaped with its "opening" toward the southwest, it is barely a half-mile long and not more than a quarter-mile wide. Two islands dot the lake, the smaller at the southern end, and the larger at the inside bend of the horseshoe. Steep hillsides form much of the shoreline, rising one hundred feet and more from the water. The campsite is on the north end of the lake.

Our early arrival gave us a welcome sense of leisure. Before pitching tents and setting camp in order, we enjoyed a relaxed and lengthy lunch, lounging in the sun as we observed our "private" lake. Private though it was, it did have some inhabitants, and we had front row seats! We were spectators to the entrancing activities and haunting cries of a family of loons, a male, female, and young fledgling.

Of all the creatures of the northern wilderness, none is more fascinating than the common loon. The mature birds weigh from five to nine pounds and measure from twenty-eight to thirty-four inches in length with a wingspread of five feet. In summer plumage their back and sides are black with white rectangular patches arranged in a nearly checkerboard pattern. The breast is pure white, bordered at each side by narrow streaks of black that extend upward to a broad black band encircling the neck like a bow tie. The head is greenish-black with a large dark bill and red eyes.

In the water, loons ride low, with only head, neck, and low profile of back seen above the surface. Powerful feet attached far back on the body, enable them to swim to depths of two hundred feet, sometimes using its wings as well, staying submerged for up to a minute or longer. The agile birds catch fish and other aquatic animals with ease. In the air, they are strong fliers, able to exceed an astonishing one hundred miles an hour when aided by a tailwind. On land, however, they are nearly helpless, shuffling along on their breast and deep-set feet, unable to take-off in flight. Even on water, they need a long flapping run to become airborne. Such beautiful and unusual birds would be interesting if only for their appearance and abilities. It is their utterly captivating calls, however, that make them unique among God's wild creatures.

To those who love the wild and solitary enchantment of the far north, nothing symbolizes its alluring magic as does the music of the loons. Four specific "melodies" are used by the birds. The simplest - scarcely musical at all - is the hoot, a single brief tone used to communicate with other members of the family group.

The other three calls are far more complex. The wail, tremolo, and yodel are eerily fascinating to the human listener. The wail, especially at night, is perceived by many people to be the embodiment of the haunting loneliness of the vast northern reaches. To the first-time hearer, the cry may seem mournful, sinister, or frightening, sometimes mistaken for the howl of wild wolves, which also inhabit the area. It begins as a treble cry that rises suddenly to a higher sustained pitch, and occasionally to a third note higher still. Other loons may answer with the same call, creating an unearthly chorus mingling with its own echo, surrounding the listener from every point of the compass. The wail probably enables the birds to locate one another.

The tremolo is the "laughing" voice that many consider to be somewhat "maniacal," perhaps giving rise to the expression, "crazy as a loon." It is a distress or agitation cry used when the birds are alarmed and is the only call uttered when in flight.

The yodel is the most complex call, a series of vocalizations that words simply cannot express, but that is unforgettable when heard. It is voiced only by males, especially when excited by the intrusion of another male into its territory. It may signal aggressive behavior. The tone and voice patterns of each individual yodel are unique and may serve to identify the birds to one another.

As we watched, the loons carried on a never-ceasing endeavor to feed their young chick. Taking turns, they would dive beneath the water, returning after twenty to forty seconds with a minnow or small aquatic animal, which they disgorged into the chick's bill. During the whole afternoon and evening, the adults constantly uttered the wail, perhaps trying to teach it to communicate by mimicking the parents. They seemed unalarmed by our presence and campsite activities, making no attempt to draw us away by the familiar, "injured wing" trick. In concern for their need of relative isolation, we did not attempt any close observation, but watched mostly through binoculars.

The loons' activities and constant cries in our "front yard," richly expressed the wilderness we had come to enjoy. Their striking beauty and grace, their family duties, and above all, their compelling cries, created in us not only an appreciation for such unique creatures, but also praise for the God who made them. Perhaps their intriguing calls were anthems of exaltation in His ears as well. An ancient poet exhorted the wild animals, cattle, small creatures, and "flying birds" to praise Him (Psalm 148:10). We could do no less as we marveled over the wonder of his creative handiwork.

Most people find pleasure in the presence of birds. Of the 15,000 species on earth, at least a few inhabit virtually every environment on the globe. While some are quite tame, most birds take flight at the approach of an inquisitive observer. The vast majority of birds are relatively small which makes viewing them, especially while looking upward in the sky, in the branches of a tree, or in dense marsh grasses, a fairly difficult task. Even when located by their singing, they may be extremely hard to see. Large birds, on the other hand, can hardly remain hidden, a distinct help to the observer. Many of the larger birds, however, seem to require more remote habitat, territory further removed from the urban areas of earth. Distant Toe Lake was home to more large birds than just the loons. While they patrolled the water, graceful gulls roamed the sky.

Several species of gulls are found in North America, principally on the ocean coasts (thus the common designation, "sea gull,") but commonly on inland waters as well. Changing plumage affected by seasonal variation and age, and general similarity of color and shape, make identification of individual species something of a challenge to the casual viewer. Herring, ring billed, common, Bonaparte's, and Franklin's gulls are most likely to be seen in the interior of the continent. Largely white or gray with black wing tips, heads, or tail feathers, these birds range in length from thirteen to twenty-four inches, with wingspans of three to five feet.

Like their kind everywhere, the gulls of Toe Lake were graceful fliers, soaring with scarcely perceptible effort on the invisible currents rising from lake and forest. Almost constantly, up to a dozen birds could be seen, skimming the surface of the lake, drifting on tilted wing along the tree line at the water's edge, climbing above the cliffs to the east, or towering ever higher in circles rising out of sight. At times they flew in silence and at others cried in the harsh screams common to their race.

As the loons ceaselessly fished for their food, the gulls with less urgency, seized the opportunity to snatch an easy morsel, particularly a scrap overlooked by their human visitors. It seemed to us that they found simple delight in mastery of the sky, coasting aloft for the pure joy of unhindered motion. Though less exciting to us than the loons, since gulls are common near even large urban areas, our pleasure in watching them was still genuine, increasing our appreciation of the amazing and abundant diversity of life.

Although the fish entrails we left on the shoreline rocks provided a modest handout to the diet of the gulls, their normal ability to live off the land and water, like that of the loons, was a demonstration of the Biblical statement, "He provides food for the cattle, and for the young ravens when they call." (Psalm 147:9). Surprisingly, we had seen no ravens or crows, though they too inhabited the area, fed and cared for by a gracious God. Can humans ever learn such perfect balance between diligent effort and unhurried calm?

Two thousand years ago, Jesus used the birds as an object lesson to teach confident trust in the benevolent care of a heavenly Father. In His great Sermon on the Mount, He urged genuine believers in God to abandon anxiety and undue self-concern by observing the creatures of the air. The birds, making no provision for the future (and presumably not worrying about it), survive and flourish by seeking their food one day at a time. The God who so cares for His feathered creatures, has promised also to care for His more valuable beings, to whom He gives the added ability to plan and prepare for the future with its unknown emergencies.

The very behavior of the gulls underlined such trustful confidence. As if they were famished, they swooped in quickly, totally devouring any fish entrails. With far less energy, they would occasionally plunge from the air to take something from the water. The great majority of the time, however, was spent in ceaseless flight, seemingly unhurried and purposeless, as if securing food was not a compelling demand. Perhaps they were fully fed. At least to us they seemed to enjoy their wilderness home as much as we did, gliding through the sky with heedless care for the needs of the future.

Rosemary was the first to see the eagles - but she was probably the only one of us actually looking for them. Unlike the loons and gulls, the eagles appeared sporadically. In fact, it may be there was only one that came and went, though a breeding pair without a fledgling was a strong possibility. Since males and females look alike, and we saw only one at a time on several occasions, we could not know. In any case, sometime in mid-afternoon the first sighting occurred. Soaring majestically, perhaps a hundred feet above the lake, the magnificent creature flew over the trees of the opposite shore, crossed the lake to cruise the eastern hills, circled back to the south shore again, then alighted in the crown of a tree.

The size of a bald eagle is simply astounding. Even from a distance, its huge form captures immediate attention. In flight, its seven-foot wingspan appears properly enormous. Perched in a tree, its body, measuring thirty-six inches from head to tail, is of equally awesome proportions. Most amazing of all is the size of the head. Whereas other birds have a smallish head in proportion to the diameter of their body, the eagle's head is huge in comparison, with a neck almost as large dropping straight down to massive "shoulders."

Of course, its stark white (bald!) head, is an absolutely distinctive identifying mark. While other birds such as the osprey have significant amounts of white on their heads, only the eagle's plumage is completely so, though not until maturity in the fourth year.

Through binoculars we watched the eagle. Sitting calmly in the tree for perhaps fifteen minutes, it took wing and flew out of sight to the south. From then on, throughout the afternoon and evening, "eagle watch" was more or less constant. At irregular intervals an (the?) eagle would appear, cruising the sky in utter mastery. We observed no attempt at hunting or fishing. To our imaginations, the eagle appeared to be the lord of the air, watching over his kingdom from on high. Little wonder that Isaiah uses the eagle as an image of power, writing,

> *Those who hope in the Lord*
> *will renew their strength.*
> *They will soar on wings like eagles,...*
> *(Is.40:31)*

Our persistent watching was rewarded most fully just after the sun had slipped behind the trees to the west, when an eagle settled in a tree a quarter mile from our camp along the eastern shore. With serene dignity, he simply observed his territory, turning his head from time to time to obtain a new angle of view. In silence and unruffled calm, he stayed at his post for perhaps half an hour, then flew away.

For his watchers it was a splendid opportunity to capture an impression of the primeval creation. The eagle, powerful sovereign of the skies, was in perfect accord with its environment, unafraid, unfettered, a fitting symbol of liberty. Untroubled by anxiety over future uncertainties, he sought his food one day at a time, dependent as the loons, gulls, and other birds, on the resources of the

Creator. Following an inner urge like other migrants, the eagle would soon fly southward for the winter, moved by mysterious instinct to seek food in a more favorable climate. Birds obey the will of God for their lives, said a prophet of old (Jeremiah 8:7). Only mankind is a rebel, defying the Creator by choosing his own way and schedule. Not so the eagle, gulls, and loons. Wild animals though they are, eating other creatures to sustain their own lives, they commit no sin but conform in unknowing obedience to the plan of their Maker.

It was while we were watching for eagles that we discovered the fourth large bird of Toe Lake. At first I thought there were several eagles circling in the sky, yet something was amiss. The huge forms were certainly "eagle-like," with great out-stretched wings and dark bodies. Seen in silhouette, the heads did not appear white, but then young bald eagles have dark heads. Golden eagles, though more common in western states, are almost identical in size and shape to their "bald" cousins, but have dark bronze feathers covering their heads.

Eventually I realized what was wrong. The heads were far too small and were attached to thin necks. Then, when they settled on a rock a short distance from our camp, I knew for sure. These large birds had *red* heads. They landed on the rock to eat the remains of a bloody carcass of some small animal. I had never seen turkey vultures before. Now at Toe Lake, three of them shared their grizzly meal as we watched.

Though nearly as large as the eagles, turkey vultures weigh only 1/4 as much, (3 1/2 lbs. vs. 13 lbs.). Perhaps the most efficient flyers of the avian kingdom, they can remain aloft for hours, floating on thermal up-drafts with imperceptible effort. Without the formidable talons of the eagles and other raptors, vultures can seldom kill live prey, depending instead on their uncanny eyesight to scavenge for carrion. Unappreciated by many for their feeding practices (widely shared by eagles as well), they nonetheless, provide a valuable function in cleaning up the wilderness.

The vultures calmly pecked at the carcass without apparent urgency, frequently standing motionless, or taking a step or two to another spot on the rock. Perhaps they were already well fed. If not as attractive as the other birds, with their naked red heads and unfastidious eating habits, they were still fascinating, symbols like the loons, gulls, and eagles, of a wondrous creation and a provident Creator.

The vultures, however, were different in one respect. They were Biblical symbols of the return of the Lord! In a thought-provoking chapter of Matthew (24), Jesus responded to the disciples' questions about the fall of Jerusalem, the signs of His return, and the end of the age. In verse 28, He told them, "wherever there is a carcass, there the vultures will gather." Full understanding of this verse is by no means easy, but relating it to the previous verse gives the general meaning. Contradicting some who were claiming that His return would be secretive and obscure, Jesus states that as a flash of lightning is plainly visible, so also is a flock of vultures circling over a carcass Even so, plainly visible signs will mark His second coming.

Eventually, the vultures finished feeding. One by one, they lifted from the rock, flapping huge wings to become airborne, and were soon out of sight. They were an unexpected treat to us, providing an opportunity to see yet another of the world's fascinating creatures.

In the morning we said farewell to Toe Lake. For less than eighteen hours, it had been our private residence in the wild. We would remember several events from our stay: the small-mouth bass we caught and ate, climbing and exploring "Mt. Vincent," a rocky cliff we named in honor of one of our companions, a brief but explosive thunderstorm during the night.

Most of all, however, we would continually recall the great birds of the air--loons, gulls, eagles and vultures. Their unhurried behavior in feeding, lack of alarm at our presence, and utter freedom in flight, illustrated with impressive emphasis, Jesus' teaching about trust in a gracious Father. As we paddled down the lake to continue our journey, we saw once more a white-headed eagle sailing above the eastern shore, a fitting farewell from Toe Lake.

Chapter Ten

INTRUSION OF GLORY

They will see the glory of the Lord,
the splendor of our God.
Isaiah 35:2

The unexpected! That is one of the most compelling attractions of wilderness. I never thought about it in my younger years. I simply went to the woods to hike, hunt, or fish. But as I realized later, it wasn't a successful catch or shoot that was magical. It was "the unexpected" - an unusual event, a new bird or animal, the continual discovery of unknown places - like Cracker Jacks, a surprise in every box. These usually pleasant novelties break into the realm of the ordinary with unanticipated frequency. Unpredictable as the unknown must be, it never fails to catch us a bit off guard, surprising us again and again, creating a deeper enjoyment and appreciation for the mystery and wonder of the world. Despite previous experience in the outdoors, there is always more to discover, as the unexpected materializes in startling places, times, and manners. Whatever its measure, its effect is to add intrigue, richness, and awe to a world already highly treasured. While its importance may be modest or profound, it is still a significant reality.

So it was, as we were heading toward Kekakabic Lake in the BWCA. A light mist was falling, barely requiring rain gear, but veiling sight and sound in a hush of gray. We were paddling quietly with little conversation when one of these "unexpecteds" gently materialized. A loon popped to the surface beside our canoe, a mere fifteen-feet away. This was a considerable surprise since they are usually very wary and keep their distance. In fact, attempting to get near enough for a close-up view is nearly always a frustrating experience. No matter how silent, swift, or calculating the paddler may be, it is usually hopeless. The loon swiftly dives out of sight and swims amazingly far underwater. Quite probably, they can sense the turbulence of the paddles under water, for they always seem to avoid the canoeist's random choice of direction as he hopes by chance to intercept the loon's course.

This day, however, one of these incredible aquatic birds came up nearby and accompanied us. Undisturbed by our slow paddling it swam in escort beside us. Its extraordinary checkerboard plumage of black and white, brilliant red eyes, and glossy green-black head were plainly visible. For several hundred yards it stayed near at hand, then as quietly as it had appeared, it slipped beneath the surface. Was it old and defective in sight, young and inexperienced, or just curious about our splashing paddles? We could not know. We simply treasured a rare close-encounter with one of our favorite birds.

A bit later in our journey, I heard a low murmur in the distance. The next portage must skirt some fast water, I thought. As I reflected on this new awareness, I recalled that the previous evening I had heard distant whispers of white water. They had been brief and indistinct, scarcely audible above the rustling trees at our campsite, making no conscious impression on my mind. Now that I was alert to their presence, I could identify and interpret the scattered fragments of memory. Our mind and senses are amazing, yet, how much escapes our perception and understanding!

Two miles further, we landed at the portage, an uphill trail of twenty-five rods. The rapids I had heard were actually a waterfall, a series of plunging cascades dropping one hundred feet from the lake beyond. Because of the turbulent spray, the brush along either side was a luxuriant tangle of greenery, rooted in mossy rocks and covered by a canopy of trees. Even in the increasing rain, this was a place of exquisite beauty.

A third surprise was not so enjoyable. At the next portage, bypassing a slow riffle of shallow water, the others carried their canoes around, but Rosemary and I decided to walk our canoe through it. It was a poor choice. The stream was choked with rocks and fallen trees, requiring us to wrestle our boat over or around a maze of obstructions. Slipping into deep holes, we both got wet to our waists, and banged our shins in the process. The portage was there for good reason. Our unexpected and painful lesson in common sense would be a topic of laughter throughout the trip.

I had read about the hills and cliffs of Kekakabic Lake so I was not surprised as we entered its high shores. Reality, however, is not just raw facts, but a fusion of physical substance, sensory impression, mental receptivity, and perhaps other subtle influences. So even though I "knew" about Kek's steep shores, they were more than I anticipated. Now I really knew, the vague notion of imagination replaced by experience.

For all of us, a genuinely surprising, first-time event occurred further down the lake. We could see a dark object some distance ahead but in the dull light of the rainy overcast, we couldn’t immediately discern its shape. It was too high in the water to be a loon and seemed too big to be a duck. As we paddled closer, I could see two appendages projecting above a dark mass below. My hunch proved correct.

"Look," I called to the others, "it's a moose, swimming across the lake.” Like an iceberg, the huge body of the cow moose was submerged beneath the water. Only her head and the hump of her shoulders showed above the water. With ears twitching like radar antennae, she turned her head toward us, then, angled slightly away. We paddled swiftly to get a closer view, though we did not want to get near enough to alarm her.

Churning powerfully with her invisible legs, she swam silently away, heading down a long channel rather than escaping to nearer shorelines. We had hoped to see a moose on our voyage; little did we imagine we would do so in the middle of a huge, deep lake. But then, the unexpected catches one unawares, in unlikely places and times. It arrives unannounced, an unlooked-for happening to be seized for the present and treasured in the future. So it was with the unexpected of the day following.

Like those before it, the day started with an anticipation of adventure and pleasure. Yet, this day was different. For one thing, there was fog in the air, not the gloom of a lingering cold front, but an obscuring veil of mist. Water, land, and sky were cloaked in gray silence. The hush of early morning was intense, weighed down somehow under the drape of moisture. Still, the day bore promise of sunshine and warmth, for a rising blotch in the east revealed the haze to be thin, soon to disappear before the powerful sun.

A dry day would be welcome after the previous day's paddle in the rain. It had actually been a rather enjoyable experience, for the air had been calm and the persistent rain not overwhelming. Yet, by the time we had reached our campsite, we were all thoroughly wet, cold, and tired. Several hours around a blazing fire had restored our spirits and dried our clothes, but today we hoped for better weather. Our expectations were abundantly fulfilled. By the time of our departure, the sun was breaking through in bright, slanting shafts.

I had asked Jules to lead this day, guiding us through several small lakes to our destination on Lake Thomas. Since our group was now well adept at paddling and portaging, my leadership involvement was minimal. With Jules reading the maps and compass, I was free to interact with the surroundings, to absorb the awesome beauty on every hand.

Letting the others go ahead and set the pace, Linda and I brought up the rear. At first, I was unaware of anything out of the ordinary. We quietly paddled, enjoying a superb day. Then a subtle impression began to form in my consciousness. It may be that Linda's perception had initiated the process. During our infrequent, subdued conversations, she had twice remarked that early mornings were different, perhaps even better than other times of the day. The anticipation of a new day's unfolding surely added a special charm to the first hours. Maybe, too, the angled light, the bare hint of breeze, and the forest fragrance, contributed to a developing sensitivity.

This morning even the water was different. The blue depths of Kekakabic, were now replaced by the quiet shallows of Strup, Wissinni, Ahmakose, and Gerund lakes. Here the water was amber - clear, burnished, golden brown. We seemed to glide over liquid sunlight, a thin molten bronze. This description may sound extravagant but it scarcely captures the beauty of the surroundings. And to the brilliant landscape without, there was a growing perception within, a developing awareness of something unusual.

The exquisite beauty of the wilderness was not new to me, for I had been in the canoe country many times before. Lofty pine and spruce, graceful stands of birch, fireweed, water lilies, reeds, rushes, loons, mergansers, and a thousand other glories formed a living tapestry. Sound, scent, and sight converged in keen awareness, familiar, but somehow on this day, more powerful, more compelling, than ever before.

Surely the silence played a part - not an absence of sound, for we talked, the birds sang, the water splashed from the stroke of our paddles - but a reverent stillness seemed to pervade the atmosphere, as if nature itself was holding its breath in anticipation. Lakes and land were empty of people. A crowded planet was far off. We were alone in a remote paradise. And then, the aloneness was broken. There was something else. Indeed, as perception grew, a *Someone*.

How this Presence was made known I cannot say with any clarity. It did not occur instantaneously or explicitly, but came with increasing awareness through the environment. The surrounding splendor seemed to be a sacred landscape, a divine precinct pervaded by the aura of God. The midweek day became as a Sunday, a holy day. The warmth of the air and softness of the breeze had no room for improvement, but were elements of perfection. There was no physical or even subjective vision of God, only a penetrating, powerful, gripping impression of beauty, Beauty personified, like an Old Testament theophany, a manifestation of God. Moses saw a blazing bush and discovered the presence of God. The Israelites knew Him in a fiery pillar and luminous cloud. I did not see Him in literal person, yet His reality was overwhelming to the point of tears, breaking into my consciousness as an intrusion of Glory.

Each morning we had read the fortieth chapter of Isaiah. Now, within and without, the words were coming true, "the glory of the Lord will be revealed." Often in the Bible, glory - the manifestation of God - is symbolized and displayed by light. Except for the previous day, we had reveled in the glitter of the sunlight on water. At night, a half-moon gleamed brightly and countless stars blazed in the dark. By whatever means, radiant glory pierced my soul that morning, searing its way into the depths of my being, unsettling me, overwhelming me.

It is difficult to convey in words what I felt and thought. To my physical senses there was only our group in the wilderness. Yet to my inner and certain consciousness, there was a compelling conviction that God was immediately near, as if we had approached His very throne. This sense of His presence conveyed through the beauty of the surroundings was one of sublime majesty, of awesome splendor, not abstract or formal but intensely personal. *He*, not *It*, was distinctly real to me, as person to person. The impression of His living reality, His nearness, His incredible grandeur, His relationship to me as Lord and God, made a stunning impact on my heart and mind. How long this awareness lasted, I am not sure, several minutes at least, perhaps half an hour. It was dispelled by our landing at the next portage, but its effect lingered for days.

Was the experience real? Was God truly present in a way that I had never known before? Indeed, is it even possible for sinful humans to have a living encounter with the divine Being?

The answer to the last question will surely be affected by our presuppositions. The materialist of whatever stripe will say, "no," for he rejects the notion of any reality beyond the physical. To some who *do* believe in a spiritual order, the answer may also be, "no," since for many, god is an impersonal force or power. Still others, believing only in a god far off, will attribute such experiences to an overactive imagination, hallucination, neurotic fantasy, or some other aberration of reality.

History, however, especially in the Judeo-Christian tradition, has recorded similar accounts repeatedly. Certainly wild and extravagant claims have been made by the mentally and emotionally unbalanced. Nonetheless, men and women whose rational faculties have commanded the highest respect, have reported experiences of meeting with God. The greatest men of Judaism - Abraham, Moses, Isaiah, and others - claimed to have seen Him, actually and personally. First-century Christians risked their very lives in tenacious witness that in Jesus Christ they had encountered none other than God Himself. Believers of subsequent generations have continued this testimony, some claiming intensely real, personal encounters.

I am in good company then, in affirming the reality of a significant spiritual experience. To be reborn, as Jesus describes in the Gospels, is to discover that He is truly alive, and knowable as a living person. As growth in Christian maturity develops, so does an ever-increasing awareness of the Living One.

For many, unfortunately, the risen Christ seems to remain far distant in heaven. Even in worship, His presence may seem vague and unreal. Is it even possible for the ordinary believer to have a genuine encounter with Him, such that he can say with bold assurance, "I have seen the Lord," at least with the eyes of the heart?

Believers throughout the ages have said, "Yes." The vision of God has been a quest of intent searchers in every generation. The testimony of Augustine, Saint John of the Cross, Theresa of Avila, Juliana of Norwich, Frederick Faber, Robert Murray McCheyne, and other passionate Christ-lovers, lights the way for our own venture of faith. In more recent years, A. W. Tozer has lamented the millions whose eyes only dimly behold Him, but he invites and challenges us to a more vital pursuit of God.

God Himself desires it! Again and again in the Scriptures, a gracious Savior invites a daring and bold approach by the sinful but trusting seeker. Old and New Testament alike commend the faith that humbly but earnestly seeks to behold Him. Will He not grant the request of those who persist, demanding neither a predetermined manifestation nor a certain timetable? In some way that abundantly satisfies, He will surely answer the yearning expressed by Moses, "Show me thy glory."

So it was for me on that memorable morning. The ordinary routine of human existence was shattered by an awareness that I can only explain as the presence of God Himself. I saw no form and heard no voice, only a compelling, overwhelming sense of beauty, majesty, *Glory*. Sky, water, trees, and companions were all completely normal, yet there was a gripping apprehension of the extraordinary.

The camaraderie with my companions - Jules, Vince, Bob, Linda, Vickie, Rosemary, and Janet, - was deeply satisfying. The loveliness of the summer day was superb and the weather could not have been finer. The beauty of the wilderness was breathtaking. Quiet solitude allowed an unencumbered mind to be receptive to the subtle influence of spiritual realities.

All these things combined in an over-powering impression that cannot be explained by details of time and place. There was an extra something, or as I believe, a Someone, that invaded the senses of my mind to create a splendor I can only describe as "glory."

What after all did Moses see on the mountain top (Ex. 33)? God said he could not behold His face and live. He was permitted to see only the back of God, as His "glory passed by." No further description is given. The result, however, was a radiant glow on Moses face. The presence of light is surely suggested. So, too, when the glory of God's presence rested upon Sinai as God spoke with Moses, it appeared to the Israelites as a consuming fire. When God entered the tabernacle, a luminous cloud enveloped it. As the New Testament reports the birth of Christ, a shining display accompanied the angelic announcement to the shepherds, and in its final book, the resurrected Savior appeared in brilliant splendor to John (Revelation 1).

It seems appropriate to me, then, that a genuine and forceful apprehension of God should be associated with beauty, light, love - in a word, *glory*. In describing my experience I do not mean to suggest any obligation for others. My only purpose is to express more fully, what occurred to me. In fact, the purposeful seeking of extraordinary experiences is not without danger. God wants us to seek Him, not the sensation that may happen. My private encounter may be too subjective, too individual to have any meaning for others.

I do know this. God is far greater than we have yet understood or experienced. He dwells in unimaginable splendor, clothed in light as a garment (Psalm 104:2), yet, incredibly, He eagerly awaits the approach of His children, as countless Scriptural exhortations indicate. If to our senses His presence is remote and obscure, it is surely not because He wills it so. In His time, in His way, He desires to reveal Himself. If we seek His face in earnest, humble faith, we may truly behold Him.

So Psalm 27 invites us with precept and promise.

One thing I ask of the Lord, this is what I seek:
that I may dwell in the house of the Lord
all the days of my life,
to gaze upon the beauty of the Lord
and to seek Him in His temple.
For in the day of trouble

He will keep me safe in His dwelling;
He will hide me in the shelter of His tabernacle
and set me high upon a rock.
Then my head will be exalted
above the enemies who surround me;
at His tabernacle will I sacrifice with shouts of joy;
I will sing and make music to the Lord.
Hear my voice when I call, O Lord;
be merciful to me and answer me.
My heart says of you, "Seek His face!"
Your face Lord I will seek.
Do not hide your face from me,
do not turn your servant away in anger;
you have been my helper.
Do not reject me or forsake me, O God my
Savior.
Though my father and mother forsake me,
the Lord will receive me.
Teach me your way, O Lord; lead me in a
straight path because of my oppressors.
Do not turn me over to the desire of my foes,
for false witnesses rise up against me,
breathing out violence.
I am still confident of this:
I will see the goodness of the Lord
in the land of the living.
Wait for the Lord; be strong and take heart
and wait for the Lord.
Psalm 27: 4-14

Are there any conditions for an in-depth encounter with God? I am not sure. He is sovereign. He may, and some have so claimed, simply break into a person's life. For most, however, time is needed, and quiet. Worshipful music may be an asset. For me, beauty was the catalyst, even the essence. The wilderness locale may well be significant, for many of the Biblical experiences also occurred in the wild and lonely places.

One requirement above all the others, however, is critically important – namely, a seeking heart. Openness, expectancy, and worship characterize the Biblical revelations. One apparent exception is that of the apostle Paul, an avowed enemy of Christ and his followers. Many scholars, however, are convinced that Paul's consciousness was prepared for his encounter with the risen Jesus, by his immediately prior involvement with Stephen, whose dying words described a vision of Christ. At least some inner sense of need would seem to be a necessary requirement.

And if the urgent seeker should actually behold the living God, what then? Would not such a momentous happening tend to unbalance the person so favored, perhaps creating a sense of superiority or pride? The possibility must be real for Paul warns the Corinthians about it. Yet, the more usual result seems instead, as it was for Paul himself, to be a new sense of humility and dependence. Human weakness, limitation, and sin, as Isaiah's revelation demonstrates, appear glaringly visible in the brightness of His perfection. Happily, this very awareness enhances further service to God since the need to utilize supernatural resources, so vividly now illuminated, are more apparent than ever. The end-result, then, of a greater awareness of His living reality, is an increased conviction of human fallibility but also of a gracious divine endowment.

Seek the Lord, then, with all your heart. Hunger and thirst to know Him, engage your soul with Him. Do not settle for the lesser goal of seeking His gifts in place of Himself. If the encounter is delayed, do not abandon the quest. Sometime, somewhere, He may break into your consciousness with an awesome awareness of His majestic presence. For you, too, there may come, an intrusion of glory.

Chapter Eleven

CHANGES

He changes times and seasons. Dan. 2:21

The fire snapped with glowing heat and the trees rustled in a moderate breeze. We were making a fair amount of noise ourselves, chattering in cheerful companionship, when in the distance, I thought I heard something. Then a second time, a sensation seemed to breach the focus of my perception, but was still too faint to be identified. The impression was vague, barely crossing the threshold of my consciousness. I dismissed it in favor of the sounds and sights near at hand.

In another minute, there was no uncertainty. Above and behind us, still some distance to the north, the staccato cries pierced the dark night, rushing ahead on the wings of the wind.

"Listen," I said, raising my hand to arrest the conversation. "Wild geese!"

Instantly our voices were still as we directed eyes and ears to the sky. For a few seconds there was nothing, then the hoarse, haunting music came gliding through the air. "Ker-ah, ker-ah, ker-ah," in moderate treble pitch, with the second syllable uttered about two notes higher than the first, the unseen flock called out in the silence. Were they informing each other of position, encouraging one another for the long flight ahead, or simply "talking" among themselves as we had been doing? If only we could know.

On and on they came, their disembodied voices filling the sky with wild melody. Through the black night we strained to see, but to no avail. With faint hope, I stared at the nearly full moon rising behind the trees to the east, eager to catch their dark forms against the bright disk, but it was not to be. Flying far above the early moon, they passed beyond us, winging steadfastly to the south. Their plaintive calls faded in the distance, until we heard them no more. In stillness we waited, but the wild song was gone. Convinced that the music had ended, we resumed our own gabble.

On this last night of our fall canoe trip, the call of the geese was a pleasant farewell gift, a parting serenade for themselves, for us, and for the season. As if to herald the changing season, all over the North, ragged lines and shaggy "V's" of migrating geese were calling to the earth below, punctuating night and day with cries of warning. Summer was gone, indeed. The days were in swift decline, in urgent transit toward winter soon to come.

We had been mindful of the turn of the seasons in planning for our trip, scheduling a late September date for the specific purpose of catching the height of fall colors. Knowing full well that other changes could be expected, we hoped we were ready for whatever might come.

So, on the last Monday of the month, we embarked from Moose Lake Landing on a glorious Indian summer afternoon. The bright sun, high blue sky, and warm southerly breeze made it seem like July. However, there was a startling difference. The familiar evergreens were interspersed with dazzling gold and scarlet, the autumn colors transforming the summer forest into festive castle halls.

Two other differences were starkly apparent. The first was a nearly complete absence of fellow canoers. Though Moose Lake is the most popular entry point of the entire Boundary Waters Canoe Area, (fifty groups being allowed daily access, in addition to day-use fishermen), we saw only two boats at a distance, and one elderly couple in a canoe returning to the landing. We would have no scrambling for a campsite or crowded confusion on the portages. The empty wilderness was nearly ours alone. With a helping wind at our back and the eager zest of anticipation, we made good time in getting to our campsite near Prairie Portage.

A second strong difference appeared soon after setting up camp and beginning our dinner. Before our dinner was finished cooking, the autumn sun had vanished. Fall's short twilight was barely long enough to finish our meal and clean the dishes. Even with the help of daylight saving time, it was fully dark by 7:30. If we were deprived of summer's long evenings for fishing and exploring, we had the alternative benefit of lengthier time around the fire. More than ever, the blaze was a strong magnet, drawing us to its luminous glow, binding us within the circle of its spell. For Jim and Rosemary, Ron and Karol, Jan, and me, the quiet hours of darkness were a welcome respite, medicine to heal the ravages of hectic summer labor, giving us time to relax, refresh, and recharge in welcome calm.

At length, the hurried departure, long day's drive, and hours of paddling, took their toll. Conversation dwindled and bodies sagged. Jim and I lingered at the fire as the others headed for the tents, but soon, we too, yielded to the lure of foam pads and warm sleeping bags - all by the outrageous hour of 9:30, another benefit of fall camping.

Before starting the next morning, Ron read Psalm 104, a majestic hymn in praise of God's creation and care. We would read it at the beginning of each day to set the focus of our thoughts, directing our attention to the great Designer of the majesty through which we traveled. After a brief prayer, we dipped our paddles into the new day's adventure.

On the north shore of Prairie Portage, we stopped at Canadian customs, prior to entry into Quetico Provincial Park, but the remote wilderness office had closed for the season. Following the instructions posted at the site, we deposited our wilderness camping fees in the metal box provided, then headed northwest across Bayley Bay on Basswood Lake. The helping breeze of yesterday was gone, replaced by a bracing wind dead ahead. Though the sun behind us glittered on the flashing waves, the air was charged with the distinct sharpness of a new season. Bending our backs to the challenge, we stroked our way into the advancing waves, making slow but satisfying progress. An hour later, we stopped for our first "goody break" in the lee of a rocky islet before starting out on another open reach.

Another hour of paddling into the wind brought us to a brief portage into Sunday Lake, a shortcut on our way to a northerly portion of sprawling Basswood. Despite several puddles and stretches of mud, the change of pace from paddling to walking was refreshing, even under the burden of packs and canoes. In a few places along the trail, huge round tracks indicated the recent presence of a moose, which we hoped (but failed) to see. Embarking again at the far end of the portage, we paddled a short distance on the lake to a nearby island for our lunch. Then, it was back in the canoes once more. Paddling into the teeth of the powerful breeze required determined effort, but made it easier to keep on course. At the far side of Sunday Lake, a short carry brought us to Basswood's North Bay.

My original idea had been to paddle across and find a site in the hidden recesses of Lost Bay, but one look at the white breakers roaring from the northwest dictated a change of plan. An appealing island a quarter mile away was a sound alternative. In less than half an hour, we were making camp at an attractive site, sheltered from the driving wind but open to the bright sun and water of the lee shore. In contrast to the relative confinement of established campsites on the U.S. side of the border, Canadian officials allow camping wherever you choose. Our home for the night had been used before, but had plenty of space, allowing us to disperse our tents at some distance from each other.

This night we did not have the luxury of fresh meat as we had the previous evening, but a freeze-dried oriental dinner, complete with fortune cookies, was a great success. Dessert did not come out quite as well, since in repackaging for our trip, I had not included all the directions. Rosemary's "guesstimate" of how much powdered milk to add to the mix was much too generous. Still, cheesecake *soup* didn't taste bad, even if it was almost easier to drink than to eat with utensils.

After marveling over a spectacular sunset, we spent a pleasant evening around the fire, roasting marshmallows and making small talk. We shared a powerful kinship of similar faith in a living God, and now more than ever, a towering appreciation for the splendor of His world. The glorious wilderness around us was not simply material substance; it was a vivid expression of His nature, alive with His presence, needing only the sensitivity of faith to experience His nearness.

The next morning was sunny like the day before, but colder, and still windy. Looking over the sheltered channel as we ate breakfast, I could not determine how high the waves might be on the open expanse of the lake. We would have our hands full in even a moderate breeze, since our route back into U. S. waters was generally southwestward. West to northwesterly winds would require strong and skillful paddling. We would soon know.

Karol was my partner for the day, an eager and sturdy paddler. Leaving the protection of the island, we headed across a mile of open water where we found significant but manageable waves, allowing for steady progress. From time to time I looked back to check on the others. Ron and Rosemary were struggling a bit but doing all right. Jim and Jan seemed to be having a hard time, driving erratically from one side to the other, yet continuing in the general direction. Jim was six feet five inches of muscular strength and I had confidence he would soon master the canoe in the strong quartering wind.

In a half hour we reached an island that broke the force of the waves and we clustered together for a breather. Only then, (and later as they amplified their story), were Jim and Jan able to tell us of their desperate labors to keep their craft on course. Loaded too heavily toward the bow, it was almost more than Jim could do to keep the nose of the canoe on course. At the top of their lungs, they had shouted at us, but the buffeting wind had drowned their voices. Rearranging the packs would improve the maneuverability of the canoe, and our further travel would often be sheltered by more islands. Best of all, a change in direction would put the wind nearly at our back for a while.

Soon we were under way again, now riding the waves as though we were on an exciting roller coaster or a spirited horse. The surging waters hurled us onward, rising and falling as the waves hissed and boiled along our flanks. All too soon, we skirted another island, altered our course once more into the wind, and settled down to methodical stroking for the rest of the day. By mid-afternoon, we were well into our own country, though no markers, boundary line, or customs office indicated the juncture of two sovereign nations.

What I now wanted to find, was no ordinary campsite, but a superior one, a site that was truly superb since we would be spending two nights in the same location. I hoped for a south facing rock ledge, elevated somewhat above the water, with an open expanse of at least half a mile to the east, south, and west, but none that we passed filled the bill. Tired from our toiling in the wind, we landed at a flat, low site with a westward view but full exposure to the breeze. I was not satisfied, but did not want to haul the troops any further in a perhaps fruitless search. While the others rested, however, Jim and I set off to explore nearby Washington Island. In half an hour, we were successful.

Returning to the others, we shouted, "We've found it. It's not exactly what we've been looking for but it's wonderful. Let's go!"

Once again, we headed into the wind, but the expectation of a magnificent camp at the end of our full day gave us added strength. Soon we were near and I shouted, "Here it is, Waikiki!" Stretching before us was a lovely sand beach, perhaps a hundred yards long and twenty feet deep, backed by a gently sloping "lawn" of grass sufficient for several tent sites, all surrounded by a shimmering backdrop of green and gold. A narrow point blocked our view to the west, but we had an ample sweep of vision to the south, and east. And here we were out of the wind, the mighty blasts from the northwest blocked by the island's bulk.

Though the air was hardly warm, Rosemary and Karol could not resist. Within minutes of pitching the tents, the (fool?) hardy mermaids were into swimsuits, ready to test the water. The illusion of summer was rudely shattered by 52-degree water. Shrieking in frigid gasps, they stayed in the chilly lake barely long enough to get wet. Sun bathing on the warm sand was a more sensible option than swimming.

After dinner, which included a successful dessert of coconut cream pie, we remained around the fire, reviewing the day and contemplating our private thoughts. Well before ten o'clock, we headed to the tents. The sky was now overcast, though the air seemed nearly calm, but not for long.

I had been sleeping only a short while when I was aroused by the fierce shuddering of the tent which I had pitched on the smooth sand at the back edge of the beach. With no firm anchoring soil, the flapping nylon had pulled most of the stakes out of the ground. Only the weight of my body kept the tent from blowing away. Crawling out into a raging gale, now shrieking from the *southwest*, I struggled with great difficulty to secure the tent, roping it to nearby trees and piling some boulders on the corners. Adequately braced, I dove back inside, incredulous that the wind had not died, but had changed direction and force.

Later in the night, I woke once more. If anything the wind was stronger still, buffeting our now exposed camp with furious gusts. Concerned for the others and for the canoes, I unzipped my warm bag and hurried out again into the wild darkness. Janet's tent seemed o.k. though the waves were slapping the shore just a couple of feet away. The other tents, somewhat screened by trees and bushes, were in no trouble, and the canoes were all there, though one had flipped over. While the direction of the wind was off the water and onto the land, I decided not to take a chance that a freak gust would somehow snatch a canoe and hurl it out on the lake. Dragging all the boats higher up the beach, I tied each one to a sturdy tree.

For a few minutes I stood at the edge of the water, braced against the onslaught of the storm, fascinated and unaccountably excited by the fierce weather, awed by its untamed power. Being wet or cold is not fun, but for me there is a distinct sense of alertness and anticipation in direct encounter with nature's violent moods. Perhaps, as to a prophet of ancient Israel, storms somehow convey a sense of God's near and powerful reality. "His way is in the whirlwind and the storm, and clouds are the dust of His feet." (Nahum 1:3). My wondering contemplation was soon cut short by the piercing cold and I made a dash to the shelter of the tent.

The next day was a pleasant interlude of individual pursuits, subject only to meal times, and the incredible variability of the weather. A damp, gray morning gave way to clear skies and bright sun by noon, followed shortly thereafter by more rain, then clearing skies, another shower, brilliant sunshine, and so on through the day. At least four times the unstable weather sent us running for cover, then, lured us out when the fickle skies brightened once again.

Perhaps the highlight of the trip was the discovery of a special hilltop a short distance from camp. A magnificent grove of white pines spread in orderly procession over the slope, rising fifty feet and more to a lofty green ceiling through which the light softly filtered. These were not the two hundred-year-old monarchs of former days, ancient pillars, three to four feet in diameter, and over a hundred feet tall. Only scattered remnants of such trees can now be found, having escaped the ravaging saws and fires of the early century. These instead, were handsome young trees, only a couple of feet thick, whose maturity protected by federal regulations, lay decades in the future. It is probable that a governmental program of fifty years earlier had actually planted them, for here and there, almost buried in the duff, were weathered gray stakes with lettered metal markers, perhaps evidence of Civilian Conservation Corps labors from the 30s.

Cathedral Hill, as I called it when showing Rosemary, was an exquisitely appropriate name. No undergrowth obstructed the aisles, for competing shrubs and trees could not survive on the meager light penetrating from above. The only clutter upon the thick carpet of needles was a few twenty-foot spindles, four or five inches in diameter, mere stalks of trees that lost the race for survival. Within the sacred precincts, the wind was stilled, and on this day at least, all sounds were swallowed in reverent silence. Here indeed was a worthy place for worship, a God-grown temple fit for quiet praise.

Quickly my mind flew from this natural place, not far distant from Ely, Minnesota, to a man-made counterpart, 6,000 miles away in Ely, England, where Shirley and I had visited a year earlier. Ely Cathedral, not as imposing as soaring St. Paul's in London, or as stunningly ornate as Westminster Abbey, had been our favorite, perhaps because it was the first we visited, and returned to see again. Its nearness to Cambridge where we were staying was a factor, and it was where our friend, Ellis, was honored by the Queen, herself, in a traditional ceremony recognizing retired lay people for significant service to their church.

Built in the twelfth century, Ely Cathedral is successor to churches dating back to before the beginning of record keeping in 673 A.D. Structures maintained for more than thirteen centuries give impressive visibility to the reality and vitality of faith.

Young as the Cathedral Hill trees were, they conveyed a significant sense of permanence, as did the limestone pillars in England. While not enduring *individually* for a millennium and a half, all over the globe, lofty trees for countless generations have formed impressive wilderness sanctuaries. In their continuity, they highlight God's declaration, "I the Lord do not change."

Even more than the trees, the ancient stone of the Canadian Shield upon which they grew, gave silent witness to an enduring God. The exposed greenstone of the Canadian Shield formation is some of the oldest rock on earth, the basal "stuff" of creation. Here was permanence, indeed, a foundation resistant to the passage of time. The continuing pines and the bedrock upon which they grew were helpful, hopeful reminders that upsetting turbulence would not triumph.

We needed such lessons. Even in our brief retreat, beautiful and satisfying as it was, we carried with us from the outside world, the turmoil of unsettling change. At best, we could gain only a temporary reprieve. Even the changes in our wilderness voyage were reminders of alterations in the world to which we must return. The wilds could not eliminate them, but gave a useful breathing space and helpful perspective.

I needed such a message. In my own mind, there had been a disconcerting "heaviness," lurking beneath the surface. I was drained and flat, needing a fresh charge to continue to serve. The cathedral grove was for me a helpful encounter, a useful image of renewal and stability. The massive destruction by early century loggers would not be permanent, for the forest was renewing itself. The pines were returning as the premier growth of the ecosystem, creating rustic cathedrals everywhere in the vast tracts of the Superior-Quetico forests.

On our next to the last day, we paddled again in strong winds and chill sunshine, clear signs of the new season at hand. We could not halt the advance of the year nor would we do so if it were possible. Summer is a glorious season, but so are the others. We had hoped for a week of "Indian summer," but if it had been more blustery and cold than anticipated, the trip had still been a wonderful experience, in fact, a "revelation" of an all too fleeting time, one seldom experienced by typical fair-weather campers. We enjoyed our late season trip immensely and would remember it with pleasure.

Reluctant to surrender our autumn interlude, we lingered around our final campfire, far past the serenade of the geese. Like them, we would head south in the morning, back to busy schedules and uncertain futures, to the full arrival of fall and winter. As if to underline the relentless passage of the year with its inevitable change, the next morning we received a vivid reminder of what the geese knew was surely coming - our leftover lemonade had turned to solid *ice.*

As we paddled the last few miles back to the cars, questions filled our minds - would we ever again share such a marvelous week, would we even return to the north country, what surprises might await us in the "outside" world, what did the future hold for each of us? These things and many others were beyond our ability to know in a world beset by constant change. One thing was certain, and for us it was enough; our God was the unchangeable foundation for our tomorrows. Whatever might come in the unknown years, we could rely on the One who said,

"I the Lord do not change." Mal 3:6

Chapter Twelve

LOST, AND FOUND!

"he was lost and is found." Luke 15:24

The emotional storm of being lost is barely describable. It may come as an instant awareness with a rush of terror. Or it may creep up slowly from the subconscious, first with an uneasy sense that something is amiss, followed by growing apprehension, then total bewilderment. Adrenaline pours through the body, preparing for immediate and vigorous action. Failure to control this physical response may account for those who go nearly berserk, tearing off their clothes, running in circles, and doing other bizarre things. To be lost is a profoundly intimidating and disorienting experience.

My first recollection of being lost was during a grouse-hunting trip in my teen years. My brother Tom and I were hunting with our friend, Leonard, in an area with which he was familiar. Following him, we gave no thought to where we were going or how we would get back. Late in the afternoon, however, Len discovered to his dismay and our acute discomfort, that he was not at all sure where we were. I had no idea where we were or how to find our car. Climbing a tree to discover our way was no help at all. Eventually we struck out blindly in a direction that seemed as good as any other, though we had no confidence it was right. How often does dumb luck attend the way of the careless or uninformed? In only ten minutes, we were back on the road we were seeking and, again by chance, followed it in the right direction to reach our car shortly thereafter.

While temporarily frightening, being lost in the wilderness, is usually inconsequential. In most cases, we eventually find our own way or someone else locates us relatively soon. Sometimes, however, losing the way can have tragic consequences. Since getting lost is easy to do, being prepared with a map and compass makes good sense when out in the woods, as I discovered on one particular occasion.

During college years, a group of us decided to go bow hunting for deer. Along a rural road, the five of us lined up in a row about forty yards apart, intending to walk through the woods toward a river a mile and a half away. I was next to the last person on one end of the line. As we proceeded, working our way around trees, bushes, and fallen logs, that person and I gradually got quite close to one another, and then, actually switched places. This put me on the far end of the line.

Picking my way through the thick brush, keeping an eye on the other hunter, and trying to spot a deer, were demanding tasks. Eventually I lost sight of the other man, which did not trouble me too much. I kept forging on for about twenty minutes, until with utter shock and disbelief, I found myself back on the road where we had started! At least in this instance, the familiar notion that people in the wilderness travel in circles, proved to be true. I had wandered in a half circle, 180 degrees from my intended direction. It shook me more than I can tell. I bought a compass before my next trip.

My worst taste of being lost was when I was hunting grouse on Blueberry Mountain in northeastern Washington State. Confident in finding my way and never thinking of bringing a compass, (some people are slow learners!), I had been walking through the bush, heedless of being lost. Plunging down a hillside under a dense canopy of trees, I suddenly wondered, "where am I, where do I go?" Thinking about heading back toward the car, I realized I didn't know how to get there. Nothing seemed familiar. The rush of blood, the surge of emotion, the bewilderment of not knowing where I was and how I would find my way, came crashing into my consciousness. My mind was flooded with surging fear and panic, while my feet were rooted in indecision. Perceptions, questions, and impressions, roared through my brain without resolution.

All thoughts of game birds vanished. The wilderness beauty was obliterated. “Where am I?” screamed in my mind. “How did I get here? How do I get back?” coursed through my head. There were no clear sightlines in the area, only forested ridges and gullies that did not run in a single direction. Nothing was familiar or made sense. I was badly disoriented, the mental map in my mind no longer matching the terrain around me. I was truly lost.

In a couple of minutes I began to calm down and started to think, trying to recall my route to where I now stood. I had started from the car on a clearly defined logging road, that later narrowed to a thin trail. As it mounted higher on the slope, it had become fainter, and overgrown with bushes. Somewhere, I must have stepped through a screening fringe of bush that closed behind me, obscuring the way back. I was lost for sure.

Taking calmer notice of the morning sun, I knew I was now facing east. Since the road and trail I had been following headed generally northward and uphill, I knew I had to go down the slope to the south. The terrain before me sloped roughly east and south, to a valley below. I was relatively certain this would intersect a more familiar area, somewhere close to where I had started. Ignoring the uncertainties, I made my way through the trees, now hunting my car instead of grouse. Within an hour I came to the road and soon found the car.

This briefly terrifying experience taught me a critical lesson, one that I should have learned long before - always take a compass and a map when out in a forest. Losing even a well-defined road or trail is a genuine possibility.

The Seattle Mountaineers have titled their classic textbook on mountain climbing, *The Freedom of the Hills*. The book is emphatic on the need to use maps and compass competently, for even in mountainous terrain where distant landmarks are often clearly visible to provide direction, they may be obscured by rain, fog, or snow. The Mountaineers have identified eight other essentials for wilderness travel that should always be taken when venturing off the beaten track. Beside map and compass, they include extra food, extra clothing, some emergency shelter, sunglasses, first aid kit, matches, fire starter, and a knife. These will provide a margin of safety for the unexpected events in the wilds.

Even boating enthusiasts should take advantage of the safety provided by a compass and map as they travel on larger water. Lakes can be greatly confusing when studded with islands, or when fog or darkness hides crucial landmarks.

More frightening than being lost myself, was when one of our companions was lost. For a time it threatened to devastate our wilderness trip.

We were in two groups this time. My son Scott led a group with his father-in-law Lee, brother-in-law Mark and his son Marc, and two other couples, Craig and Chris, Mel and Robin. In my group were some veterans of previous trips, Janet, Bob, Jim and Rosemary. Rosemary's sister Janice and brother-in-law Laurie, and Dick, an old friend from years before, were all newcomers to the canoe country. I was especially eager for Dick to encounter the marvels of God's wild places. For him it was a dream of a lifetime, finally coming true at age 67. We had not crossed paths for over 30 years, but our re-connection bridged the lapse of time. As we paddled our canoe together, we eagerly recalled times past, updated each other on the intervening years, and shared the delights of God's world.

Under gray skies, we started from Gull Lake Landing, on the Gunflint Trail. As we paddled westward, rain and wind did little to dampen our spirits. Late in the afternoon we set up camp at the west end of the lake. Scott's group was camped across a small bay, a half mile distant from us. We had made prudent provision for the rain, bringing three-pound bags of charcoal to get our fires going for our first meal. In half an hour, the steaks were grilling over the coals. Au gratin potatoes, freeze dried peas, French bread, and cheesecake completed a great meal and a wonderful day.

Still, we hoped for sunshine the next morning, and were not disappointed. With great pleasure, we began breaking camp under bright skies, anticipating a delightful day. I was about to paddle over to Scott's group to tell them to set out ahead of us, when Dick volunteered to go. He wanted to try paddling the canoe alone. I had some slight misgivings, for he had very limited experience in a canoe, but the short distance seemed manageable. I returned to the tasks of dismantling our campsite and preparing to set out again. After twenty minutes or so, I began to wonder if Dick had returned and went to check on him. I saw a canoe far off in the distance, far from the campsite of our other group, and too far to tell if Dick was the paddler.

Returning to our crew, I called Jim to help me look for Dick. Quickly we launched a canoe to begin our search. Though it was less than five minutes from my sighting of the lone canoe, it was now nowhere to be seen. With alarm and worry, we paddled quickly over to our other group. Their words confirmed our fears. Dick had never arrived at their campsite. Searching with binoculars toward the east end of the lake, we failed to see a canoe anywhere.

As we left the shelter of the bay, we discovered the winds of yesterday were still blowing strongly from the northwest. A single paddler would have great difficulty in handling a canoe.

As we pulled furiously on our paddles, we saw a boat with three occupants heading toward the far South shore. When we drew near enough, we asked if they had seen a solo paddler in a canoe. To our joy, they said they had, though it had been quite some time before.

Leaving them, we paddled further east, searching desperately for sight of him. Though the waves were surging, it seemed unlikely they were high enough to obscure a canoe. Why couldn't we see him? Our unspoken worry was that he had capsized. That was a thought too dreadful to contemplate. How I reproached myself for letting him go alone. Anxiety scourged me and drove my paddle faster and deeper.

As we stroked onward, we spotted another canoe, but unfortunately, it carried two paddlers. It was along the shore to the south and east of us, and we frantically paddled to ask them if they had seen anyone. When we were close enough for them to hear us, they said, “yes,” they had seen a single man paddling off to the northeast. As they tried to tell us where, they caught sight of him and directed our view, until we, too, located a distant paddler. Surely, it had to be Dick, for only rarely in the Boundary Waters do you find a solo paddler.

Off we flew again, paddling with our might, but now greatly relieved that in all likelihood, our friend was safe. At last, we pulled beside him. With gratitude too deep for words, we tied our craft to his and prepared to head back toward camp. Dick's warm smile for our rescue effort was deeply heartfelt. I was grateful that he did not appear upset or anxious. He was actually calm and cheerful, admitting that he had not had the right direction to the other campsite. As I had expected, the winds were too much for him. Once out of the sheltered bay, he could not make headway in the face of the winds.

The saying that "all's well that ends well," has a great measure of truth in it. At least I could take comfort that our fright of a couple hours duration was only that. Dick had simply stayed with the craft, letting the canoe run with the wind, a prudent course of action since he would eventually have drifted to shore. At least now, he was safe. We joyfully thanked God for a good outcome of this misadventure. With Dick's canoe tied behind us, we eventually drew near to our campsite.

How our comrades cheered the return of our wilderness wanderer. It was like the return of the Prodigal Son that Jesus told about in Luke 15. Celebration is essential, the Father said, when the rebel returns to the family, when a sinner repents and is restored. As a long-devoted follower of Jesus, Dick had made that spiritual commitment to God years before, but our joy at his recovery from physical peril was profound.

In due time, our group was underway again, the blue-green wilderness calming the anxieties of our frightening experience and giving us great pleasure. Dick was moderately chagrined, and from time to time, made laughing reference to his ineptness. Fortunately, it was not enough to dull his appreciation of the trip and he wrote a daily journal to share with his family when he returned. He expressed hope that in the future, his sons and sons-in-law could join him in a similar experience. On my part, I could muster no hilarity like the others, in the mild bantering over this episode. Our desperate search for our friend was too serious for humor, reminding me of Jesus' life-mission in coming to earth, to "seek and to save the lost, (Luke 19:10).

Two days later, we came to awesome Lake Saganaga, the third largest, and the deepest lake (280 ft) in the BWCA, where we would spend two nights before making our way back to civilization. That gave us a free day to do whatever we desired. Scott's group settled on a site a couple of miles distant and planned to use their day for fishing. Our crew found a pleasant campsite, and decided to use the next day to visit Silver Falls, across Cache Bay on the Canadian side of Saganaga.

Setting out the next morning, we checked in at the Canadian ranger station where they told us of some pictographs in Lost Bay. Since it wasn't marked on our map, the ranger gave us verbal directions. I sketched these as best I could on the border of the map sheet, and off we went.

With only one false probe of an incorrect bay, we soon found the right one, a closed cove with no outlet. There on an exposed rock face was a set of faded red markings, two stick figures and several short lines. The figures are called, "Mamigwezi." In Indian lore, they are somewhat like the leprechauns of Ireland, mischievous creatures that delight to play tricks on unwary travelers. To the Indians and early French Voyageurs, the Mamigwezi were thought to be responsible for minor mishaps, such as when canoes unexpectedly tipped at places of no real danger.

As I pondered the images and others I had seen across the canoe country, I wondered about their significance, and why this place had been called Lost Bay? Had some accident occurred at this place, or some tragedy? Was it the bay itself that was "lost," a location that was not found by someone who set out to travel there? Was it a person who was missing, perhaps an Indian unaccountably stranded at this spot, maybe even perishing? Or was it bygone fur traders who made their way to this dead end when they intended to go somewhere else? So many ancient mysteries linger in this great wilderness.

These musings were banished from my mind as we arrived at thundering Silver Falls, a magnificent torrent gushing from the lake. In breathtaking beauty the water rushed and hissed over a rocky defile, falling 50 feet into the river below. The sunlight broke into a spectrum of colors in the lofted spray of water which drifted over us. Venturing near the lip, we crossed small side channels over fallen logs to get closer views. In the midst of this spectacle, real danger was present. Surely over the centuries of travel by the Indians and then the fur traders, people had narrow escapes if not genuine loss of life at places like this. Some of the journals of the fur traders recount such incidents.

Explorer David Thompson, in the early 1800's recorded an occasion further northwest in Canada. With two Indian companions, they encountered near tragedy when his canoe was swept backwards over a waterfall. He escaped with his life but severely injured his foot. Losing all their goods, they endured grave hardship in making their way back over many miles in bitter cold weather, with no food and only the clothes on their backs. Though not lost in direction, they lost most of life's necessities and nearly life itself. Thompson expressed profound gratitude to God for preserving his life.

The next day as we paddled toward our final campsite, Jim led the way. He had been hopelessly confused during our first day of travel, because he was misinformed about our starting point. We had intended to set out on the Sea Gull River and travel south into the main lake before turning west, but changed our minds and departed from the public landing at the east end of the lake. Throughout the day's travel, he was vainly trying to make sense of our direction of travel from where we had originally planned to launch our canoes. Now he had a more satisfying experience. Keeping a careful eye on the chart and frequently checking the compass heading, he successfully guided us through the islands.

In early afternoon we came to a great campsite, as did the other group on the opposite side of the same island. Regulations prevented us from camping together or even traveling on the water in a compact group, but at least with near proximity, some of us from our group could join a couple from the others for fishing. In the evening, we spread our bags and mattresses on a rock shelf at the north edge of our campsite to behold the skies, contemplating the marvel and beauty of the distant stars. It was an awesome sight, a fitting climax to a fine week in a splendid wilderness.

Our journey home the next day was filled with recollections of delight. I was especially grateful that Dick’s misadventure seemed to be taken in stride. Our brief experiences with being lost were only temporary. We had found our way and were on course, for this world, and the next.

Chapter Thirteen

THE MOON

God made two great lights...
the lesser light to govern the night.
Genesis 1:16

Do you remember what you were doing the night of July 20, 1969? Of course, many people were not yet born at the time, but for those who were, the date itself may have little impact. Like other momentous events, however, such as the assassination of John Kennedy or the destruction of the World Trade Center, there is for most people an indelible image of event and place attached to it.

I was directing a week of summer camping for fourth through sixth grade boys, at Pine Lake Camp in central Iowa. Because of their youth and the schedule of vigorous activity, our normal evening events gradually wound down to a relatively early bedtime. This night, however, would be special, in fact, a night like none other in all our lives, justifying a drastic change in routine. So we altered the order of the day, keeping the kids up far past their usual lights out, and contrary to all precedent, allowing them to watch television!

Borrowing a set from somewhere, we placed it high on a table in the dining hall. Following the regular events of the evening, we seated the kids before the screen. In breathless suspense we watched, as heavy boots descended a spindly ladder and then crunched the dusty gray soil. The forever-memorable footprints of Neil Armstrong were clearly visible on the moon's virgin surface. For the first time, humans had set foot on soil beyond their earthly home, a "small step for man, one giant leap for mankind."

The impossible had now been achieved, technology triumphing over unimaginable obstacles, the ingenuity of man surpassing all previous exploits. No longer would tales of the man-in-the-moon and green cheese provide material for casual humor. The mystery, wonder, and searching questions stimulated by the moon, were changed forever by images of hard reality transmitted from a quarter million miles away.

Or so, perhaps, it seemed at first glance. Who would discount the marvel and magnificence of the achievement? To dig beneath the lunar surface, to explore its cratered landscape, to cavort in its feeble gravity, even playing a bit of lunar golf, and bringing back loads of rocks for experimentation were astounding accomplishments, tributes to mankind's mastery over the environment, now extended beyond his native planet.

Yet what a brief and shallow impact has been made on the moon itself. To earthbound watchers, no trace of this incredible activity is visible at all. Except for a modest number of scientists, the moon remains as distant, unknown, and mysterious as ever. In silent orbit above the earth, it continues as an object of beauty to those who travel about in the hours of darkness, a darkness made a bit less foreboding by the borrowed light of the hidden sun.

It was in the light of a full July moon that John and I discovered the magic of Iowa's wilderness. Yes, wilderness, even in Iowa! It can be found, in fact, anywhere in the world, even in great urban centers inhabited by millions of people. Of course, it is not the wilderness of the northern forests or western mountains, but it is genuine nonetheless. It's essential character is "wildness," not remoteness, (though in the hours of darkness, even that may be discerned to some degree). Every city has wooded parks, greenbelts, and other areas left in natural cover. No state is so completely agricultural, urban, or commercial, that it does not have literally thousands of acres of trees, grasslands, seacoast, swamps, and other terrain left in a natural state. And no matter how small they may be, or how surrounded by residential or industrial tracts, they are inhabited by wild creatures that venture forth at night.

The occasion of our discovery was a Fourth of July paddle down the Wapsipinicon River. Putting in at Troy Mills at about ten a.m., we set out for a great day of family fun. Four-year-old Mike, wearing a football helmet and swinging a tiny 24-inch paddle, helped his parents, Jim and Sandy. Barb and Janette assisted their Dad, John. Forest and his son, Steve, shared a canoe, and Dave and Judy another. Ken and his boys, Steve and Jeff, paddled together, as did Roy and his sons, Paul and Karl. Shirley and I paddled the sterns of two canoes, helped by our kids, Scott, Leigh, and Karen.

Our journey was a pleasant mixture of relaxed paddling, lazy floating, swimming, laughing, singing, and good-natured horseplay. At one place, as Scott was bending over the bow peering intently into the water, Dave, in the canoe alongside, gave our boat a sudden shove. Scott went overboard in an instant. His sudden ducking was a surprise, though not an unpleasant one. Later, nudging against an overhanging tree, Judy discovered a snake, and nearly capsized her canoe in haste to get away. As the rest of us were maneuvering around the tree, a small bass, perhaps disturbed by the commotion riling the stream, jumped out of the water and landed in a canoe! It was a delightful day of wholesome fun.

Late in the afternoon, we arrived at our destination, a streamside picnic ground, where we were joined by some spouses and children who had not come along for the day's paddle. Our cookout and games lasted well into the evening hours. As we drew things to a close and families departed, John and I were reluctant to end a fabulous day. The weather was perfect, the water was still inviting, and a huge full moon was rising in the velvet sky.

"What do you say about paddling down to the next bridge," John asked me. "The wives can drive a car down and leave it for us, and then go on home. It's only about six miles so it won't take too long. What do you think?"

There was really no decision to make, for the prospect was irresistible. Off we went, into the unfamiliar world of night, through fringing woodlands that seemed as boundless and remote as the far North, into a true *wilderness* created by the transforming darkness, a darkness that also unloosed the daylight's hidden creatures.

We floated down a sinuous dark ribbon. Overhead a leafy silhouette brushed a blue-black sky. We were helped on our way by an occasional glint of moonlight piercing the foliage but often we navigated by varying degrees of shadow. How feeble our eyesight seemed as we watched for lurking obstacles, which fortunately, were very few. As the darkness inhibited sight, hearing assumed greater prominence.

The quiet was impressive. Of course, we now had no noisy companions. Though the river flowed with the same volume as in the earlier hours, it now sounded different, voicing a muted warble of soft undertones we had not noticed during the day. Paddling in attentive quiet, as if fearful of breaking the enchanted hush of night, we were attuned to unknown sounds of a different world. Our infrequent words were barely more than whispers. The waters murmured their gentle song, insects hummed in unseen flight, a subtle breeze rustled the leaves, and now and then, small "cracks" and scurryings along the banks, signaled the presence of lively creatures going about their nocturnal business. Then from somewhere overhead came the disembodied refrain of a whip-poor-will, repeating its name again and again, filling the silvery night with its call.

As we continued our quiet journey, a sudden splash a few yards ahead startled our meditations. A dimly lit wake on the water ended in a spreading ring of turbulence. A short way downstream our supposition was soon confirmed, as we watched a beaver snorkeling through the water, its broad tail trailing behind. Drawing a bit too close, it disappeared with a resounding "splat," of its broad tail upon the water, indignantly disapproving of our intrusion and warning its companions of our threatening presence. Though we strained our eyes for further glimpses, the creature had vanished into the darkness of night and water, a phantom from the age and land of the fur traders. But the beaver was real, its presence in a farm state like Iowa powerfully underscoring the existence of wildness even in the tame and settled areas of the country.

Brief as it was, our encounter was sufficient, a final pleasure to crown an evening of delight. The elements had been in perfect harmony. Sight and sound, the easy thrust of our paddles in the gliding stream, the humid smell of summer vegetation, joined in wondrous complement, a subtle reality unknown and unknowable in the stark brightness of day. It had been an enchanted time in a magic place. But even magical journeys come to an end, as ours did at the appointed rendezvous.

The passing years and realities of a hurried and mechanical world, however, have not erased that singular night from my memory. It springs into fresh existence when the pale light floods the rustling trees and gleaming waters. It awaits re-discovery whenever the moon rides high.

Of all sightings of the moon, surely an eclipse is the most spectacular. They are frequent enough that nearly all adults have seen one, but still rare enough to be special. One was especially noteworthy for me, because it happened when I was in the backcountry.

I was with a group of teen-age back packers in the mountains west of Anaconda, Montana. This was a first-time experience for most of them. The leader, Bob, had planned just the right kind of route, neither too easy, nor too hard, in an area of magnificent scenery. To top it off, he informed us one morning that an eclipse of the moon would be visible that evening. It was a surprise to me since I had somehow missed the usual newspaper and TV announcements of the pending event. It would also be the first time I had ever observed one in a wilderness setting.

With no light pollution in the mountains, the moon that night was more brilliant than ever, the bright glow an environment of wonder, casting a silver-gray sheen upon everything. With no roof over our heads, we had an unrestricted view of the eclipse's entirety. A dent at the moon's edge grew to a curving cutout, continued to a missing quarter, and finally, a vanishing white sliver, when the familiar disk had completely darkened. The eclipse's methodical progression was irresistible, forcing our attention to conform to its deliberate pace. Other activities could not overcome its spell, for the eclipse was compelling, demanding continued observation, forcing contemplation of an awesome universe and its lively bodies. Especially intriguing was the dramatic change of color when the earth shadow had completely covered the moon, shifting from dark gray to orange-red. Then the restoration sequence followed, until the familiar moon was whole again. It was an eerie, moving, and beautiful spectacle.

In former ages, eclipses caused great anxiety over these heavenly displays since their cause was largely unknown. In our sophisticated, scientific era, of course, there is no longer any worry about supernatural forces or baleful influences from the moon. To us it is merely a dim light source at night, a feeble reflection from a distant sun gleaming beyond the far side of earth. Yet, reports are still made of strange human behavior during the days when the moon is full. And how can we explain the persistence of phrases like "moonstruck," and nervous humor about the effects of a full moon? Not everyone seems to be confident with factual knowledge about the moon.

It may well be that wild creatures react to moonlight in special ways. While wary animals like deer display extra caution when the moon is bright, others seem to act more boldly. Whether wolves and dogs truly howl at the moon may be impossible to prove but it certainly appears so. Reports of weird behavior apparently triggered by moonlight have been given for other animals.

A fascinating example is an incident described by Sigurd Olson in his book, *The Singing Wilderness*. Camped out on a night of brilliant moonlight, a rustling on the side of the tent attracted his attention. Peeking out, he observed a mouse scrambling up one of the guy ropes. Making its way along the ridgeline, teetering in precarious balance, it suddenly jumped off, doing a "belly flop" down the sloping side of the tent. To his amazement, the mouse returned to the rope, walked out on the ridge, and launched out once more down the slippery slide. Then, again, and again, each time with more skill and abandon, the tiny beast repeated its daring act, appearing to its astonished observer to do so for sheer enjoyment. What other explanation could better account for such extraordinary behavior? Was the moonshine a factor? Who can tell? But it did happen in the moon’s full light.

Whatever the actual effect of moonlight, most humans find it appealing and beautiful. The subdued light, which merely brightens rather than dispels the darkness, is appreciated more for its pale allure than for any significant illumination. Since moonlight is 400,000 times less bright than sunlight, the cone cells in our eyes cannot distinguish colors in its light, though for some people, objects under moonlight seem to take on a bluish cast. For me, the surroundings are transformed in pearlescent light, the bold colors of day muted and altered to tones of silver and grey.

While we treasure sunlight, embracing it as our essential environment and reveling in its warm comfort, we are not able to gaze at its blinding brilliance. It is not so with the moon. The moon is a congenial friend to man, directly observable in contrast to the blazing sun, and in perception, larger and nearer than the distant stars. Peering intently at its scarred surface, the moon provokes searching, wonder, and in former times, even worship. To many, in fact, behind the enjoyment of the moon and other natural splendors, there is an awareness of something greater still, a powerful sense of a great Creator to whom the material realm gives witness. Little wonder that the Psalmist wrote, "the skies proclaim the work of His hands," (Ps. 19:1).

Creator and creation were in my mind on a singular night in the canoe country. We were near the end of our travels, camped for a final night on an island in Disappointment Lake. Though revealing only a portion of its face, the moon's light was surprisingly bright, dimming the stars, but brightening the dark forest and water with its soft silver. We did not need flashlights for camp chores this evening, as the "moonshine" bathed the land.

Rosemary and I could not resist a late evening paddle, easing across the water in alert silence. Loons punctuated the stillness with their stirring calls. Across the black water, a silver ribbon stretched to the western shore. The wash of moonlight covered everything, transforming the world with its luster. We were pleasantly "moonstruck," caught in its otherworldly spell. It was quietly thrilling, magical, enchanting, yet elusive, a fleeting time and experience that could not be detained, only treasured in mind and memory. The moon made the difference.

Of the Biblical passages referring to the moon, none is more intriguing to me than Ps 89:36, 37. Concerning His promise to establish an everlasting Kingship founded on the line of David, God says, "his throne will endure before me like the sun; it will be established forever like the moon, the faithful witness in the sky." It is clear by these words, that the sun and moon were meant to be signs of unchanging permanence, even to eternity. In appearance, both bodies circle the earth, year after year through the ages. While we now know that they are both undergoing change, for comparative purposes, they are essentially everlasting. Like them, the Messiah, ultimate ruler of the Davidic dynasty, will reign forever.

While some translations construe the sentence to include both sun and moon as witnesses, most single out the moon alone as a witness. But what is the significance of the moon's characterization as a *faithful* witness?

It may simply be a reinforcement of the statement, meant to convey that the unfolding fulfillment of the promise is constantly visible, like the never-failing moon. This makes good sense. As the rainbow continually serves to recall the promise that God will never again send an earth-destroying flood, so the moon never falters in its task as a visible reminder of His plan. But that function is true also of the sun, so what significance is there in highlighting the moon in a special way?

What intrigues me as a possible answer, is the moon's special relation to the crucifixion and resurrection of Jesus. Passover/Easter is a highly unusual, perhaps unique, religious season because of its variable date, always tied specifically to the full moon of spring. Passover starts with the full moon of the Hebrew month of Nisan, late March to early April in the western calendar.

On the night of Jesus' arrest, it is likely that the sky was clear, since the rainy months of January and February were past. A large crowd in the high priest's courtyard stood around a warming fire, improbable if it was raining, and the sharp cold a likely indicator of a cloudless sky. Under the moon's revealing illumination, Jesus' nighttime arrest and trial could not be hidden by darkness. People who were there could see what was going on because of the full moon's light.

There may be still more in this text. It suggests to me that the shining moon was a celestial observer of the events on earth, an eye in the sky, so to speak, offering reliable and truthful testimony of all that happened to Jesus, since it occurred outdoors and in full view from above. At the tragedy of the crucifixion, the sun withdrew its light, but the moon was steadfast, lighting the dark scenes and watching all that went on.

The watchful moon was a witness as well, of the resurrection. While even the posted guards failed to see His emergence from the tomb, the unblinking witness above saw it clearly. When the women came to the tomb early in the morning of resurrection Sunday, John's gospel says it was still dark, since the sun had not yet risen. If the moon had not yet set, its light helped them as they made their way to the place of great discovery.

Whatever the precise meaning of the passage may be, the full moon at Easter continues as a faithful herald, reminding us year after year, of the resurrection of the Lord. While we treasure a warm, sunny Easter Sunday, the lesser light of Easter eve should be treasured as well.

It has been some time now, since I have been under the moon in the wilderness, but I see it now more than ever. Our new home faces the east from a slight elevation.

When the moon is full or nearly so, I see it rising above the horizon in its lovely brilliance. Despite the several hundred times I have seen it in my lifetime, it always attracts my attention. It is never merely ho-hum. In the week of its near fullness, Shirley and I usually remark on its beauty several evenings in succession.

And now, more than ever, its critical importance should be appreciated. While the sun's necessity for human existence has been known for centuries, discoveries in the past few decades demonstrate that all animal life is also dependent on the moon. Moon-generated tides are crucial in preventing life-essential nutrients from being buried in ocean depths. The moon is also necessary to stabilize earth's tilt axis as it circles the sun, preventing earth from becoming uninhabitable because of extreme temperatures. Further, the moon serves as a brake on the earth's speed of rotation, slowing it from an earlier 5-hour day to our present 24, and reducing unlivable wind speeds of 1000 miles an hour, to the familiar ones of present-day experience. Other factors, too, reveal the moon to be not only "the governor" of the night, but a very preserver of earth-life itself. "*And God saw that it was good.* And so it is, indeed.

Chapter Fourteen

HIGHWAY IN THE WILDERNESS

...make straight in the wilderness
a highway for our God. *Isaiah 40:3*

We heard it in the quiet of evening, an unexpected, out of place murmur in the east, faint, but undeniable. Except for the piercing call of the loons, ordinary night sounds were hushed and irregular, the soft slap of a wavelet against the rocks, a tremor among the trees, an unknown rustling in the bushes.

During the day, we had not been conscious of the distant noise since campsite activities and the daytime exuberance of nature were enough to cover so subtle a sound. In the silence of night, however, it was surprising how far away the river rapids could be heard. Though we were more than three miles from its foaming turbulence, there was no mistaking the presence of Curtain Falls. Perhaps even Rebecca Falls added its voice to the dark melody, for it was less than another mile distant from Curtain. I was inwardly pleased to hear the falling water for it could help our navigation, guiding us by ear to the portage around it.

When morning came, however, the sound had vanished, smothered somehow in a dense fog that obscured every object beyond our immediate campsite. Now neither sight nor sound was available to help in finding our route. While I was hopeful the fog would lift by the time of our departure, I was still somewhat concerned. I had four magnificent maps of various portions of our route, but where the maps joined one another, a sliver of territory, precisely where we had to travel to the falls, was not shown. It would be difficult enough in clear weather; in the fog we could easily miss a narrow opening between islands and points, perhaps losing our way in a deep bay with no outlet. That would eat up time and energy, and could create disorienting confusion. We would have to take our chances and hope for the best.

Our experience of the day before intensified my unease. To begin with, we had made a mistake in following a wrong portage. The first of our canoers approaching the west shore of Gull Lake saw a portage in plain sight. Well acquainted with the routine, they quickly unloaded the boats, shouldered packs, and started out on what was supposed to be a very brief carry of 35 rods, no more than five minutes. When no water had appeared after twenty minutes, it was obvious that something was amiss. As one of the last to arrive at the carrying place and start down the trail, I was surprised to see them coming back with their loads. "This can't be the right portage," they said. It was time to re-check the map.

Sure enough, two portages were marked on the map, a 35-rod portage at the northwest end of the lake, and another of 240 rods just a short distance from the first. Unfortunately, the long one (wrong for us) was clearly visible from out on the lake. The one we needed was hidden in a narrow, deep inlet that was out of sight. With groans for the extra labor and wasted time, we soon found the right path.

The missing map segment caused the second trouble. Arriving at Iron Lake after a long day of travel, we slowly forged our way through acre after acre of dense wild rice, but were unsure of our location. The small map did not show enough detail to identify landmarks with certainty and we could not find any campsites. Weary as we were we struggled on, dividing into separate search parties in an attempt to locate an established site among the many bays and long shorelines. After an hour without success, I led our dispirited crew to a long rocky spit where we could pitch our camp at an undesignated spot. I was tired myself and unhappy that my failure as a guide had caused the others unnecessary labor. At least some food perked up our spirits.

As we neared the end of our meal, I continued to search the distant shores with binoculars hoping to discover one of the permanent campsites where we could legally stay for the night. Half a mile to the north, a likely looking place seemed promising. Recruiting two of the more energetic men for the task, I sent them off to investigate. They returned shortly with good news, leading us to one of the most magnificent sites I have ever found in the BWCA, so good in fact that we decided to spend two nights enjoying its amenities, giving us a day without travel to make up for our hard previous day. We enjoyed our unscheduled day of leisure immensely.

Now we had to move on. Thankfully, the fog lifted by the time we were under way, but with a shift of the wind, we could still not hear the falls. Working carefully with the compass and filling in the "missing" map data with my best judgment, we found our way with satisfying accuracy. Now we could finally hear the powerful roar of falling water.

Some men were standing at the shore. As we greeted them, we failed to notice subtle signs of swift water. Fifty yards from the landing, a powerful rush of current from the nearby falls unexpectedly roiled the calm, flat water of Iron Lake. The lead canoes were suddenly gripped by the surging stream. Vigorous paddling and attempts to adjust the angle of advance were too late as the canoes were shoved sideways and backwards. There was little real danger, just a bit of unexpected embarrassment in the presence of the bystanders on shore. Mercifully, they said nothing, perhaps realizing our conversation had caught us off guard.

A recent discovery has cast a new light on this small incident. Reading a book about this historic canoe route, I learned that the great North American explorer and geographer, David Thompson, had a similar experience at Curtain Falls. He recorded in his journal that in 1797, when approaching this precise spot, he too "very near upset" in the "strong Current." If an experienced canoe man like Thompson could have a narrow escape, perhaps novice paddlers should not be too hard on themselves over a similar result.

We quickly made successful second tries, arriving at the portage with a new appreciation for the force of slanting water. As we carried our first loads of canoes and packs up the slight incline, we heard the increasing rush of water, pulsating and throbbing through the air. Suddenly, where the trail crested a low rise, we could see the vast pool of Crooked Lake escaping in pent-up fury over a narrow sill of rock, exploding in gushing bounds to the riverbed thirty-five feet below. It was an entrancing spectacle, stopping us in our tracks. After a brief glance, we quickly turned to complete our portage so we could properly view the falls and give serious attention to the water.

We pressed to the very brink of the falls, fascinated by the water's transformation from blue tranquility to frothing white savagery. It was possessed, thunderous, and unbridled, gripping us with its power and taunting us to come nearer. To capture its vitality was impossible. We resorted to taking pictures and splashing in tributary rivulets as a feeble response. After half an hour, we reluctantly returned to the canoes to continue our travel.

The beautiful vistas of Crooked Lake were wonderful, new to us but comfortably familiar in their similarity to the North Country's countless other lakes, great glacial gouges filled with crystalline water. Moving water, to me at least, was another matter, compelling, somehow mystifying, especially in its most dramatic expression at waterfalls. It was obvious that the water came from the higher impoundment and fell to a lower basin, but for all the thunderous escape of myriad gallons, the upper levels seemed undiminished. Why did the waters not stop? How could it possibly continue to flow? How could a vast lake like Crooked, often surging *eastward* in raging waves continue to slip *westward* through the gap at Curtain Falls? Gravity, of course, is the simple answer, but a seemingly inadequate one. The questions lingered in my mind as we once again gave serious attention to navigation.

Crooked Lake is aptly named, a huge lake strewn for a dozen miles along the international boundary, with deep projecting bays to the south and north – (from west to east), Sunday, Saturday, Friday, Thursday, and Wednesday on the U.S. side, and an equal number in Canada (of which, unaccountably, only one, Gardner, is named on my maps). Careful attention to the map and compass would be needed to keep us on course, for the bold streak on the map dividing the two countries was invisible in the real world of blue and green through which we traveled.

As we neared the tip of an island, an unusual noise arrested our attention. Halting our paddling, we listened to hear it again. In a few seconds, we heard a high- pitched squealing that varied in tone and intensity. Bev wanted to investigate immediately but I decided against it. If it were a couple of bear cubs as I supposed, or less likely, a litter of wolf pups, it would be best not to disturb them, or their mother! It would remain a lingering mystery to recall in years to come.

Reasonably sure of our route, we had stopped for lunch along the southern shore when one of our crew noticed a strange object on top of a rock. Closer examination revealed a six-inch tall brass obelisk embedded in the granite, with numbers and letters inscribed on its four sides. "U.S. Boundary" it read, "568.” As we pondered these findings, sudden awareness struck me. "Of course," I burst out with a laugh. All along the black line on the map, marking the location of the International Boundary, were little squares with numbers. In this area on the U.S. side, were 565, 566, 567, 568, and so on. We were paddling a water highway used for hundreds of years and these were modern-day signposts! At least in this portion of the wilderness, we could be sure where we were. From Grand Portage on Lake Superior to the western edge of the state on Lake of the Woods, the 547-mile border between Canada and Minnesota was clearly posted. My worries about finding the way were as unsubstantial as the early fog; the joke was on me and I fully appreciated the humor of it.

That evening, camped on a west-facing site only a hundred yards across the water from the Canadian shore, someone got the bright idea to swim to another country. It was strictly illegal, of course, if we actually stepped on the shore, but the notion seemed irresistible. Soon several bodies were churning the water to swim to our northern neighbor. As souvenirs, some of the swimmers brought back exotic foreign flowers to those who stayed behind. Whether anyone actually stood on Dominion land is lost in the dust of history.

In ancient days, there were no such national entities and finding the way was by slow trial and error. Bit by bit, the first humans in the area had to learn their way around. Now called Paleo-Indians, they entered the area 10,000 years or more ago, after the retreat of ice-age glaciers. Intriguing remains of their presence continue to be uncovered.

Once when several members of our family were spending a week in a cabin south of Ely, Leigh and I visited an archeological "dig" at McDougal Lake near Isabella, MN. About six people were carefully scraping the soil from a small pit. They showed us an arrowhead that had recently been uncovered from a layer of earth estimated to be about 8500 years old. Other recent finds have provided evidence of human occupation as long as 11,000 years ago, including a Clovis style spear point from a site north of Duluth.

With no roads or trails, the Indians had to navigate by the stars and terrestrial landmarks, making mental maps and probably drawing them with charcoal on birch bark. These early inhabitants developed marvelous skills, enabling them to travel through thousands of miles of dense forest without the help of a compass.

When Europeans arrived with compasses and sextants, they drew exacting maps as they explored and traded. Early explorers and fur traders made note of natural landforms to help find their way. When such features were lacking, they often trimmed the lower branches from prominent tall trees, leaving a conspicuous tuft at the top as a route marker. These "lob-pines" continued to show the way long after the fur trade was abandoned.

The best routes became permanent since they provided the quickest and easiest access through the area. They became literal highways, though not paved with concrete or asphalt as in modern times. Using water routes wherever available and primitive trails where portages were necessary, they traveled from Lake Superior into the far interior of Canada and the western territories of the U.S. In most cases, these routes followed those developed centuries before by the Cree, Sioux, and Ojibway Indians. For centuries, water routes and anchorages had been called "roads." The most common thoroughfare through the border country was called The Voyagers Highway.

Sometimes early travelers missed the road and got lost. In July, 1823, while trying to determine the exact location of the boundary, American, Major Joseph Delafield, and Englishman, Dr. John Bigsby, members of the International Boundary Commission, got lost more than once among the islands of Crooked Lake, even with the help of Indian guides. Their work established the "customary route," which became the international boundary, utilizing the best, easiest, and shortest way between the two nations. Portages were sometimes on what became the American side, and other times on the Canadian. The Webster-Ashburton Treaty of 1842 settled the route of the boundary and granted free passage to all travelers on the unguarded border.

Long before this official determination, nearly as soon as the fur trade began, Catholic missionaries began traveling the water routes to teach the Indians about faith in Christ. The "black robes" poured out their lives to teach about a coming King, Jesus. All of these men, often of considerable learning (Marquette mastered six Indian languages), were surely mindful of Isaiah's text about a wilderness highway. In the New Testament gospels, the passage was applied to the work of John the Baptist who prepared the way for Jesus' ministry. The priests could not have failed to see themselves in an identical role as announcers of the King.

As the prophet Isaiah had urged, they were to prepare a highway, metaphorically filling valleys and leveling hills for His arrival. In the ancient world, kings often came to be honored by his subjects. Roadways were smoothed for the Sovereign, rolling out the red carpet, so to speak. The enduring application of the text is that responsive people are to prepare energetically for the return of the Lord. It is significant that Jesus called himself, "The *Way*" (John 14:6), and the early Christians were called "followers of the way"

That was a significant purpose in our trip, too. While we paddled the wilderness highway, finding refreshment of body and mind, we were there as well to encounter the Creator through the medium of His creation. We left behind the mountains and valleys of civilized clutter, to let loon calls, sunsets, flashing water, and the smell of pine resin smooth the bumps and holes in our inner beings. Each morning we read from the Bible and prayed, often singing His praises. Through the day as we paddled, it was impossible not to connect with His presence.

Except in short segments used by recreational paddlers, the Voyagers Highway now seldom functions as a long distance thoroughfare. Instead, the huge area of lakes and forest has been designated the Boundary Waters Canoe Area Wilderness on the U.S. side of the border, and the Quetico Provincial Park on the Canadian side. Multiple thousands of outdoor lovers enjoy the glories of the area, mostly following loop routes of a few days duration. The guidebooks by Robert Beymer describe nearly a hundred popular "roads" through the wilderness. In the BWCAW, entry is restricted to a modest number of access points, the most popular of which can be quite congested at times, much like heavy traffic in the city. Once beyond a day's paddle, however, the waterways are virtually empty, providing a marvelous opportunity to experience creation as it must have been before the coming of mankind.

So we traveled down the highway. At Lower Basswood Falls, the portage around the fast water was on Canadian side. Further east, near marker 765, we left the main highway, turning south on a secondary route through the Horse River, Horse and Fourtown Lakes, and returned to Ely. Driving south on paved highway 169 and Interstate 35, we traveled past woodlands, farmsteads, small towns, and great cities. Not too long before, even these modern roads had been scarcely more than pathways through virgin wilderness.

Some of us returned to the Voyager's Highway a few years later. Traveling west through several lakes, we entered lovely Knife Lake and turned east, picking up the customary route of the voyagers along the International Border. The sky was bright and the wind at our back, making paddling a breeze. At Little Knife Portage we carried across a short, rocky trail, then launched into Ottertrack (or Cypress Lake, as it was named by the French voyagers because of the many *Cedar* trees lining its shores. Names in the North country are often the confusing contribution of Indian, French, English, and American travelers over centuries of usage).

Along the south shore of the lake, we came to the home site of Benny Ambrose, one of the last permanent residents of the BWCAW. Though the house has been removed, the place is marked with a plaque. He lived for over sixty years in a small, one room cabin, guiding, trapping, and prospecting for gold, and where he and his wife raised two children, over fifty miles from the nearest town. Originally from Iowa, he hauled sacks of topsoil from his native state to enhance his garden in the Minnesota forest. He died in 1982. Flowers that he planted still bloom at this historic spot.

As we continued our journey, the memories of these bygone travelers lingered in our minds. To have names, dates, and life-details of previous sojourners in the wilderness added depth and charm to our experience of the country, giving substance to remote history.

A few miles and two portages later, we paddled into Lake Saganaga, dotted with nearly 300 islands. At American Point, we found a fine campsite in a beautiful little bay where we stayed two nights, giving us a day to spend as we pleased. Two events were especially memorable, one bad and one good. While we were all away from camp during our "free" day, someone visited our site and stole one of our single-burner gas stoves. It was irritating, but at least our loss was small.

The positive experience was a baptismal service. Mark senior had asked if I would baptize him in God's wilderness where His presence was so powerfully alive to people of faith. I was pleased to do so. All of us clustered around and I read the pertinent Biblical instruction. Mark related how he had invited Jesus to reign in his life as Lord. Fully immersing him in the water, then standing him up, completed a picture of burial and resurrection. As he shook the water from his eyes, his companions broke into spontaneous cheers of approval. Though it will never appear on the maps of the Voyager's Highway, "Baptism Bay" lingers in my mental image, a fitting place and an appropriate action to mark the King's wilderness highway.

Chapter Fifteen

ANIMALS AT OUR DOOR

Every animal of the forest is mine,
and the cattle on a thousand hills.
I know every bird in the mountains
and the creatures of the field are mine.
Ps 50:11

Alyssa calls us from upstairs, "There's a deer outside."

"What?" we ask.

She says it again as she comes downstairs, "There is a deer across the street."

Peering out the window, we see nothing unusual. Joining us, she says, "See, at the corner of the garage across the street. Now it's moving."

Then we see it too. Hesitantly and cautiously it moves into the cul-de-sac. It stops, looks back, takes a few steps forward, stops again, looks around, then continues into our driveway. It looks back across the street again, then proceeds to our front walk.

We all chatter quietly, looking through the window at the deer just twelve feet away. The deer does not appear alarmed, but is alert, seeming to inspect the bush in the front yard. Then it walks out of sight in front of the garage, perhaps checking the bushes growing on the other side.

"Look," Alyssa exclaims, "there are two more!"

Sure enough, across the street are two smaller deer stepping hesitantly toward the street. Now the first deer, almost certainly the mother of the twin yearlings, walks back into our view. As the youngsters cross the street, the mother walks out to join them. They follow her as she walks between our house and that of our neighbor, disappearing from our view. Hurrying to a rear window, we catch a glimpse of them again before they angle out of our field of vision.

It is an unusual but not extraordinary event in our neighborhood, a first ring suburb of Des Moines. Four hundred homes surround the fairways of our golf course community. Wooded areas line several of the holes. Extensive natural areas surround a modest creek less than a mile away. It is probable that the deer are searching for food. It has been a nasty winter with frequent snow and freezing rain. Ice lies thick under the snow cover. In all likelihood, many homeowners will lose shrubs and plants to hungry deer before spring arrives.

Many deer live in close proximity to the half million people who live in metropolitan Des Moines. I see them occasionally when I ride my bike along the trails. A few weeks ago, one crossed the street in front of me in broad daylight. Last week, as I drove to the grocery store one evening, another ran along the edge of the road. Just east of town at the edge of Interstate 80, I recently saw nearly forty deer feeding on corn stubble. Community officials estimate that 90 deer per square mile inhabit our town. In many states, there are more deer now than there were when Europeans first began to inhabit America.

There are other wild creatures where we live. The winter snow is crisscrossed with bunny tracks, as well as those of other wild creatures. They live in comfortable co-existence with urban dwellers. During the past summer, mallard ducks often waddled across the lawn, though the nearest ponds are a couple hundred yards away. Dozens of Canadian geese are residents in the community. Smaller birds, too, will soon join the winter sparrows, cardinals, and crows. Barn swallows will doubtless endeavor to build nests under our deck, a gold finch couple may settle again in our birch tree, and hopefully, the ruby throated hummingbirds will return.

In some of our previous residences, except for the common rabbits and squirrels, we did not have many four legged visitors. Fences keep pets in, but generally keep wildlife out. The birds, of course, are not restricted. In Spokane we were frequently visited by Valley (or California) Quail, beautiful plump birds about 8 inches tall, largely gray in color but with a black face and a white necklace, chestnut flanks and a black plume curling over head. I never tired of seeing them or hearing their distinctive call.

In our former Des Moines home, the resident male cardinals were eye-catching in their brilliant red coats. They were also extremely optimistic, beginning their mating calls as early as mid January – or were they simply trying to hurry the arrival of spring? Closer at hand, however, were the house finches, sparrow-like birds with a pale red wash on their heads. With astounding determination and persistence, they endeavored nearly every spring to build a nest over a light fixture or in a wreath by the front door. They usually laid a few eggs, but frightened by the paper carrier, visitors, and lawn mowing, they were often unsuccessful in hatching the chicks.

Beyond their sometimes extraordinary beauty, what is it that makes wild creatures so interesting, so commanding of our attention? Surely, it must be their lively motions, their ability move from place to place. While plants are often beautiful and well worth our interest and study, because of their immobility, they become almost part of the too-familiar background. We see them constantly and thus give them little notice. The lively birds and animals, however, catch our focus because they move into or through our visual field, interrupting our attention by their sudden appearance.

Further, their freedom of action, their own choice of when and where to travel, is part of their charm. They are wild and independent of humans, endowed with movement, physical strength, intelligence, and self-determination. They are co-inhabitants of our planet, created by God who made them. The wise man, Job, urges us to learn from them:

But ask the animals and they will teach you,
  or the birds of the air, and they will tell you;
In His hand is the life of every creature
  and the breath of all mankind. Job 12:7, 10

When we lived Florida, there were no fences in our community. Most of the homes were built adjacent to long ponds and wetlands, almost like living in wild country. There were many small birds, but the large ones were compelling.

On our second day after moving in, we were enjoying the sunny and balmy December weather, reading on the patio. Suddenly there was a loud, piercing cry, very close at hand. Jumping up from our chairs, we were confronted by five, tall, sandhill cranes, calmly walking toward us. Standing about four feet high, they were gray in color, except for a red patch on top of the head. A feathered "bustle" covered their tails.

I had previously seen sandhills from a great distance in Wisconsin, but here the birds were making their stately way across our back yard. They were not in the least alarmed by our presence, approaching as close as ten feet without hesitation. As they moved along, their eyes scoured the ground for edible seeds and insects. They seemed as much at home in the community as we did, though their nesting areas were out in the wet areas surrounding our streets.

We never tired of their company, though their harsh cries were arresting, especially as they flew overhead like some airplane fighter squadron, head and long necks thrust forward, and gangly legs trailing behind. Occasionally they came to the windows of our family room, and pecked at the glass. It is unlikely they were looking in at us, but were probably responding to the bird reflected in the window. Most fascinating to watch were there springtime mating dances, when they would strut, prance, flap their wings, and spring into the air. Newborn chicks grew to adult size in only a few weeks.

Other tall birds lived among us. About the same size were the great blue herons, more gray and brown than blue. They were familiar friends from the northern states and much quieter than the cranes, uttering only a rare croak when alarmed. They often stood as silent sentinels at the edge of the water behind our house, waiting to spear a passing fish. I frequently called them, "Henry," though we were unsure of their sex, and if it was one or several individuals. He/she would often stand nearby while I was fishing, hoping I might share my catch.

Their relatives, little blue herons, looking much like the greats but about half as tall, sometimes made an appearance. Less frequently, tricolored herons came to fish. They are all beautiful birds. Unlike the sandhills, the herons fly with legs tucked beneath their bodies and with their heads pulled close to their shoulders, their necks forming a "u" in front of their breasts.

A third tall bird was the great egret, like the others, about four feet tall, but dressed in white plumage, with long trailing “aigrette” feathers drooping from its breast. Also like the others, it was a shoreline feeder, walking the bank in hope of a finny meal. It was a rare day that none of these birds came to call.

On a few occasions we were visited by smaller cattle egrets, about 24 inches tall, almost completely white except for some yellow-beige feathers on the breast, crown, and back of breeding adults. These birds have migrated to the western hemisphere from Africa and the Spanish-Portuguese Peninsula only since the 1950’s, and are now spreading to many places across the U.S, and even into Canada.

Another similar bird was the White Ibis. It, too, was about 24 inches tall, with white body coloring, black wing tips appear only when the wings are extended, and red face, legs, and long down-curved, 8–10 inch bill.

One species of bird new to me was the limpkin, both fascinating and irritating. About 24 to 28 inches tall, it was mostly brown with white spots and streaks, and had a distinctive eight-inch down-curving bill. It is named for its curious walking motion. Its piercing cry, which can’t be reproduced by words, is unusual enough that it was used to create a jungle atmosphere in early Tarzan movies filmed in Florida. While the cry is certainly novel, when repeated for hours during the night, it makes sleep very difficult.

Another bird new to me was the fish crow. It was completely black like its northern relatives, but somewhat smaller. It perched in the trees or on the streetlights, calling out, “ah ha, ah ha.”

A more fascinating black bird was the anhinga. It swam in the water with powerful webbed feet, diving below to find small fish. When partly submerged, its streamlined head and bill attached to a long neck was all that could be seen, swiveling like a periscope or a snake. Not surprisingly, it is often called the snake bird. Getting its entire body wet, requires it to dry its wings, so it would find some branch in the sunshine where it spread them out like shields, remaining utterly still for long periods of time.

Much the same size and color were the common cormorants that seemed to be seasonal migrants. Like the anhingas, they also spread their wings to dry, but their sharply hooked bills were distinctive identifiers.

One large black bird never went into the water. I saw it mostly in the sky, effortlessly tracing huge circles overhead. When one caught my attention, it was usually accompanied by a few others. With a wingspan of five feet, the common vultures were champion fliers, scarcely moving a wing while staying aloft for many minutes in search of a meal of carrion. Occasionally they would perch in a tree, or even rest quietly on the grass in our backyard.

Once in a while we saw a bald eagle, with its unmistakable white head and tail. They are now fairly common in Florida, recovering from near extinction.

A bit more common in our neighborhood were the ospreys, almost as large as the eagles, but with a brown tail and brown and white streaked head. It was a thrill to see their acrobatic flight along the canal and their plummet into the water to grasp a fish.

In the Midwest, it is a common thing to see various species of hawks flying overhead, cruising over fields and forest, or perched on rural fence posts. What was surprising at our Florida home, was to see a red-shouldered hawk resting on the roof of our neighbor's house, or in our back yard. In all likelihood, it was our community's proximity to the surrounding wetlands that made these unusual sightings so frequent. For me it was a delightful coexistence.

A smaller but spectacular bird, was the pileated woodpecker which appeared some winters. About the size of a crow, with brilliant red, black, and white coloring, it had a pointed cockade of red feathers extending back from its head. It probed for insects as it hammered away at the bark of the trees behind our house.

Once as I sat beside the water's edge I turned to scan the trees across the pond and saw a surprising sight. In a large tree about 75 yards away were ten wood storks. These birds, too, were about four feet tall, with white bodies, and grey head, necks, and huge beak. During the two hours of my watching, I also saw a red-bellied woodpecker, a mourning dove, a snowy egret, a common gallinule, and a sandhill crane.

Perhaps my favorite feathered neighbors were the barred owls that lived near our back door. Nocturnal creatures that they usually are, I often heard one calling in the mid-evening, "whoo, whoo, whoo, whoo," nearly always four "whoo"s, with a slight break after the second, and a modest emphasis on the fourth, then repeated once again. It is often called the hoot owl, and by some, the "eight hoot" owl. It was enchanting to have them living so close by, since I thought of them as deep woods creatures, having seen one only once before in a Minnesota forest.

Sometimes I saw a pair of them, even in the day time. Like the other neighborhood birds, they, seemed unafraid. One day I saw one in a low branch just behind our house. I grabbed my camera and started shooting. After each picture I stepped closer. It simply stared at me, seemingly unperturbed. This lasted for three or four minutes. When I had approached to about ten feet, it finally flew to another tree about 40 feet away, but I didn't purse it any further.

All owls are fascinating and have marvelous capacities that distinguish them from other families of birds. While they are well known for extraordinary vision, as much as 100 times more acute then that of humans, owls' ability to hear is also incredible. At least some species can successfully hunt in absolute darkness by hearing alone.

Barn owls can locate mice under three feet of snow by hearing their heartbeats! In the kingdom of birds, the Creator has made truly magnificent creatures.

There were other birds, of course, each of them brimming with life and beauty, flying marvels crafted by the hands of a great Artisan. Perhaps they are created for some earthly purpose, but then, again, it may simply be for our delight and enjoyment – or more likely, *His*.

Not all of the animals at our Florida door had feathers. At least in our first couple of years, the rabbits were there as they had been in our previous places. Then they disappeared, or at least became fairly scarce. Perhaps other creatures were the cause, or maybe they found greener pastures.

The squirrels were a major nuisance. They lived in the oak trees at the edge of the water. I don't recall ever seeing them in our three palm trees. They ran across the roof of our house, up and down the screens of our lanai, and with fiendish agility, raided the bird feeders. Again and again, I tried various strategies to foil their thievery, with only sporadic success. When temporarily stymied, they would often jump from the roof, about twelve feet above a tiny platform holding the feeder. Only once did I see one slightly miss, dangling by one paw before falling unhurt to the ground. Irritating as their depredations were, their athletic feats demanded admiration.

During the warm months, green anoles, slim lizards, also ran across the walls and screens, and occasionally managed to get into the house. They were very quick and hard to catch. We liked them better on the outside.

There were turtles in the canal, about fifteen inches long. They were usually submerged, only occasionally raising their small heads above the water. Females came on land to lay their eggs, as one did digging a shallow depression in our lawn. When the hole was large enough, she started dropping the eggs, As she did her work, the crows were watching. When she had finished, she pushed sand over the eggs, and waddled back to the water. In less than a minute, a crow came, then another. Raking through the sand, they uncovered and took every egg. Another season, two turtles across the canal, laid eggs at the same time, with the same result.

Our yard was a dinner table for other creatures too. Often the turf was torn up, with small holes here and there. My suspicions were confirmed one night when I heard a rustling in the foundation plantings. Taking a flashlight, I soon found the marauder, a twelve-inch armadillo, looking for grubs in the soil. A sprinkling of red pepper flakes over the lawn seemed to discourage them.

One night I heard a strong rustling in the trees and went out to investigate. Shining a light in the leaves, I discovered a raccoon, probably looking for eggs in the bird nests.

A few snakes appeared from time to time, one climbing up our front wall to go after the eggs in a bird nest. I removed it and set it free in another place. Not all snakes were so fortunate. Our neighbor, Fred, beheaded a four-foot diamond back rattler that he discovered in his front yard shrubbery.

The end of our street was on the outskirt of our community, surrounded on three sides by undeveloped wetlands, where several times, Fred saw a bobcat sitting among the trees. Jeff and Theresa, just a few doors away, often saw deer and wild turkeys. Supposedly, someone claimed to have seen cougar tracks in the freshly leveled sand of a new foundation on our street, but that seemed highly unlikely to me.

But what about the alligators? This was wild Florida at our door. The previous owner told us that they showed up occasionally, but week after week went by without any sightings by us. It didn't occur to me that the water in the canal was only in the 50's when we moved in. At this time of the year, the alligators were almost dormant in the mud back in the reeds.

But it finally happened. Looking out our windows I saw something moving in the water. I grabbed the binoculars and confirmed my suspicion. All that was visible were the nostrils, eyes, and a bit of tail. In the still cool water it moved slowly along. Quickly I went out the back door to get closer view, a live alligator virtually at our door. After watching it for several minutes, it sank slowly from sight.

How appropriate is the Bible's poetical description of the closely related crocodile,

I will not fail to speak of his limbs,
his strength and his graceful form.
Who can strip off his outer coat?
Who would approach him with a bridle?
Who dares open the doors of his mouth,
ringed about with his fearsome teeth?
His back has rows of shields tightly sealed together;
each so close to the next that no air can pass between.
They are joined fast to one another; they cling together and cannot be parted. Job 41.

I always enjoyed seeing the alligators. Through the warm months we saw them every few days. Once I saw three of them at one time, doing a lot of splashing (mating?), but they were usually solitary. We were especially delighted that nearly always when we had visiting company, a gator seemed to be at hand for our guests to enjoy.

Most of them were four to seven feet long, but once in a while larger ones came around. Late one fall as the temperatures were dropping, a ten-footer lay on the opposite bank for about four days before disappearing. The smallest I saw, at the edge of the water, was about ten inches long.

On one occasion, I discovered a four-foot gator in the street at the edge of our driveway. It had been raining for days, and water in the canals was very high, the gutters in the streets were overflowing, and run-off areas between some houses were filled. After several minutes the gator slithered slowly back to the canal.

While the alligators often look docile and torpid, they are dangerous wild animals. Once as we saw a commotion on the water, the binoculars allowed us to see a life and death drama. An alligator had a great blue heron in its mouth. For long periods they were still. Then the bird would struggle a bit. Next the gator would thrash and submerge for awhile, then rise to the surface. These cycles were repeated for about fifteen minutes until, the alligator, with the heron still locked in combat, swam around the bend beyond our sight. The final outcome was not much in doubt.

Watching the death of an animal often seems painful and sorrowful. We enjoyed the herons for their beauty and stately presence. Why should they die for a gator's lunch? Yet the herons patrol the water's edge and gobble baby gators in an instant. It is God's plan for the animals. There is no sin involved, for the creatures obey the Creators plan implicitly. Only humans disobey His design for their lives.

Even the stork in the sky
knows her appointed seasons,
and the dove, the swift, and the thrush
observe the time of their migration.
But my people do not know
the requirements of the Lord. Jer. 8:7

The wild creatures, however, honor their Maker, living their lives according to His divine plan. The "wild animals, cattle, small creatures, and flying birds," (Ps. 148:7-10), also praise Him, demonstrating the brilliance of His ingenuity and skill in executing their multiple designs. Whether in the remote wild places, or just outside our doors, the untamed animals reveal the glory of the Lord.

Chapter Sixteen

THE OCEAN

How many are your works, O Lord!
in wisdom you made them all:
the earth is full of your creatures.
There is the sea, vast and spacious,
teeming with creatures beyond number—
living things both large and small.
Psalm 104:24, 25

I stand at the edge of the sea, transfixed by the ceaseless surf and boundless horizon. It is awesome, beautiful, magnetic. A tang of moist air envelops me and birds wheel and call overhead. Though boats and people move nearby, they are but specks of motion, insignificant against the vastness of the ocean. Pictures and written descriptions have failed to prepare me for this encounter. Even my youthful familiarity with huge Lake Superior has not been helpful, for large as it is, it is still enclosed by shoreline. The ocean in contrast is boundless, extending everywhere, unconfined by shorelines, enclosing the very continents as great islands. It is truly beyond conception.

Our first encounter with the ocean was on a vacation at Oceans Shores, Washington. We had a great time racing go-carts and enjoying other family activities, but persistent fog severely limited our view of the sea. We did enjoy walking on the sand and wading in the surf. And like beachcombers everywhere, we especially treasured the shells we found, particularly the sand dollars whose usually broken remains were everywhere. Occasionally we found a whole one, a flat whitish disk about four inches in diameter. We brought several home with us.

A couple of years later Shirley and I were back at Ocean Shores to attend a conference. This time the weather was more cooperative. As we walked on the beach, our eyes were drawn across the awesome spread of restless water. Beautiful, alluring, and overwhelming, it defied comprehension. Its magnetic attraction drew us back whenever we had brief periods of free time. Future encounters would be needed.

One novel discovery whetted my desire even more. On our last morning, I went for an early jog on the beach. Just beyond the edge of the waves, I came upon a dark mass, about 30 inches wide, and I guessed, about six pounds in weight. Its kite shape made it instantly recognizable as a member of the ray family of fishes. It was dead, presumably washed ashore in the surf. When I returned home, I did some research and concluded it was most likely an animal called a skate. My first-time discovery underlined the mystery and attraction of the ocean. What other wonders lurked within its dark water?

I knew, of course, that some of those wonders were more common fish, many of which are fun to catch and good to eat. So a time came when I went fishing in a charter boat with Shirley's business partner, Bill. With a dozen others we boarded the boat at about eight in the morning. I headed for the bow to enjoy the bouncing ride to the fishing area. On the way we saw an intriguing bird floating on the water. It was a tufted puffin, a 15-inch black sea bird with a white face, thick orange-red bill, and strands of yellow feathers extending back from its head.

For inland residents like us, it was a treat to see another of the fascinating and delightful birds inhabiting the earth.

I also noticed something that puzzled me as we churned across the water. Looking down I saw a blue-black streak flash by the side of the boat, a few feet below the surface. This happened three or four times, but I didn't know what to make of it and dismissed it from my mind.

After an hour we slowed down over the captain's selected fishing spot. Each of us hung a baited hook over the side and waited expectantly – but suddenly I didn't feel very well. In fact my whole body ached and my stomach felt wretched. Asking Bill to watch my rod, I started for the lavatory. As I made my way below, the captain hollered, "Don't toss your cookies in the 'head'. Go over the side." Fortunately, or not, I never did upchuck, but felt miserable the whole while on board. In due time I went back on deck to find I had caught the first fish of the trip. Or at least my rod hooked the first one, which Bill had hauled in. It was a beautiful six-pound silver salmon.

Throwing a fresh bait over the side, I sat against the cabin wall with little enthusiasm. It wasn't long before my rod began to bend again. "Oh, no," I thought. "Now I have to get up and haul in another fish." As I did, I saw more of the blue streaks go by. Then I understood. The streaks were fish, swimming incredibly fast, much faster than the boat. We were trolling above a large school of salmon. It would have been much more exciting if I wasn't feeling so crummy.

At last we returned to shore, each with our limit of three, sleek, silver fish, weighing five to eight pounds each. They would provide several delicious meals. By the time we arrived back home my seasickness had worn off. Now I knew by personal experience what the Bible calls the "restless seas." Thankfully, Bill was not troubled at all.

Shirley and I went back to Ocean Shores a few years later, staying at a lovely beachfront condominium. At the shore we came across a black sea bird about fifteen inches tall, probably a cormorant that may have been injured or ill. It allowed us to come quite close before shuffling away.

Shirley wrote, "I love you!" in six foot high letters in the sand. A wonderful highlight was celebrating our 25th anniversary at a cliff-side restaurant overlooking the sea. Holding hands, we watched as the setting sun gilded the water 100 feet below. It was a romantic evening made even more so in the splendor of the surroundings.

We found other opportunities to see the ocean: another visit to Ocean Shores, a ferry trip through the San Juan Islands to Victoria, British Columbia, and a conference on Mexico's Baja Peninsula. Always the water was compelling. As Melville describes it in the first paragraphs of Moby Dick, wherever water is found, people are irresistibly drawn to it.

Then we went to Hawaii. At least twice before, Shirley and I had made tentative plans to go, but each time important events changed our agenda. Now we were finally under way. As the plane soared across the sky, we could see the endless expanse of blue, six miles below. Hour after hour slipped by but still the water stretched out of sight, not surprising since the Hawaiians are the most distant of any islands from a mainland, and the Pacific Ocean covers 1/3 of the earth's surface, larger than all the continents together. The Psalm writer said it perfectly, "there is the sea, vast and spacious."

Almost certainly the writer of the Psalm was thinking of the Mediterranean Sea, no small body of water to be sure, covering almost a million square miles. More awesome still, however, is to ponder the other seas on earth, covering 71% of the earth's surface, 216 million square miles, a staggering immensity. Yet, flying across an entire ocean does not help very much in sensory understanding, since time and distance are diminished by speed and altitude.

In an attempt at better comprehension, I tried a mental exercise. In my mind's eye, I visualized standing before a cubic mile of water (or better, a solid block of ice). This enormous "chunk" of water, containing 1.2 trillion gallons, towers 5,280 feet overhead, extends 2600 feet to each side, and a mile in depth. Then I imagined stacking two more such blocks upon the first to approximate the average depth of water in the oceans. Finally, to somehow grasp the total volume of the seas, I tried to picture millions and millions of similar cubes, 310 million of them. But, of course, I could not. "Vast and spacious," indeed!

And of the great Being who formed the oceans, of whom the Scriptures speak, "Who has measured the waters in the hollow of his hand?" (Is. 40:12), I am overwhelmed. No wonder the writer of Psalm 104 begins and ends his majestic poem with exultant cries of "Praise the Lord."

In our brief Hawaiian vacation nearly all our activities were oriented to the sea. Every day we went to the beach, strolling the sands and swimming (or stumbling) in the surf. In a drive around the island, it was the water more than anything else that commanded our attention. On our final night we sailed out in a catamaran upon the shifting waves themselves. Sitting on a thin web of fabric, three feet above the water, it was a bit eerie to contemplate the depths below. How quickly did the bottom fall off from the shoreline, how far down did the ocean descend in the mid-Pacific, what creatures swam barely out of sight. Perhaps to the island residents such questions pose no novelty, but to me they were provocative and the sea utterly absorbing.

In later years we had opportunities to visit the ocean in Florida. Friends Erv and Katherine had a condo on the Gulf coast that they kindly let us use. The sands were soft and the waters warm. Beach fisherman pulled in a variety of fish including small sharks. As we waded in the surf, small schools of stingrays would sometimes swim in front of our feet.

Gazing across the waves, I often hoped to see the spout or back of a whale, perhaps unlikely so near the shore, but who knows? We often saw their smaller cousins, bottlenose dolphins. They appeared fairly frequently. A nearby waterfront boardwalk provided a great viewing stand as their dorsal fins and arching backs quietly broke the surface.

"There's one!" – "no, two of them", Shirley exclaims. "Look, there's a third."

We can hear the whooshing exhalation of their breath as they surface, reminding us that these marvelous creatures are not fish at all, but air breathing mammals like ourselves. Truly, God's creative handiwork is astounding.

One of the best times Shirley and I had on the Florida waters was a boat ride with friends Ed and Joyce, their son Shane, and friend, Dave. We spotted some dolphins in the distance, so the boatman attempted to get us much closer. As we roared along at high speed, a dolphin suddenly rose from the water and crossed the wake behind the boat. Then another arched into view. This happened repeatedly. For a full half hour these marvelous creatures cavorted in the wake of the boat as we watched in awe. How appropriate is the Biblical statement about the sea: "there the ships go to and fro, and the leviathan (probably whales or dolphins) which you formed to frolic there" (Psalm 104:26). Frolic, indeed. What an expressive description that is, and how appropriate to the dolphins, for they seemed to be enjoying their aquatics as genuine play or sport.

As we strolled the beaches, the countless shells were irresistible, 7,500 different species inhabiting Florida waters. Who can restrain the impulse to inspect, marvel at, and carry home such treasures? Yet, the living reality is more wondrous still as Brittney and Cameron discovered when they came to visit.

Scooping a handful of watery sand, they uncovered several ½-inch long Coquina clams. As the water drained away, the living creatures suddenly turned upright and attempted to escape between their fingers. Their ability to quickly burrow in the sand is amazing.

Florida shorebirds were not the same as those up north. Here were red ibis, roseate spoonbills, oyster catchers, black skimmers, ruddy turnstones, whimbrels, and many others. Not only were there many species new to me, but some flight patterns, too, were novel.

Flocks of small shorebirds, sanderlings, perhaps, especially entranced me with their synchronized flight, fifty to one hundred birds flying with their backs to me, and then in instant precision, turning edge on and become nearly invisible, only to turn again in perfect unison, reappearing in a different pose. It was an exquisite aerial ballet, marvelous for its intricacy, and mysterious in its unknown choreography. How do they know when and where to turn, who gives the command, how is it received, and how is it executed in a blink of an eye? I never wearied of watching them.

The time came for our retirement and we moved to Florida. Now the sea was more accessible. Our closest local beach was only 30 miles away but the water there was fairly shallow and the shoreline rocky with little walking area. So from time to time, we went with Fred and Marion or Dick and Judy to Ponce Inlet beach on the Atlantic Coast. Here were miles of great sand, moderate waves, and not too many people. It was a wonderful place to play in sun and water and to ponder the sea and its creatures.

Gulls and pelicans patrolled back and forth over the sand and surf. The latter were especially interesting, large brown birds with enormous beaks. Like prehistoric beings they sailed above the waves with wings outstretched, their eyes searching the water. Then they dropped like thunderbolts, raking the water with open bills and filling their great pouches with fish. What were they catching? Anything available, I suppose.

As we wade into the water we stride boldly at first, but as it deepens, the waves mount higher. We are aware of the increasing surf but also wonder what may be swimming near our legs, unseen and maybe dangerous. I can see small fish flashing by, too quick to identify but I guess they are mullet. A short way down the beach two men are casting hand nets, enclosing dozens of five to ten inch silvery fish at each throw. In a short while they fill several ice chests with the tasty creatures from the sea. The pelicans like them too, and while the men do their work, the birds sail along and take their share.

I am also mindful of other animals and keep a wary eye on the surface. Just two miles south is New Smyrna Beach, site of three shark attacks in one recent season. The odds of being bitten are infinitesimal, only a few dozen incidents a year among the nation's millions of beach-goers. Still, three at one location is sobering. Even more astounding, in 2008, nineteen people (23 according to some sources), were reported to have been bitten (none fatally) by sharks in the waters of New Smyrna Beach! Happily, no dorsal fins appeared during our visits.

We found them later, however, when Bernie, George, Fred, and I went fishing on the Gulf Coast. Putting in at the Fort Island boat launch, we made our way down the Crystal River, at first past beautiful homes, but then along increasingly wild shores, marshes, and islands. After ten to twelve miles, we stopped the motor and let the boat drift in ten feet of water. Using fresh shrimp for bait, it wasn't long before something was hooked. Was it a snook, a grouper, or a red fish? No such luck. We caught only a few small sea trout and some sheepshead, throwing them back.

Then Bernie had a strike, not big but vigorous. He quickly reeled it in, a strange fish with a spade shaped head and a prominent dorsal fin. Its eyes were located on the extreme sides of the head. It was thrown back, too. I later identified it as a bonnethead shark, related to the more familiar hammerheads.

Then I hooked something fairly lively. It was a couple of feet long and perhaps four pounds. It was blue-black on top and white on the underside, had a mouthful of teeth, and black tipped fins. That was the key, a blacktip shark. It went back as well.

After some time, Fred hooked something, strong! He reeled in line when he could but often the fish stripped it away. Following the fish from one side of the boat to the other, and from end to end and back again, Fred cranked his reel. The rest of us had pulled our lines in so he wouldn't get tangled. After twenty minutes or so the fish was near the boat. Using a gaff hook, Bernie hauled it aboard – another black tip shark about twenty-five pounds. It was a lot of fun for fisherman and spectators alike, though probably not for the fish. Since they grow to about seven feet and a weight of sixty or more pounds, we sent it back to grow to maturity.

I enjoy fishing in freshwater lakes, but the presence of very large fish adds a special dimension to salt water. And you do not always have to be fishing to see them. Like the dolphins, fish sometimes jump. An incredible internet picture taken of a surfer off New Smyrna in 2008, showed a six-foot blacktip shark in the background, jumping completely out of the water!

The ocean can be enjoyable and exciting, especially in a small boat. The early Indian dwellers of Florida launched out on the sea in small canoes. That is still popular with modern Floridians, including several of our neighbors. As might be expected, we often joined them. Six of us went together on one occasion to paddle the Chassahowitzka River. Fred, Marion, Brian, and Mary used solo kayaks, and Shirley and I paddled our canoe.

We set out from the county boat launch and began our paddle downstream. The water was crystal clear from its source in a limestone spring just above the put-in place. This strong fresh water flow mingled with salt water tidal surges, allowing both salt and fresh water fish to live in the same river. Alligators and otters also lived in the water and Florida black bears inhabited the surrounding woodlands.

We were pleased to have the river nearly to ourselves since there were not many other boaters on the water. We passed a few homes along the way, most looking quite ancient, gray, and weathered. Mossy trees lined the shore and tall reeds stood in the water. As we progressed further along, the dwellings thinned out and the water opened wider to the Gulf. Low islands appeared, barely higher than the rise of the tide, covered by marshy vegetation.

After a couple of miles, the river banks disappeared. Only the invisible flow of fresh water beneath our boats resembled the rivers we usually knew. To the eye we were in the shallow margin of the huge Gulf of Mexico, not yet in open water, but penetrating its shaggy fringe. Now small islands were everywhere. It would be easy to paddle a winding channel into a dead-end. We hoped we were following the right course.

Our objective was Dog Island, where there was a boat dock, picnic shelter, and primitive rest room. We paddled onward, sometimes clustered together, but more often spread apart. Conversation was limited. Mostly we were immersed in our own aquatic world. Sitting virtually upon the water, with island vegetation higher than our heads, it was easy to feel utterly alone, lost in the enormous earth ocean. Except for the quiet dip of the paddles, there was no noise.

Suddenly our silent reverie was broken. A huge splash sounded just ahead of Shirley in the bow. She almost jumped from her seat and stopped paddling. A great circle of water spread out in front of the canoe. I was startled too. "What was it?" I asked. "I don't know," she replied. "I didn't see it."

What could it have been? Whatever it was, it was huge to make such a disturbance. Could it have been Dog Island Joe, a twelve-foot alligator reputed to inhabit the area? Or a six-foot, 150 pound tarpon, great fish that cruise the coastal shallows? Or a twelve-foot, 1,000 pound manatee, common residents of western Gulf shore, or some other of the sea's "teeming creatures beyond number"?

We didn't know and could never find out. It was a briefly scary event, and a continuing mystery, in our minds adding to the unknowns of the sea.

In due time we arrived at Dog Island, enjoyed a pleasant lunch and a needed rest. The way back was uneventful and tiring. We were not as young and strong as in former years. But the day was well spent.

Now I stand again at the edge of the sea in the darkness of night. The water is dimly visible, the surf ceaselessly washing the shore in endless waves. From where do they come? I keep waiting for a lull in the sound, at least a brief moment of silence, but there is no interruption. Even between the breaking swells, there is a continual murmur of movement, the advance of smaller surges and the whisper of temporary retreats. The sea is alive, restless, and unfathomable, a stunning creation of an astounding God.

Chapter Seventeen

SOLITUDE AND SILENCE

Be still and know that I am God. Ps 46:10

It was a crazy idea. After all, it was twenty degrees below zero! I'm not sure now exactly why I wanted to go, whether it was to see the stars in remote brilliance (probably) or to experience true silence (possibly). In either case, I got both of them.

We were visiting Shirley's family in Duluth over the Christmas holiday when the notion sprang to life. My plan was to drive to Greenwood Lake north of Two Harbors, and then walk out on the ice. It would be about an hour each way in the car, and an hour (or less!) in a frosty stroll. The family thought a dinner together sounded like a much more sensible activity. Since I had not planned for a winter excursion, I had to borrow snow boots and mittens from my father-in-law, Erv.

By late afternoon I was on my way. Darkness was coming on and the cold air was doing its best to freeze the holiday sparkle. Fortunately, there was little wind. By the time I had reached Two Harbors, it was fully dark and traffic was sparse. Turning north on highway 2, I found the road nearly empty of cars. Everyone was sensibly ensconced in their warm homes, enjoying holiday leftovers. What was I doing on this fool's errand? At least the car was warm and I was comfortable at the moment.

The headlights probing ahead revealed no cheering summer landscape, only a harsh winter scene, frigid, lonely, and empty. Still, I was upbeat about this outside-the-box escapade. In my sheltered city life, and even in my warm-weather outdoor ventures, I had limited opportunities to see the nighttime skies under the clarity of ultra low humidity. As for silence, there was almost zero chance of any noise out on the ice.

I passed no more than six cars going south. Crossing the Gooseberry and Cloquet Rivers, I began to look for the Greenwood Lake parking area. Bypassing a few driveways into scattered private properties, I came to the short spur to the public access. Now, did I really want to leave the warm car? The temperature outside had probably dropped another five degrees since I left town. But if I didn't go out, the whole trip was wasted, simply a ride in the dark. I had to follow through.

Turning off the engine and headlights, I was plunged into darkness. I waited in the stillness for my eyes to adjust. The car uttered strange, irregular noises as its metal shrank in the bitter cold. Changing my shoes for the boots, zipping my parka, and pulling on leather mittens with wool liners, I stepped out into the frigid night.

Arctic air gripped my exposed face like a vise, freezing the moisture in my nose. I had forgotten how intense the cold really felt in a northern Minnesota winter.

No tracks marred the pristine snow on the icy lake. What would someone think if he followed my destination-less tracks onto the ice? Probably that I was a fisherman who decided that sitting beside a hole on the lake was a dumb idea. In any case, the next snowfall would cover my footprints.

Before setting out on the lake, I stood still and simply listened for several minutes. I heard absolutely nothing. No traffic noises came from the nearby highway, no bird or animal sounds were audible, and not a breath of wind rustled by my ears. It was a strange and eerie silence, an alien experience.

Standing still in frigid winter air is a chilling event, however, even when dressed in warm clothes, so I started walking. At each step, the silence was broken by the distinct crunch of snow being compacted under my boots. The noisy footfalls were inescapable - crunch, crunch, crunch - whenever I placed a foot, a sound uniquely different from any others, triggering memories of winters past. In other seasons, and on compacted snow, it is possible to walk almost soundlessly, but now I could not escape the squeaky intrusion on the silence I had come to encounter. It was a noisy irony.

As I made my way onto the ice, I expected to hear it crack and creak with contraction from the cold, but the frozen lake was silent. Perhaps the fifteen inches of snow was sufficient insulation from the frigid air to shield it from further shrinkage.

Soon, however, I heard another sound beside that of the crunching snow. My breath was whooshing from my nostrils as I plodded further from shore. I was chugging like a steam engine, faster and louder the further I went. Warm air from my lungs spurted into the frosty night air and froze in pale clouds, faintly visible in the near darkness.

After a few hundred yards, two new sounds began to reach my consciousness. I was a bit puzzled at first, stopping quietly and turning my head to discover their source, then foolishly realizing they were my own heartbeat and the rush of blood in my eardrums, subtle noises seldom heard in the clamor and slower pace of daily routines. What a wonder that in the vast wilderness around me, *I* was the only source of sound.

In such quiet, it was surprising to me that I could hear no distant sounds, for without any nearby noise, I expected something from farther away. Perhaps the frigid air restricted the propagation of sound waves. No wolves howled, no owls called, and no dogs barked. All the people, animals, and machines on earth were stilled, as if they had moved away, or ceased to exist, and I was alone in an empty, frozen world. It was an intriguing sensation.

The dark sky above me was splattered with stars, glinting sparkles of brightness, and a pale swath of Milky Way, enough to reflect some illumination back from the snow on the lake. In the brittle cold there was no shimmering of the light, only unrelenting pinpricks of brilliance piercing the awful vastness of space. I had never seen them in such fierce intensity,

As I scanned the distant canopy, I was surprised to see a small, blinking dot at the edge of my vision. Turning my head, I watched it more carefully. In total silence, it drifted slowly through the star field, a ghost aircraft, too high and far to be heard, and in a few moments, out of sight as well. It was the only interruption of the solitude, a brief hint that the world was alive with people and activity. With its disappearance from view, I was alone again in a silent, seemingly empty land.

I did not search for any special phenomena, and except for the unavoidable dippers, I paid no attention to the other constellations. This was not a discovery expedition or a study session. I simply wanted to apprehend the sky in its full brilliance, undiminished by obscuring, man-made illumination, to see it like wondering, awe-stricken night people of earlier generations. The radiant stars were breathtaking. Little wonder observation often leads to worship.

A shepherd of earlier centuries, often alone with his sheep, had similar opportunities to behold and ponder the stars. His poetic response serves well yet today.

The heavens declare the glory of God,
The skies proclaim the work of his hands.
Day after day, they pour forth speech,
Night after night they display knowledge.
Psalm 19:1, 2

The splendor of creation, and its witness to the Creator, is present everywhere on earth.

How long did it take to see the stars and to sense the silence? Not long at all. With the bottom falling out of the thermometer, twenty minutes was more than enough. I turned around and retraced my trail in the snow, the silence as pervasive as ever. Only the clinging crunch of my footsteps and the chuffing of my breath broke the stillness. Even as I neared the car, I still heard no traffic on the road. The silence was profound, the solitude immense. But it was time to go.

The trip back was uneventful. The sound of the car engine was comforting and unobtrusive, the quiet hum of the heater warmly appreciated. Somewhere another car appeared at last, and urban sounds broke through as I entered civilization. Back with the family, I fully enjoyed the customary chatter and activity of normal life, and would never want to give it up. But I returned home with my special gift, a slice of utter quiet and solitude, a treasure in the mind and memory as significant as those that came wrapped in a holiday paper, one that would never be lost, broken, or worn out.

Over the years, the great majority of my encounters with solitude have been in the wilderness but in temperatures that were more hospitable. While it is possible to engage in mental and emotional isolation even in great crowds, it is not easy. Frankly, I have always enjoyed the rush of vast urban areas, and even when complaining about the crush of traffic in the Twin Cities, Chicago, Tampa, or Atlanta, I marvel at the energy of millions of nearby people. Still, like most people, I instinctively crave periodic withdrawal from crowds and activity. It is a necessity in my psyche that demands regular outlet.

Often it had to be in little snatches captured from a busy lifestyle, a quiet walk in the neighborhood, or a visit to a community park. These brief forays were helpful, but insufficient. More extended time was necessary, at least occasional whole days were required. In my earlier years, hunting was often the occasion. If I was successful in the hunt, well and good, but if not, the quiet pleasure of the fields or forest was fully satisfying.

Once I went bow hunting for deer southeast of Ely, Minnesota. Driving on Highway 1, I parked on a short gravel spur branching from the road. As I shouldered my gear, I noticed a weather-beaten board nailed to a tree. It read, "Civilian Conservation Corps." During the depression a couple decades before, the Federal government had hired legions of unemployed people to do various construction jobs to ease the financial crisis. These workers built many of the roads and trails in the Superior National Forest.

They were long gone now. As far as I could tell, the forest around me was empty. I had it all to myself. I walked through the trees until I found a likely spot. A faint trail, hopefully made by a deer, meandered ahead of me. Finding a somewhat clear area where I could get an open shot, I sat in front of a tree twenty yards from the track, and settled down to wait. Hunting usually requires a lot of waiting.

It was a beautiful morning. Bright sunlight filtered through the golden leaves of birch and aspen, a pleasant contrast to the dense green of spruce, balsam, and pine. A light breeze fanned the leaves, but was quiet enough not to obscure faint animal sounds. I waited eagerly, an arrow placed on the bowstring, listening and looking intently for my quarry. All was in readiness, but I saw and heard nothing.

Knowing that I needed to be alert and prepared for instant action, I tried to stay focused. I continually scanned the field of view, while keeping my own motions as still as possible. Straining my ears to hear any unusual sounds, I heard only the muted flutter of the leaves. I stole a glance at my watch. Ten minutes had gone by. This could be a long day.

Inevitably, my attention wavered and my mind wandered. I continually reveled in the perfection of the day and the glory of the little glade. It was like beholding an artistic masterpiece in a great museum. Questions percolated through my mind as they would before such a picture. How did the painter conceive his composition, what determined his choice of colors, why use the particular brush strokes he employed, how did such genius come about?

Other technical questions arose. What were the names of the small plants growing around me, or the bushes and trees of which I was ignorant? What about the geology of this North Country, where the ancient Laurentian Mountains had been ground to meager hills by successive glaciers, and where iron ore and quartz are found in various places?

I savored the natural canvas around me, even as I pondered the questions it raised. It was deeply enjoyable, at least as much as the anticipation of shooting an animal. The enforced silence and aloneness allowed me to enter a state of mental and emotional awareness of the fabulous creation. While my visual field was confined to a handful of yards, it was not like looking at mere rocks, shrubs, and trees. It was as if I were seeing an astounding wonder under a microscope, a minuscule portion of a stupendous display. I did my best to keep looking and listening for a deer, but it was a continual effort to stay fixed on my intended objective.

An hour passed. I was not bored, for my active mind continued to pursue its mental pathways, even as I waited for a deer to show up.

Then something in the picture changed. An animal appeared, not where I expected, chest-high at the edge of the clearing, but low down, just in front of me. A mouse was searching through the grass, five feet away. It seemed oblivious to my presence, steering back and forth through the vegetation, but generally closer to me, its sharp nose testing the air for anything edible. It continued to come closer until it reached the toe of my boot, where it crawled up and across, then down the other side, still unaware, or ignoring the large creature in its territory. It soon vanished under the plants beyond me. It was a surprising but delightful encounter. What might we discover if we spent more time sitting quietly in the woods? I continued listening and looking for a larger animal.

More time passed. At last, I heard a scuffling of the leaves, deeper in the trees in front of me. It was intermittent, but seemed to be coming closer. Perhaps it was a red squirrel, a tiny animal that is often surprisingly noisy, though I heard none of its usual chattering. The rustling of the leaves continued, not methodically, but hesitantly closer. Though it was not the bouncy, explosive bursts typical of squirrels, I still thought that was the most likely source, but readied my bow in anticipation.

My pulse raced in expectancy. Would the animal come into the clearing? Could it be a deer or some other large animal? I swiveled my head a bit, trying to see through the brush. The waiting was excruciating.

Then I saw it, a deer for sure, and it saw me in the same instant. Before I could pull the string to full draw, the animal reacted with a twisting, sideward leap, and vanished with crashing bounds back into the trees. Shaking a bit, I relaxed the bow, and waited for my heart to slow to normal. The disappointment in failing to get a shot was genuine, but not overwhelming. The actual, sudden encounter had been thrilling and fun, a fitting climax to my patient wait in the woods, a reward for successfully choosing a meeting place to confront a beautiful creature in the vast forest.

Too late in the afternoon to find another spot, I returned to the car. As always when I was not successful in the hunt, I soothed my failure by the thought that at least I didn't have to skin and clean an animal.

It had been a productive day for physical, emotional, and spiritual refreshment, a profound and beneficial change from the usual demands and activities of city life. I had not thought specifically about God, but there was no question in my mind that I was enjoying His world. The mouse and deer were His creatures, residents of His wilderness. By spending a quiet day in their habitat, I was helpfully reminded that I, too, was His being.

Philosopher-theologian, Dallas Willard, identifies solitude and silence as having "primacy and priority" among the spiritual disciplines that enable people to gain strength as followers of Jesus. Moses, David, John, and Paul, were leaders of the faith, who found significant spiritual benefit from wilderness retreat.

Jesus himself left his busy public ministry for remote, quiet places to converse with His Father. Luke mentions that *"Jesus often withdrew to lonely places and prayed," (5:16).* He spent time alone in the wilds, especially before great events in His life. When starting His ministry, he spent forty days in the remote country, then, overcame the

Tempter. He prayed on another mountain before choosing his disciples, and did likewise before his arrest and trial.

In a clamorous world filled with noise, distractions, pressure, and calamitous news from an entire globe, to seek solitude and quiet in the natural world has great benefit. Relaxed engagement with nature is a helpful environment for easing tension, restoring calm, and gaining perspective, never more needed in an era of continual babble on television, cell phones, internet, and video games. For many people, solitude and silence may be a foreign and fearful prospect. Younger teens and early adults, especially, often seem uncomfortable when alone, ill equipped to enjoy their own company.

Extended time in remote places is not essential, though such experiences offer unique opportunities. Even an hour among the trees and flowers of a local park, sitting quietly at the edge of a stream or lake, or a walk under a nighttime sky can provide the benefits of silence and solitude. On a purely secular level, an occasional engagement with the natural world has proven to be a helpful restorative of mental and emotional wellbeing.

For Christians, it is also an open door to the spiritual realm, an easy entrance into the presence of God himself. Surrounded by His glorious creation, composed through chosen solitude, and responsive in quiet listening, His Being is inescapable. *"The Lord is in his holy temple,"* wrote the prophet Habakkuk, *(2:20)*. Not merely the building where we customarily go to worship, but the whole world is His temple, for *"heaven is my throne, and earth is my footstool,"* said the Lord *(Isaiah 66:1)*. Habakkuk continues his counsel, *"Let all the earth be silent before Him," (2:20)*.

In seclusion and stillness, especially in His wild places, we will be more alert to the wonders of His creative artistry, and specially prepared to meet the Artist Himself.

Chapter Eighteen

FALLING WATERS

Deep calls unto deep in the roar of your waterfalls.
All your waves and breakers have swept over me.
Why are you downcast, O my soul?
Put your hope in God, for I will yet praise him,
Psalm 42:7, 11

Southwest of Duluth, Minnesota is Jay Cooke State Park, a very popular place for family picnics. In a beautiful forest setting, the main attraction is the St. Louis River, which flows through a gorge about 100 feet below the surrounding area. For youngsters the chief thrill is to cross the river on a suspension bridge spanning the canyon. Swaying and moving with each footstep, it is a mildly exciting walk while looking through the cable stays at the racing water below. Up and down the stream are a series of rapids and waterfalls. Four (perhaps five) generations of our family have enjoyed this scenic locale.

An equally popular place is Gooseberry Falls State Park, just 45 minutes north of the city along Highway 61. The area has been known for centuries, first appearing on a map in 1660. It is not clear if it was named by the

Indians for gooseberry bushes growing at the site, or if it was named for explorer, Medard Groseilleirs, (whose French last name means gooseberry), who with his brother-in-law, Pierre Radisson, were the first Europeans to visit the area, in 1658.

The Gooseberry River flows from the hills above, falling 100 feet down a rocky channel, in a series of two minor and three major cascades. In the spring it is a rushing torrent, but in a dry summer is only a modest stream filled with boulders, making it possible for agile people to step across the rocks from one side to the other. A gift shop and small museum are of interest, but the streaming water is the major attraction.

Our family went there frequently during my childhood. It was also a popular destination (cheap date) for young couples. During high school years, Shirley and I went there often, once with Glenn and Betty on spring "skip day", and on another occasion with a different Glen and Shirley's sister Carol. Other waterfalls and rapids on North Shore streams were also popular places to visit, including the Split Rock and Baptism Rivers. All the falls are beautiful but fairly low in height, since the elevation of the hillsides surrounding this section of Lake Superior's shoreline are not greatly elevated.

A much higher and more spectacular fall was just a few miles away in Wisconsin, at Pattison State Park. Big Manitou Falls on the Black River is 165 feet high, the highest waterfall in the state, and the fourth highest in the country east of the Rocky Mountains. Once on a picnic, a family friend dropped her purse over the falls. My Dad retrieved it the next day, using a long rope to help in climbing down and back.

When we moved out West, we had many more opportunities to view waterfalls. Steep mountains and flowing water combine to create awesome cascades. Over the years it was our privilege to see some of the spectacular and well known western waterfalls. Multnomah Falls in Oregon was not too far away, a splendid surge of water, plunging 620 feet into the Columbia River. More than 70 other waterfalls are also located on the Oregon side of the Columbia gorge.

Of course, the waterfalls in California's Yosemite National Park are world class in beauty and variety. Our visit there was too short by far to see the Parks many wonders. Yosemite Falls, at more than 2400 feet in height and the highest waterfall in North America, is a simply stunning sight, which no view for me was long enough to satisfy. It falls in three separate sections of 1,430, 675, and 320 feet. While not a huge volume of water, its shimmering, plunging stream is captivating in beauty.

Yosemite has many other remarkable falls that are outstanding. We visited Bridalveil Fall, whose gauzy flow of water seems to flutter down its 620 feet, suggesting its name. Vernal Fall, 317 feet high, is a broader ribbon dropping over its ledge in a symmetric flow. Like most tourists, we took pictures to record their glories but nothing is sufficient except an in-person encounter.

Yellowstone National Park's astounding thermal features tend to overwhelm its more ordinary spectacles, including the Grand Canyon of the Yellowstone River with its impressive waterfalls. As is true for most visitors, Old Faithful geyser, bubbling mud pots, the surrounding mountains, and free-roaming animals amazed our family. While there are more than 200 waterfalls in the park, with its incredible abundance of competing spectacles, the waters often take a backstage position. We did take time to see thc splendor of the Upper and Lower Falls, 109 and 308 feet high. The surging torrents pouring through towering rock walls, were truly awesome, and are the largest by volume in the Rocky Mountains. The lower cascade, though much narrower, is twice as high as Niagra.

While not world famous, many waterfalls were much closer to home, the nearest of which was in downtown Spokane itself. The original name of the community was Spokane Falls, for the city was first settled where the Spokane River plunges over a rock sill, dropping 75 feet to the gorge below. Nearly every day I drove across the Monroe Street Bridge, spanning the river just west of the falls. Standing on the bridge sidewalk and looking down into the fierce torrent of spring snowmelt was an impressive sight. An even better viewing location is from the platforms near the powerhouse. Leaning over the railing to stare into the boiling rush of water was nearly hypnotic; the fury of the river in its thunderous leap seems to draw the viewer with it in its fierce urgency to join the Columbia River on its journey to the Pacific. During the Spokane World Fair in 1974, a gondola ride was erected at the site, allowing people to ride in cars suspended over the very brink of the falls. It continues as a permanent operation of the park.

I was not expecting waterfalls when I set out one spring day on a quick hike in the North Cascade Mountains. I had to be in Seattle for a morning meeting on the day following, so leaving Spokane at about 4:00 a.m., I drove to the hamlet of Index Junction on U.S. Highway 2, then turned north a few miles to the trail to Lake Blanca. It was a good path but aggressively uphill through magnificent trees. After an hour or so, scattered patches of snow appeared, and after another hour, the entire trail was buried. At 4,600 feet of elevation I reached a crest. A mile in the distance, nestled in a circle of beautiful peaks, was Lake Blanca, still frozen in solid ice.

As I continued onward, I met an outdoorsman returning from the lake, his fly rod over his shoulder. He would have to wait a bit longer to try for ice-out trout.

When I arrived at the lake I faced a dilemma. I had chosen this jaunt because I wanted to explore a glacier, a first time experience for me. Across the frozen lake, the Columbia Glacier stretched from the peak above to the lake shore below. With some effort, I could make my way around the rocky shore or, considerably easier, I could walk across the ice. But was it safe? There was a narrow band of melt-water next to the shore but the ice three feet out seemed solid. Using a fallen branch, I hammered at the ice with no visible effect. Next, I walked out a bit and stamped on it with my feet. It seemed hard as rock. Still, with melt water flowing down from the slopes above, and unlikely, but possible, hidden springs, I couldn't be totally sure. Nonetheless, it seemed reasonably safe. Just in case, I carried my open knife in my hand. If I did fall through, I could jab the blade into the ice as an anchor and hopefully pull myself out.

As I walked toward the glacier, the majestic spires of, Columbia, Wilmon, Kyes, and Monte Cristo peaks stood in a semicircle before me, impressive and beautiful. What really took my breath away, however, were the ribbons of water pouring over the rim surrounding the Blanca basin. Ten separate falls cascaded downward from the melting snows on top. None of them were roaring torrents, just glinting silver braids, leaping and curling down the cliffs. It was surprising and enchanting. I had been expecting a pristine blue lake but found ice and snow instead. The falls were more than adequate recompense.

Crossing the lake, and in front of the snout of the glacier, was an area of muddy silt filled with pockets of water that had required careful navigation. Successfully across, I came to the foot of the glacier, many feet thick. Rivulets of water flowed from several caverns melting out of the glacier front. At one side, I walked up onto the ice which was covered with grayish grit. Walking on the ice was not much different than walking on ordinary compacted snow. Of course, in this case, the ice was *moving*, though perhaps not at this specific moment.

Glaciers slide inexorably downhill, a conveyor belt of frozen water, slipping from its temporary resting place, in imperceptible creeping oozes, or sometimes, in explosive shudders. As I looked into narrow cracks scarring the surface, I could hear the murmur of water below. Melting rills were percolating through the ice and flowing through unseen channels to reach Lake Blanca.

There was much to investigate but little time, certainly not enough to hike to the head of the glacier. I soon began my long journey back.

One more delight awaited. Half way cross the lake I took a brief rest on some boulders along the shore. As I was drinking some water I heard a loud buzzing, actually ducking my head a bit. It came again and I caught a glimpse of something a few feet away, thinking it was some large flying insect. Was it a large bee? No. When I got a clear look, I saw it was a rufous hummingbird, quite unalarmed by my presence. Its rust colored head and body with a white breast flashed in the sun as it flitted here and there. It was a lovely jewel, a fitting gem for a magnificent landscape.

With a last glance at the streams tumbling from the surrounding cliffs, I turned my back and continued down the trail. Seattle was many miles away. It had been a long, tiring effort but was well worth it, though the pain in my legs the next day made walking (hobbling!) more than a challenge.

By far, however, the western waterfall that was most intriguing to me has no water at all! Located ninety miles west of Spokane, Dry Falls was once the largest waterfall ever known on earth, 400 feet high and *three and a half miles wide*, many times the size of Niagra Falls. It was formed at the end of the last ice age, when an ice dam blocked the Clark Fork River, creating Glacial Lake Missoula in Montana, impounding thousands of square miles of water. When the melting ice could no longer sustain the enormous pressure, it gave way in a catastrophic flood that obliterated the landscape for hundreds of miles to the west.

A horrendous wall of water, *one thousand feet* high and traveling at forty five miles an hour, poured westward down the Clark Fork and Spokane River drainages, leveling hilltops, ripping out blocks of columnar basalt, creating the present day channeled scablands of eastern Washington, and scouring the Grand Coulee and lesser canyons. When the deluge reached the area of present day Soap Lake, Washington, it dropped over a ledge and began eroding backward, as Niagara Falls is doing today. Rocks were torn loose and dropped into the furious maelstrom, the brink stretching wider and wider, carving an ever-deepening channel. Water covered the site of today's Portland, Oregon to a depth of four hundred feet. Draining in as short a time as 48 hours, its flow has been estimated at 60 times greater than the Amazon, and 10-15 times the volume of all the rivers of the world. The noise must have been beyond comprehension.

All that is left of this incalculable torrent are a few remnant lakes surrounded by sheer cliffs and rocky rubble. It is a somewhat eerie, almost Martian-like desolation, yet beautiful in blooming spring. The present channel of the Columbia River has moved several miles away.

Were any early migrants from eastern Asia present to hear what must have been a truly earthshaking roar? Could any have survived if they were? The evidence of this awe-full phenomenon has gained general acceptance only in the past fifty years. This little known but mind-boggling event raises tantalizing questions and deserves much greater study.

When we returned to the level terrain of the Midwest, the waterfalls were of a more familiar scale, more comprehendible, and intimate. Most of the fast waters were "rapids," sloping cascades, rather than actual falls.

They were often nuisances on canoe trips, requiring a portage - unloading the canoes, carrying everything around the turbulent water, reloading the canoes - and then setting out again, sometimes three or four times in a half mile stretch of river. Still, the rapids were charming, for the water sang and danced, delighting the ear and eye, and often providing good fishing. There were places, however, where the waters dropped over a vertical ledge, sometimes in an unhindered plunge, and sometimes in successive steps. They too, required portages, and always commanded attention and appreciation.

After a hard day's paddle on one trip, our crew couldn't resist camping at the foot of Lower Basswood Falls. While I fully enjoy waterfalls, I prefer not to camp right beside them. I like the quiet of the night, but my comrades were thrilled to hear the rush of the water, expecting it to lull them to sleep. After setting up our tents, and putting the "kitchen" in order, the gang was soon clambering over the rocks at the edge of the falls, a drop of about 20 feet. Sitting in little side channels was a pleasant way to cool off after a very warm day of paddling under a bright sun. It wasn't long, however, when a wailing cry pierced the air, and a lean white body went careening down the rocks. With a great splash, Vince plunged into the pool below, but quickly surfaced to the relief of the others. Except for a few scrapes on the shins, he was uninjured. He had not meant to body surf the falls, but had slipped on slick rock and lost his balance.

It was precisely at this location that at least one canoe had capsized, perhaps two hundred years earlier. Accidents at such sites have happened across the centuries, since the days of the fur traders, and probably before. Journals of the early voyageurs relate capsize incidents, where furs and trade goods were lost in deep water, and occasionally, someone drowned. In 1800,

Alexander Henry reported losing a canoe full of goods at such a site.

In the 1960s, some enterprising historians thought that underwater exploration at the foot of such waterfalls might be productive in discovering artifacts of the fur trade. Using diving gear to explore under the rushing water was initially unproductive, recovering only fishing gear and modern refuse. Moving somewhat further downstream from the brink of South Basswood Falls was hugely successful, however, as significant materials were recovered from their long years of burial. Nesting copper kettles, axes, chisels, trade beads, lead shot, plates, etc were recovered, and are now on display at various locales in the canoe country.

Searching at other locations revealed a pattern. Artifacts were usually found on the west side of a moderately dangerous spot. Rapids with mild turbulence seldom resulted in an upset, while the clearly impossible places were never attempted. It was the tempting middle choices that often proved to be unwise. Since the north or westward traffic was loaded with goods to trade for furs, it is these articles that have remained in the water to be recovered after so many years.

Waterfalls certainly added to the labors of river travelers, and occasionally had their financial and human tragedies. Rather than a sight of beauty and wonder, the sad experiences and memories likely produced a somber melancholy associated with the treacherous water. As is often done today where fatal auto accidents occur, it was customary then, to erect a wooden cross to mark sites of a death along the waterways. Such tragedies continue in modern times. As recently as 2002, a teenage girl from Iowa drowned at Upper Basswood Falls, along with a young man who attempted to rescue her. Beautiful waterfalls can conceal deadly peril.

The single Biblical reference to a waterfall is Psalm 42:7, quoted above. It is not clothed in wonder and beauty but is drenched in doubt and darkness. The incident, geography, and emotions are foreboding and troublesome. The author is far from home, isolated physically and emotionally from accustomed worship in the temple at Jerusalem. In a generally parched and barren land, he desperately thirsts for spiritual refreshment. Probably near the southern foothills of snow-covered Mt. Hermon, where the Jordan River begins its noisy rush and fall over the rocks, he is overwhelmed by waves of bewilderment and fear. The tumbling waters threaten to submerge life itself, rather than alleviate intolerable thirst.

Still, in the face of a dangerous, unresolved future, he counsels himself to continue trusting in his faithful God, believing that He will bring him into a land of safety and praise. The very waterfall that triggered such currents of doubt and foreboding, may well have prompted hopeful anticipations in their fresh, life-giving vitality. As other Psalms reveal, even when overwhelmed in trouble, the believer can find a glint of sunlight and a satisfying sip of refreshment for the days ahead. It is helpful to note that the Psalm writer regards the waterfall, the waves, and breakers as God's possessions. He is in his Master's territory and circumstances.

In most Biblical references, water is a symbol of life, a divine gift from a faithful God, provided for the sustenance and enjoyment of His people. In the Bible's final chapter is a luxuriant picture of a sparkling stream flowing from God's very throne, pouring through His majestic city, and nourishing a life-giving tree that bears fruit every month of the year, a feast for the eye as well as the body. Flowing and falling waters entrance human attention, as well as maintain life itself.

One waterfall with a foreboding name was enticing to me, long before I saw it in person. At the north end of

Lower Pauness Lake, the Devil's Cascade was marked on maps of the western Boundary Waters. The name conjured up images of horrific turbulence, jagged rocks, and deadly danger. For years it lurked in my mind as I planned various trips to the canoe country. At last, the opportunity arose to paddle that way. It was finally time to see it and encounter its mystery.

With a group of nine others, we set out for a loop going up the Little Indian Sioux River to South Lake, east to Lac la Croix, and back down the Nina-Moose River. Driving northwest on the Echo Trail, we began our trip with the half mile portage along Little Indian Sioux River, and paddled through Upper and Lower Pauness. From the latter lake, a beautiful portage winds through trees edging a rocky gorge. Before carrying our gear over the trail, we walked unencumbered to see the falls.

The Devil's Cascade was not quite as exciting as its name, but was still an impressive place. The stream was about thirty feet wide, rushing through a rocky channel between forty-foot walls, until it surged over the brink, falling twenty-five feet to the Loon River below. It was an exciting visual spectacle, stirring my imagination to wonder about its name. Had something occurred in decades past to label this chasm with such a dark name? Or was some disgruntled canoe-man simply fed up with still another portage, venting his ire with a frustrated name? I am still in the dark, as I have found no historical material that gives a clue.

One unseen waterfall still calls to me from the storied past - Pigeon Falls and its Grand Portage. For a variety of reasons, my canoe travels have never led to the far northeast, where the great brigades from Montreal met the wintering traders from the interior. Nasty enough to prompt intensive search for a better route, it proved to be the most practical of all, despite its backbreaking *nine-mile* portage. Pigeon Falls itself is insignificant and I am certainly not now going to carry my canoe over nine miles of mud, boulders, tree roots, and puddles. If I were younger, I would not hesitate to walk the eighteen-mile round trip. But I would still like to see it, and walk along it for a ways, recalling the unheralded men of the past who carried huge loads of goods and furs across its length. Someday, perhaps.

For now, whenever I walk beside quiet waters, or a roaring waterfall, I am mindful they are His creation, deep calling to deep, of danger sometimes, but beauty most often. As for most people, they are for me, places of delight and refreshment, where my soul is restored by a wonderful God.

Chapter Nineteen

WATCHER OF MY WAYS

O Lord, you have searched me
and you know me.
You know when I sit and when I rise;
you perceive my thoughts from afar.
You discern my going out and my
lying down;
you are familiar with all my ways.
Psalm 139:1-3

When you are a young child, finding the way to a destination is always the responsibility of an adult. Youngsters do not need to pay attention to where they are going, or how to get back home. Later, with adult guidance, simple routes to school and neighborhood locations are mastered over time. Finding the way does not acquire great significance until teenage years and the securing of a drivers license. Then a personal age of exploration begins.

So it was for me. Finding my way around the 26-mile length of my hometown was a pleasant challenge. Even more exciting was the probing exploration of the country and forest roads beyond the city. Somehow, I always managed to find my way back home. Fortunately, I had sympathetic parents who generously let me use the family car and did not inquire too closely about my whereabouts. On rare occasions, my Dad raised a vigorous protest that the gas tank he had filled the day before was now almost empty. After all, it was expensive at 27 cents a gallon!

It often seemed to me that I was born in the wrong century, since discovery of unknown territory was intoxicating. Driving the back roads to find a new place to fish or hunt grouse was as compelling as the fishing or hunting itself. My brothers often came with me, but when I was by myself, I relished the keen pleasure of solo discovery.

Sadly, my wandering days were short lived. Working my way through college and seminary, plus marriage and family responsibilities, greatly restricted my explorations for several years. The locations of my first two pastorates were also limited in opportunities for wilderness discovery. When we moved to the west, however, vast, enticing places beckoned.

Early in our residence in Spokane, I often used a day off to investigate the exciting geography of our new state. Sometimes with the family, but often alone, I drove the roads and trails of NE Washington. I discovered that snow lingers on shaded mountain roads long after city streets are clear, creating hazardous steep driving, but I survived without mishap. I loved the lonely forests and mountains with deep intensity. Better by far than driving, was hiking primitive roads and trails. Surprising discoveries seemed to occur with some frequency, as on a shoulder of Mica Peak, where the road glittered with flakes of the shiny metal, I found an abandoned homestead with many fruit trees including apples, plums, and pears.

In many areas, fool's gold (iron pyrites) glittered on the ground, but someone told me real gold could be found in Lost Creek, north of Spokane. Unfortunately, I didn't find any. Instead, I followed a nameless trail up the slope through a forest logged decades before. I came across a moldering log cabin, its roof falling in. Who lived there, I wondered, and how long ago? How did he, or they, make a living? Probably by hunting, mining, or logging, I supposed. Coming back down the trail I found a rusty five-foot saw blade, the handles rotted off. I carried it back home. Perhaps someone would want to clean it up and paint on it, as many craftspeople like to do.

A typical excursion was a jaunt to Calispell peak, a refreshing getaway after many weeks of people work. Driving an hour north of Spokane to the hamlet of Cusik, I followed a primitive road westward for a few miles until it withered to a rough jeep track. Leaving the car, I set out on foot. It was a lovely spring day, the sky was clear, the forest fragrance tantalizing. I had no agenda and a whole day to spend. As mountains invariably do, the track led upward but not steeply so. An occasional bird flew across the path but the hillside was mostly silent, an inviting quietness to see, listen, smell, and feel the texture of the wild creation. The cones on Ponderosa Pines were opening, exposing little red buds. Fiddlehead ferns flourished in runnels at the edge of the road, where water seeped from under the vegetation. There was much to investigate, always something to examine – the twisted trunk of a fallen tree, exposed rock formations, new or familiar flowers of white, yellow, blue, and pink - paintbrush, lupines, shooting stars, sheep sorrel, penstemon, and bluebells.

As I walked along, I came to a clearing at the edge of the road, where a six-inch-thick birch log, about six feet long, lay on the ground. It would have been unremarkable except I had seen no birch trees anywhere on the mountain. I concluded that someone must have camped at the site and left a chunk of firewood brought from elsewhere. I continued onward, marveling at the mysteries that appear in the wilds, but quickly reverted to mental meandering, triggered by the powerful presence of the natural world.

As I continued upward, I once again pondered the sensation of aloneness, but not loneliness. It was not fearful, only an acute sense of separateness from the world around me, and distance from its many inhabitants. No one knew where I was, and I had no human company. I was alone for a time, free to explore, investigate, and interact with the wild world of the forest and mountain. It was a rich prospect.

After another hour of hiking, the trees thinned out, evidence of logging years before. In the distance I heard a noise and stopped to listen more closely. When I heard it again, the sound was unmistakable, the bellow of a cow, 6,000 feet up on the mountain. Open range livestock was disconcerting in a land of deer, bears, cougars, and elk. This has been a century-old practice in the West, but jarred my Midwestern sensitivities, where market animals are fenced in and confined to private property. Domesticated beasts wandering unrestrained on government land, a mountain at that, rudely bruised the aura of isolation and remoteness, even though they soon wandered out of sight, back into the trees at the edge of a clearing.

The top of the peak (6,837 feet), offered some good views of the Kaniksu National Forest, and at least an impression of remoteness. I rested a while to treasure the scenery. Picking up a stone as a memento of the peak, I started down the hill. When I came to the clearing with the birch log, I thought it would be perfect for our fireplace, so I put it on my shoulder to carry it to the car. Half way back, it seemed much heavier and more trouble than it was worth, but since I had already lugged it so far, I decided to take it all the way home. It did make a lovely fire on a cold evening.

Sometimes my explorations were to small but beautiful mountain lakes, usually nestled in a bowl of forested hills. Some of these were sites of forest service campgrounds with swimming areas, where we sometimes went for a day of family fun. The higher peaks, however, held the greatest attraction for me, as they did for my friend Gus.

"Be careful," Shirley said as I departed for another venture on a bigger hill. Gus and I were going to climb Borah Peak, Idaho's tallest mountain, in the Lost River Range. It was not a technical climb, only a lengthy scramble, though some places were a bit "hairy." Shirley was not really worried. Her words were merely the automatic response for any member of the family leaving on a trip. It was her way of expressing the bonds of love, asserting the ties that knit us together as a whole. She had confidence in my judgment and competence as an outdoorsman, and was never afraid for my safety. Her words, however, did underscore the uncertainties of wilderness outings.

Leaving Interstate 90, we drove south on Idaho Highway 93, to Birch Springs Road, then east for several dusty miles, arriving by late afternoon at the foot of the mountain, elevation 7,200 feet. After a quick bite of food, we started up the slope. We had a geological survey map but it showed no trails. A friend of Gus's had verbally described a general route but the details were sketchy at best. Following a faint path from where we parked, the route soon forked, leading to either side of a deepening canyon. I thought the left trail to the north looked best, but Gus thought otherwise. Since he had received the vague directions from his friend, I readily submitted to his choice.

Gray-green sagebrush dotted the dry landscape. Looking back across the basin to the west, the peaks of the Sawtooth Mountains receded in the distance. To the southeast were the crags and spires of the Lost River roadless area, home to antelope, elk, and bighorn sheep, none of which we were fortunate enough to see. To the east and north, Borah and its subsidiary peaks rose above us.

In the silence of our private thoughts, we forged upward, high enough to leave the sage and enter some sparse trees. As the incline became steeper, switchbacks in the vague track became necessary. Soon the trees gave out as our elevation passed 9,000 feet. Looming above us were the craggy jumbles of Chicken Out Ridge where we would encounter the greatest challenge of the trip. That would wait for the next day. For now, we would pitch our tent on the west end of an adjoining ridge, hopefully at a reasonably level place.

Five hundred feet above the tree line, we found a suitable campsite with superb views. Since no water was available, we drank from our canteens and ate some previously prepared food. As we lay in our sleeping bags, we read from the Bible and thanked God for the splendor of His wilderness. We also prayed for our families back home, asking God to keep them safe in our absence.

Our families were praying for our safety, too. Of course, as was always true of our rambles in the wild, they had no way of knowing precisely where we were. They knew generally where we would be and when we planned to return, but specifics were impossible. Not only did they not know, no one else did either.

In my usual world, the notion that my whereabouts were unknown never crossed my mind, but in the wilderness, it often captured my attention. Of earth's billions of people, except for my immediate companion, no one knew, or could know, where I was. This was never an alarming sense of aloneness or isolation, only a keen awareness of human separateness, of our essential independence. With modern technology, it is now possible to be in touch with others wherever we might be. Mountain climbers call family members even from the top of Mt. Everest. Shortly after getting my first cell phone, I remember calling Shirley from a woodland site where I was watching wild geese on a lake. If we wish, however, it is possible to be completely isolated from other people. That may be one of the charms of wilderness. At least for a while, we can escape the delights and demands of social interaction to investigate more intensely the natural world in which we live.

There is one great exception. God always knows. That was always a satisfying and encouraging thought to me. His watchful eye kept track of my most obscure meanderings. On one occasion, that notion gripped me with fierce intensity. Carrying my canoe across a portage, under a dense canopy of foliage many miles from civilization, and at that moment, unseen even by my trip companions, He knew exactly where I was. A few days later, back in the routine of the populated world, I heard the words of Scripture, "You are familiar with all my ways," (Ps. 139:2,3). Immediately, my mind flashed back to that portage trail. What was true of that moment was true of every moment, and for every person. The omniscient God knows us perfectly and intimately

After a quick breakfast the next morning, we resumed our climb. Blocks and slabs of stone obstructed our way but provided good footing until we came to the crux of the entire route. We were on top of Chicken Out Ridge and now we discovered why it was so named. Before the final summit pitch, a fearsome gap confronted us. We had to climb down a twelve-foot vertical section of rock, to a narrow snow bridge that fell steeply down on either side. It was only about fifty feet across, but the abyss on each side was truly intimidating. Hesitancy would only create greater anxiety, so with cautious steps we inched across the yawning chasm.

Safely across, a steep quarter mile brought us to the top of Borah Peak at 12,662 feet above sea level. It was a satisfying accomplishment. The tremendous views were beyond our ability to internalize. For me, it was an experience of sublime joy and worshipful ecstasy. This was the handiwork of God!

As we rested before our return, we signed our names in the summit logbook, and added, "How great Thou art." Glancing through some of the entries, we read an appeal for help in locating two hunters who had been lost in the area a few weeks earlier. Several weeks after our climb, newspapers reported that their bodies had been found.

Retracing our path, we started down. The snow bridge was as threatening as before, but with careful balance, we made our way across without mishap. A few hundred feet lower, we met a single young climber coming up. He was a visitor from France and had already climbed another peak earlier that day. We exchanged a few pleasantries and he continued toward the summit, moving quickly and confidently. Within twenty minutes, he was back from the top, passing us with amazing ease and quickness. I realized more acutely than ever, that climbing mountains is better suited to the young than to sedentary middle-agers. As Gus prepared to take some pictures overlooking a severe drop, the front section of his camera case fell off and fluttered downward, where our recent acquaintance just happened to be walking. He snatched it in mid-air, brought it back up, and then resumed his downward journey. We were flabbergasted.

Our journey back to the car took only a couple of uneventful hours. Once off Chicken Out Ridge, it was an undemanding and pleasant hike, providing quiet time for observation and contemplation. For a while, I thought of the lost hunters and wondered about what happened to them and where they were. It would be easy to lose your bearings in these mountains, mile after square mile of rocky crags with no roads and few trails. At least where we were, we had an unobstructed view and open slopes back to the car. Today, anyway, we could not lose our way.

As we made our way down the trail, it was encouraging to recall Jesus' words, that even a fallen sparrow could not escape the Father's observation (Matt 10:29). He sees all and knows all, even the apparently insignificant beings of his creation.

Over the years, I have seen the remains of several fallen birds, but two have lingered in my memory. One was a ruffed grouse I found in a snow bank. It had no obvious injury and looked perfectly healthy. As they sometimes do, it had likely taken refuge from a storm by burrowing into the snow. It had not frozen to death but suffocated when ice clogged its nostrils. The other bird was a Wilson's Phalarope that I found lying on the ground of a golf course. I had never seen one before but recognized it from pictures. It was about eight inches long, with a grey back, white breast and head, and a striking black to cinnamon streak extending from its eye down its neck. A lovely bird, even in its lifeless condition, and still seen by the eye of God.

He watched over us, too, though upon the open slopes of Borah, that was hardly a difficult task. Wherever we had been or might choose to go, we were not only under his watchful view, but were also intimately near to Him. As David continues in Psalm 139,

"Where can I go from your Spirit?
Where can I flee from your presence?
If I go up to the heavens, you are there,
if I make my bed in the depths, you are there.
If I rise on the wings of the dawn,
if I settle on the far side of the sea,
Even there your hand will guide me.
Your right hand will uphold me fast. (vss.7-10)

.

His constant presence was always at hand, whether we sensed it or not.

As we neared the car, my thoughts were no longer on the magnificent wilderness, my family at home, or on our companion, God. My body was giving me urgent signals about hunger, thirst, and rest. Food would have to wait until we found a restaurant on our way home, but a sparkling creek near the parking area gave us cool, refreshing water, Unburdened of our packs, we quickly removed our boots and socks, then plunged our feet into the icy stream. It was piercing cold, but delightful, nonetheless.

Soon we were on our way. When we stopped at a place to eat, I called home to let Shirley know we would not be back until well after midnight, but no one answered the phone. Continuing our drive, I called a couple of hours later but there was still no answer. Further along, Gus reached Kathy, but there was no answer at my house. I was puzzled and now somewhat alarmed. Finally, when we were almost home, we called once more, and at last, Shirley answered. She had been at the hospital, as our daughter Karen went through an emergency appendectomy!

How relevant were our prayers the night before as we had prayed for our families. We had been unaware of the crisis unfolding in Karen's life. Severe abdominal pains triggered a rush to the hospital where she underwent urgent surgery.

As she was about to be wheeled to the operating room, Shirley asked if there was anything she wanted when she came out of recovery. She replied, "I would like my Daddy to be here." Regrettably, I didn't make it until the next day, but thankfully, she was confident that her Heavenly Father was there, and had been with her all the while.

The God who was watching over our footsteps on the mountain, was the God who was fully aware of her developing medical crisis. Yes, He had the power to intervene with miraculous healing, but in His divine plan, He allowed the emergency to unfold. He was aware of her pain and Shirley's anxiety, watched as the ambulance rushed to her aid, and was present while the doctor operated. And with pleasure, He also saw our joyful reunion, and her full recovery in the following days, for as the Scriptures declare,

The Lord will keep you from all harm –
He will watch over your life;
The Lord will watch over your
coming and going
both now and forevermore. Ps. 121:6,7

Chapter Twenty

WILDERNESS COMPANION

The Lord God said,
"It is not good for man to be alone.
I will make a helper suitable for him."
Gen. 2:18

She was the cutest girl in a pew full of them. I had just started getting serious about God and attending church, but my interests were not only about the spiritual. In youth group activities I began to get acquainted with her and in due time we dated. Shirley was not outdoorsy, but she occasionally came with me to fish or hike. In time, we fell in love and married. Our honeymoon was at a northern Minnesota lake where we enjoyed a few days of fabulous togetherness before rushing back to begin another year of college.

In the years that followed, working full time, attending school, and raising three wonderful children, left little opportunity to enjoy the wilderness. A day now and then was all that could be spared to taste the woods, fields, and lakes. Not until well into my life work and the kids were launched on their educations, were matters settled enough for more extended experiences in the outdoors. A week at a resort on Bear Island Lake was a wonderful family event. Fishing, swimming, and games filled the days.

Shirley made pies from wild blueberries growing right beside the cabin. One evening we all watched as a bear strolled by the screen door to investigate the garbage can.

The following summer, Shirley joined me in leading a week of wilderness Bible camp at Mink Lake in Minnesota, where all of us had to sleep in tents. She enjoyed teaching a Bible class, canoeing on the lake, and hiking up a hill overlooking Northern Light Lake. While a visiting speaker was leading a session in the dining hall, a camper glanced out of the window and shouted, "A bear!" In a flash, forty boys flew from the room to see the animal, leaving the speaker with no audience. The bear's presence in the surrounding woods made them a wilderness, indeed.

However, it was when Shirley agreed to go on a canoe trip with my canoe-building buddies and their wives that she truly became a wilderness companion. The Boundary Water Canoe Area Wilderness is genuine wild country – no permanent residents, no buildings, no roads - and wildlife of many kinds. With the exception of a few hiking trails, all travel was by canoe. Everything needed for living - shelter, food, clothing, and transport - had to be paddled and portaged, sometimes in miserable conditions, (see chapter three). Through a challenging week, she was a stalwart companion, though I had grave doubts about her willingness to do it again.

When we moved to Washington State, we did some fishing, hiking, canoeing, and campground camping in tents or borrowed RVs. She enjoyed fishing for rainbow and cutthroat trout in nearby lakes, especially when they jumped out of the water as she reeled them in. Most of all, she liked paddling in sunny weather.

Local travel and trips to Seattle, Portland, and Vancouver, B.C. introduced us to the mountains and the sea. Abundant wildlife was at home in the area. From a campground on Pend Oreille Lake, we watched mountain goats cavort on high cliff faces. In Glacier National Park, marmots scampered over the talus slopes. Big horn sheep in Banff Provincial Park were semi-tame. Moose grazed in a river valley on the way to Canada's Jasper Park. The majesty of God was magnificently displayed in the wild creatures and rugged landscapes. There would be later trips to Yellowstone, Yosemite, Monterrey Peninsula, and the Grand Canyon. All were spectacular and wondrously beautiful. Encountering them with my life partner greatly increased my enjoyment of them, building a treasury of shared memories to recall in years to come.

Not everything was exotic or grandiose. Small wonders and pleasures were significant as well. Two blocks from our house in Spokane was a deep canyon forming the southwest edge of the city. A sidewalk edged its rim, five-hundred feet above Hangman Creek in the valley below. It was a great place where we often walked, enjoying the steep, natural environment. The city as a whole was also beautiful, surrounded in many areas by high rock cliffs, endowed with a lovely river, and blessed with attractive parks.

After our return from the West, some Iowa teens and adults were eager to discover the canoe country, and Shirley thought she would try it again. Jules and Bev were the other adults, and Amy, Doug, Shane, and Brent were the teenagers. We traveled a moderate loop beginning at Lake One, through Insula, Alice, Thomas, Fraser, Disappointment, and ending on Snowbank Lake. (See chapter eight for more of this trip). By her own choice and with popular approval, Shirley assumed the role of chief cook, kitchen manager, and mother superior. Since the skies were generally clear, everyone got as much sun as they wanted. With Shirley as my bow paddler and companion, the trip was great fun for me, especially since she seemed to enjoy it, despite the usual challenges of biting insects, strenuous activity, and dirty fingernails.

Catching some tasty fish, and watching a moose with two calves swim across the bay in front of our campsite, were special highlights for her.

In 1986, we shared a great adventure, a six-week pulpit exchange with a pastor and his wife from Cambridge England. Pastor Roy and Margaret lived in our house, drove our car, and ministered in our church, and we did the same in their country. It was a fabulous time for us in meeting "foreign" brothers and sisters, enjoying a new but ancient culture, the home of Wycliff, Bunyan, Wesley, Whitfield, and Spurgeon. We experienced intensive weeks of more than usual togetherness, including three wilderness experiences.

Early on, new friend Richard took us to Wicken Fen where Charles Darwin studied beetles in the early 1800s. Originally covering 300,000 acres, the fen is a unique marshland with underlying vegetation turning to peat. Wooden boardwalks gave access through tall reeds and sedges harboring multitudes of animals, birds, and insects.

On one of our free days we drove in Roy's right-hand-drive Morris automobile (on the "wrong" side of the road), about 90 miles to the east coast seashore. The drive through picturesque villages, over narrow roadways bordered by rock walls, and past thatched roof houses was delightful. Arriving at the villages of Blakeney and Cley next the Sea, we found our way to the edge of the North Sea. It was a cool, overcast day, and the gray skies and steely waves were not enticing. Only a handful of other people were about, including a wind surfer trying unsuccessfully to mount his board. Small rocks covered the gravely beach. A caution sign warned beach-goers of possible unexploded munitions that might be washed ashore from a war that had ended decades before. As Shirley wrote in her journal, I explored the shore, mindful of Continental Europe a mere 80 miles across the water to the east. When the ice age lowered the oceans, a shallow bowl of land connected England with the continental landmass. I tried to imagine early people walking across from mainland Europe, but the restless, noisy waves soon overpowered historic speculations.

Two weeks later, another wonderful experience developed. We met a fine couple from Wales who invited us to visit them at their home. We gave a polite but noncommittal reply and thought little more of it. When we received a written invitation a few days later with directions to their house, we knew they were serious. Maurice and Jean were marvelous people who had retired from city life in London to hike the mountains and shores of the Welsh countryside. Their generous hospitality made us welcome in every way. Maurice suggested we climb Mount Snowden, a modest peak of 3,560 feet, but the highest mountain in Wales. Jean stayed home, but Shirley decided to go with us.

Driving to the north side of the mountain, we set out from the youth hostel at Pen-Y-Pass in damp, foggy weather. Visibility was limited to a bare hundred feet. The grade was not steep but pitched continually uphill.

After nearly two hours, we stopped for a rest. With less than 1,000 feet to go, Shirley seemed cheerful and perky, but later said she was barely making it, yet was determined not to quit for any reason. As we toiled up the last half hour, the clouds broke up, the sun appeared, and a great landscape spread before us. The view was spectacular. A surprising number of people were present on top, where a visitor center and the terminal of a cog railway from Llanberis at the west foot of the mountain were located. We signed the logbook and bought enameled pins to commemorate our summit achievement. Since Shirley was very weary, I asked if she wanted to ride the train back down the mountain, but she was determined to make it under her own power. After an hour of absorbing the views and taking pictures, we started down a gentler trail on the south side. When we reached the highway at the bottom, Shirley and Maurice waited while I hitched a ride back to the car, and then drove around to pick them up. It had been a glorious day but an exhausting one for Shirley. I was *very* proud of her.

A couple of weeks later, we drove to Scotland with Floyd and Ila, visiting friends from the states. We reveled in the English countryside, Sherwood Forest, the Lake district, and the Scottish lowlands. In suburban Glasgow, we visited Minnie, Marie, and Bob, relatives of mine whom I had never met before. Then we drove into the Highlands, along the shores of Loch Lommond, Loch Awe, and even famous Loch Ness, where we failed to see the monster.

Outside of Fort William was Ben Nevis, the tallest mountain in Britain (4,409 ft), a training site for many world-class British climbers. Though modest in elevation, nasty weather and severe cliffs on three sides present serious challenges at times. Shirley graciously kept the others company for shopping while I climbed the hill. It was an enjoyable experience for me to ramble in the homeland of my maternal ancestors, where a great grandfather had been a shepherd in these very highland hills. A visit to Edinburg and a night in a 14th century castle wrapped up a fabulous week.

In the summers following our English foray, Shirley accompanied me on several canoe trips. Happily, she found that canoe trips were great opportunities to enjoy family interaction as well as the beauty of the wilderness.

I had discovered that in earlier years. Son Scott was a companion on my first extended canoe trip when he was ten years old. Nineteen dads and sons in two groups paddled a loop down the Kawishiwi chain. I had arranged for a veteran outdoorsman to lead us and do the cooking, but at the last minute he had to cancel. By default I became the leader, but it all came out wonderfully well. I especially enjoyed having Scott as my tent mate and bowman, the first of several trips to come.

While I had taken daughters Leigh and Karen for a weekend camping trip in their young years, I was sorry that I had not included them more often. Their introduction to the BWCA did not arrive until later.

In 1987, Shirley was my partner on a trip that included Scott and his wife, Tami (see chapter 14). It was a strenuous journey, but we had delightful weather. Fishing late one evening, Shirley and I had a great time catching several small mouth bass. Since there was enough for the whole group, we decided to clean and eat them immediately as a bedtime snack. As we ate, we observed the most spectacular display of northern lights any of us had ever seen.

The next year, youngest daughter Karen joined us to discover what the canoe trips were all about. Setting out on Nina-Moose Lake, we paddled into huge Lac La Croix. Fishing was not very productive, especially after Shirley lost Scott's last Rapalla lure. One day we went to see ancient Indian pictographs along the Canadian side of the lake, and then climbed Warrior Hill, where in long-ago years, indigenous men raced each other to the top. The spectacular view of surrounding lakes and forest was well worth the effort.

Daughter Leigh, who says she doesn't like sleeping on the ground, completed the family introduction to the BWCA a few years later.

In 1992, Shirley was willing to tackle another mountain with me. Arriving a day early for another conference in Estes Park, we decided to climb Colorado's, Twin Sisters, a few miles south of town. While the trail was not steep and was well switch-backed, it was no piece of cake. The elevation gain from the trailhead to the summit (11,428), was about 3,000 feet, about the same as Snowden in

Wales, but required far greater effort because of the reduced oxygen at its much higher elevation.

Starting out at mid-morning, with only some snacks and water, we followed a well-trod trail through moderate forest cover of lodgepole pine. We set out at an easy pace, stepping up the gentle slope, and then angling back higher, as each section of trail forged upward. Every fifteen minutes or so, we paused for a couple of minutes to catch our breath and swallow a mouthful of water. Occasionally we could glimpse the much higher peaks to the west.

After two hours the trees had thinned, spruce and fir replacing the pines. Now, open vistas began to reveal the grandeur of the snow-covered peaks of Rocky Mountain National Park. At last we broke out above the trees and the trail withered away in a five hundred foot boulder field leading to the twin peaks. Picking our way through the rocks, we reached the slightly higher west Sister. Though it was brightly sunny, the air was sharply cool and the wind was buffeting.

Arriving at last at the summit, we were happy to halt and feast on the panorama before us. Westward were the splendors of Long's Peak (14,259 ft.), Mt Meeker (13,911), Powell Peak (13,208), and Taylor Peak (13,153). Awesome, spectacular, and beautiful were inadequate words to convey the impressions formed in our minds.

What is it about steep piles of snow-covered rock that stirs such emotion in people? I have no adequate answer. Nor does repetition seem to diminish the exaltation of the vision. The inner marvel cannot be described to another and pictures are hopelessly inadequate. But on this day, Shirley, the one I loved above all others, was there to share it with me. Whether she felt and thought as I did, I did not know. But she was experiencing for herself, what was so compelling to me – the anticipation of the event, the labor of the climb, and the stunning grandeur of the creation around us. And even more than these, the One who brought it into existence.

For me, it was more than aesthetic pleasure; it was a profound engagement of worship, in a setting we had not shared before. Perhaps now she could understand a bit more clearly, the real quest in my wilderness ventures. Hiking, hunting, paddling, and climbing were enjoyable activities in their own right, but they were much more; they were windows to ultimate reality, gateways to His realm and Person.

None of these thoughts was explicit as we devoured the view. I was deeply proud that Shirley had achieved the peak, had been willing to toil up the hill, and accompany me in an activity that seems a bit far out to many people. A least a few thought as I did, for a dozen other hikers were present on the summit with us. We asked one of them to take our picture as a reminder of this memorable occasion. As is always true when reaching the top of a mountain, the trip was only half completed. At least going down was significantly easier. Retracing our steps, we made our way back. Hot showers and a luscious pizza were a fitting conclusion to a marvelous day.

Of course, these few wilderness excursions were only brief interludes in the fabric of our lives. The great majority of our years together have been filled with the common tasks of family living and our work and ministry over more than fifty years. Through ups and downs, good times and bad, Shirley has been a steadfast helper and encouraging companion, as God intended in giving her to me. Humans were designed as social beings, needing complementary companions for fulfillment and satisfaction. As recorded in the earliest pages of Scripture, the first man surveyed the wildlife, but found no suitable companion. God then made another being, one like the man himself, but with significant, beneficial differences. She was to be a helper, as wives are in many ways, but her greatest contribution was to fill the void of companionship. God himself announced that a totally solitary life was not good for Adam, or for humankind.

How good He has been in providing that companionship, generally in other friends and family, and specifically in this choice woman for me. As He intended, she has brought pleasure, satisfaction, delight, and joy to my life, accomplishing the Creator's plan in marriage. He intended that life together should be joyful, as He stated through the authors of Scripture,

Rejoice in the wife of your youth. Prov. 5:18,
Enjoy life with your wife whom you love.
Eccl 9:9.

So, whether in the glories of His wilderness, or in the routines of ordinary life, Shirley has been a pleasant, helpful companion, a gift from God, indeed. We continue to seize opportunities to treasure the delights of the wild creation, though expectations do not always materialize as we plan.

A recent trip to spend a few days with Shirley's sister, Judi, and her husband, Dick, was such a case. We had expected to enjoy the early summer days in the bright sunshine and warm weather, riding across the blue lake in the boat, but the northern Wisconsin weather did not cooperate. It was windy, wet, and cold. We spent most of our time indoors, richly enjoying our companionship, though our disappointment in limited fun outdoors was real.

There was a compensation, however. As we shared the bonds of love and family, we also shared the marvels of wild birds. Even as we were approaching their house, we had a "birdy" surprise, for a wild turkey was feeding at the edge of the gravel road. As we drove near, the huge dark bird (12-15 pounds), launched itself into the air and disappeared into the trees. It was a happy welcome to the lake. The main attraction, however, was the continual gathering of birds at the feeders, just outside the windows of the living and dining rooms.

Three feeders held sugar syrup, attracting several ruby throated hummingbirds. Their darting flights, backward thrusts, hovering in place, dipping to drink, and alarmed departures, were continually fascinating. Tiny as they were, they fiercely contested their personal space around the feeders, driving rivals away, only to be driven off by a more aggressive arrival. Very rarely two would feed at the same time. It was impossible to tell how many there were, but on one occasion there were six in sight at a single moment. We never tired of watching their incredible dexterity in flight, marveling at the blur of their wings, beating 500 times a minute.

Other birds came to the seed feeders: assorted sparrows, chickadees, house finches, goldfinches, red wing blackbirds, grackles, and brilliant orioles. The stars of the show, however, were the five different species of woodpeckers, drawn to a suet block, and like the orioles, to half an orange fastened to the deck rail. All of them were boldly feathered in different patterns of black, white, and red.

The downy woodpeckers were about six inches long with white fronts and backs, black wings, and black and white heads with a small red patch. Their cousins, the hairy woodpeckers, were almost identical in color, but half again as large. They were aggressive in attacking the suet to bring home food to their young nestlings. Redbellied woodpeckers were as large as the hairies, but had a mostly white face with a broad red streak covering the back of their necks and top of their heads. The slight red on their bellies was very difficult to observe. They were fond of the orange. An occasional northern flicker also came to dinner, more gray-brown than black, though with many black spots, and a red crescent on its head.

The most spectacular of the clan was also the rarest. It came just once while we were there, for less than a minute, but it surpassed the others by far. The glorious pileated woodpecker was nearly too big to perch on the feeder. At about 18 inches long, it was the size of a crow. Arrayed in glossy black, with a bold white stripe across its face, and a flaming red-crested head, it was an unforgettable sight, all too briefly in view, before it rocketed away. Our days on the water were washed out by unseasonable weather, but "woodpecker week" was an unexpected highlight of our time together, another of the many delights we have shared over the years.

My best chum continues to share the charms of wilderness with me, even close to home. On a recent walk on a woodsy bike trail, just two miles from our house, we enjoyed the beauty of early fall. Color was just beginning to paint the leaves, glorious under the golden sun. We had seen small animals: rabbits, squirrels, and a snake. A couple of days earlier we had heard a pair of barred owls calling back and forth from both sides of the trail. But we were hopeful of seeing a deer, as we had on earlier occasions. On our way back, we came to a bench where Shirley suggested we sit down and watch for a deer. I said, "Okay, but the likelihood of it happening is next to nothing."

You guessed it. It did happen. Within thirty seconds of sitting down, I heard a slight "crack" of a twig a short distance behind us. It was too loud for a squirrel to make, and I thought it could be a deer. We did not turn around but continued to scan the trees on the lower side of the trail. Within less than a minute, Shirley whispered, "I see something moving. Look, there's a deer!"

With great skepticism, I looked in the direction of her gaze, and to my amazement saw a deer trotting to our right, where it turned, came up the slight slope, crossed the path only ten yards from us, and ran into the trees beyond. While we were still stunned in surprise and delight, Shirley said, "There's another one!" Sure enough, a second deer followed in the footsteps of the first, crossing the trail just as closely as the first, then disappeared behind us.

The gray-brown animals were not quite adult sized and had no antlers. It was extraordinary – almost magical - to see them where she had hoped we would, to see them almost immediately, to see them so close to us, and to see not just one, but two. I suspect there was even a third deer, probably their mother, who had snapped the branch behind us, before we saw the two yearlings.

We will never forget it. And best of all, we experienced it *together*. If only one of us had seen it, neither of us could have adequately re-told the moment to share with the other. It was a richer treasure by far in enjoying it together, and in recalling it later, sometimes even sitting on that same bench and hoping for "lightning" to strike twice (which not surprisingly, has not happened). But I wonder what surprises await in the future with my suitable helper and wilderness companion. Time will tell.

Chapter Twenty-one

GRANDKIDS IN THE WILDERNESS

Children's children are a crown to the aged,
Proverbs 17:6

Scott was five years old when I took him along for his first overnight in the wilds, but he introduced his own son to wilderness even earlier. Cameron was just three and Brittney five when they came on their first family canoe trip. I was a bit apprehensive about taking the grandchildren at such a young age, but Scott and Tami seemed comfortable with the idea, so who was I to object? It was a short trip, with only a few miles of paddling, a couple of portages, and three or four nights out, so it would not be overly strenuous. Tami's dad, Lee, nephew Mark, and Shirley and I, made up the rest of the party. We were all excited about it, the grandkids most of all.

Stopping on the way for gas and goodies, Cameron came up with an expression that has become part of the family lore through the years. Eying a package of snacks that I was eating, he said, "I yike sheetoes," so I cheerfully shared my corn curls with him.

A few hours later, we were loading our canoes at the Lake One landing. Scott and Tami had brought some kid-size folding chairs for the children to use in the canoes and at the campsites. The chairs, with only three-inch legs, kept the kids off the bottom of the canoe, but well below the edge of the boat. Brittney rode with us and Cam was in his parent's canoe. They had their own small paddles to assist the grownups. Stroking when they thought about it, and gazing at the passing scenery when they didn't, they were absorbed in a new world.

Also like the adults, the youngsters shouldered their own packs at the first portage, and carried a fishing rod or a paddle as well. Their smaller steps seemed to keep pace with ours, burdened as we were by heavier loads. Without a complaint, they made a first trip, and then a second.

Paddling across a short pond, we came to our second portage, repeating the previous process. As if it was a routine event, the grandkids carried their loads to the far side, seeming to enjoy it as much as more usual summertime fun. Half an hour of additional paddling brought us to a fine campsite, out of the busy traffic heading further east toward Lake Insula.

The children did what they could in unloading the canoes and setting up the tents. When the essential chores were finished, they explored the site, visited the edge of the lake, and made themselves comfortable in their temporary wilderness home. Gathering firewood was a task they shared with me.

Each of us searched for downed and dry wood. Small pieces were broken up for kindling, but some larger pieces had to be cut into the right lengths. Under careful supervision, each of them tried their hand with the saw, discovering it to be harder than it looked. Then it was off into the trees searching for dead birch bark for tinder.

Soon they had more than enough. Placing tinder and fuel together, we lit the fire. Again, under watchful eyes, Britt and Cam added sticks as the fire burned higher.

Keeping a fire burning and staring into its flaming depths is a special pleasure for me, and so it seemed, for the grandchildren. Of course, a good campfire almost demands toasted marshmallows. So once again, they scoured the bush for the right sticks with which to roast them. Then, it was the familiar challenge to toast them without setting the treats on fire. Whether golden brown or cinder black, they ate them with zest.

It had been a long day. As the evening wore on, the youngsters strenuously fought sleep, but succumbed at last to the need for rest. They slept as well in a sleeping bag inside the tent as they did in their bedrooms at home.

Fishing, swimming, exploring, berry picking, and of course, tending the campfire, filled the next days. A big hit with the children were the lightweight hammocks that Scott had brought along, even if getting in and out of them was not immediately mastered. Cameron fell out several times, fortunately with little damage beyond a few bumps on the head. All my small uncertainties about how the grandkids would manage in the canoe country vanished. Like ducks to water, they seemed to be completely comfortable in the out of doors. And so were their parents, as far as I could tell. Soon it was time to return home, reliving the memories of the week, and eagerly anticipating next summer's trip.

In 1999, our paddle was only to Lake One. It was just a week after the great Fourth of July storm that devastated the Boundary Waters. With many campsites and portages buried under broken and uprooted trees, we thought staying put in a sheltered and relatively undamaged camp was a prudent thing to do. As I had the year before, I bypassed the joys of paddling with adult friends, for the rich pleasures of a family group. In addition to Scott's family, our oldest grandchild, Jenna joined us. She was twelve, Brittney was ten, and Cameron, seven. Since Shirley did not come, Jenna was my bow paddler. She did very well with this major task, contributing strongly to our tandem effort.

As they had on the previous trip, the children enjoyed swimming, fishing, trying to capture tadpoles with their bare hands, exploring the area around the camp, and just being kids. When it rained, discouraging outdoor activity, the youngsters had a great time in the tent, playing card games that wise mother Tami had brought. We discovered that two hammocks for three children (and three adults) created some scheduling difficulties.

The next year, granddaughter Alyssa came with us on a trip to Isabella Lake. At age eight, she fit nicely with her cousins, Cameron also eight, and Brittney, eleven. They were a congenial threesome, enjoying the fun and activity more than ever. The hammocks (three this time), were again hugely popular with the kids.

Though the fishing was not greatly productive, the youngsters enjoyed it fully, whether out in the canoes or from the rocks on shore. In years to come, Alyssa would become the most enthusiastic angler of all the grandchildren. While Scott and I were out in a canoe, Brittney, fishing from the shore, caught a Northern Pike. When we cleaned it, we were surprised to find a good-sized fish in its stomach.

With the inventive imagination of the young, the kids put together what Brittney called, an "underwater petting zoo." Building a stone corral in the shallow water at the shore, they found various creatures to inhabit the enclosure – sunfish, snails, crayfish, clams, etc. Shirley and I were awed and proud of their creativity. How happy we were that God had answered the Biblical blessing, "may you live to see your children's children," (Psalm

128:6). To spend such extended time with them in the unique wilderness setting was a priceless treasure.

Two years later, the number of grandkids on our trip rose higher yet. Because of busy personal schedules, our plans were late in development, missing the deadline for the usual BWCA entry permit. We were restricted to camping only on Brule Lake. Unfortunately, several weeks of dry weather had created a severe fire hazard, prohibiting open burning. Since we always used white gas camp stoves for cooking, it did not hinder meal preparation, but with no campfire, it made evening activities significantly less enjoyable.

On this trip, Brittney and Cameron were now seasoned veterans. In addition to their parents, Scott and Tami, and Shirley and me, our daughter Leigh was along, with her daughters, Jenna, and Christie. The four children had a blast, especially since we had brought a hammock for each of them. They sat in the hammocks, read in them, swung in them, and learned to wrap themselves and (briefly) lie upside down in them.

A highlight of the trip was an initiation ceremony for rookies Leigh and Christie, inducting them into our family order of voyageurs, as the fur traders of ancient days did for novice paddlers crossing the height of land separating the waters flowing to the Great Lakes from those entering Hudson Bay. Scott blindfolded each one as they stood before us, put into their open hand a smooth rock, urging them to feel its texture and hardness, a reminder of the bedrock of the country and the need to overcome. A pine cone came next, to symbolize the great forest and the need to use it wisely and carefully. Last, a feather was given to represent the animals to be enjoyed and treasured. Then they were sprinkled with a pine bough dipped in lake water, and pronounced a true voyageur.

Another delight was a family of ruffed grouse that paraded through the camp on several occasions, a mother followed by four diminutive chicks. They seemed completely undisturbed by our noisy intrusion in their territory.

We were alarmed, however, by a much larger intruder in *our* space. We were all in our tents at about 11:00 p.m., and I was just dozing off when Shirley hissed, "There's a bear outside!" She had thought that on other occasions and I was inclined to dismiss it this time as well, but as I listened, I concluded she was right. A bear was attempting to get at our food packs hanging in a tree just ten feet away. I started hollering at the beast, blowing a whistle, and banging some metal plates together. Unzipping the tent, I shined a flashlight around but didn't see the animal. Perhaps it was a false alarm. By now the other campers were aroused, the children eager to rush out and see the bear. Parents prudently restrained them.

The bear had vanished, but left behind unmistakable evidence. A soft-pack beverage cooler was on the ground with a corner bitten off. Claw marks raked the tree trunk from which the other packs were hanging. As the kids and parents gathered around, we were keenly alert, searching the brush with our lights, wondering if the bear was still close by. Eventually we all went back to the tents to sleep, the grandchildren taking it in stride as a novel wilderness experience. I am not sure how comfortable their parents were.

Black bears nearly always run from people. Although a bear attacked two men in the BWCA in 1987, it was an extremely rare event. During an earlier 18-year study of bear-human interactions, there were eighteen million visitor-days and not a single attack.

The next night we pulled the food packs higher in the tree and tied all our metal pots and pans on a cord encircling the trunk. We hoped hanging the "bearbells" around the trunk would be an effective bear alarm. It was - and it went off about midnight! Again we shouted and whistled to drive it away, although I think the "bells" were enough to frighten it. Kids and grownups alike were excited about seeing a bear close at hand, yet a bit apprehensive as well. But it had disappeared. Concerned that the persistent bear might possibly encounter one of the young children, and be less intimidated by their smaller size, we decided the next morning to shorten our trip and leave for home. Not being able to enjoy evening campfires was also a factor. We would come back to the wilds another year.

Our youngest grandchild, Danielle, has not been involved in a full canoe trip so far, but she did spend a brief overnight when our families rented a cabin on the fringe of the BWCA. With her dad, Lynndon, and me, we paddled a few miles into South Farm Lake. Just within the Wilderness boundary, it was not far from civilization, but was completely isolated nonetheless. We saw no other canoes. At six years old, Dani was not overly thrilled with camping out, but enjoyed riding in the canoe, fishing, and trying to lure a large snapping turtle onto the shore. A special treat was seeing a fox near the edge of the campsite.

Unfortunately, I have not had the opportunity to enjoy the wilds with Jamison and Jordan, but perhaps the future will make it possible.

Turtles were more abundant than fish during our most recent canoe trip with grandchildren. Again, Shirley and I joined Scott's family for a trip into Lake Two. Our island campsite was a popular place for several painted turtles to lay their eggs. Crawling from the water, they meandered around the area looking for a suitable location. This was not too easy, since our campsite was mostly solid rock and soil coverage was very thin. Eventually each turtle found a spot to scoop out a shallow depression where it dropped its eggs, then covered them with soil, and returned to the water. How many there were is uncertain, but one evening three of them were digging nests at the same time. In my mind, this place will always be remembered as Turtle Island.

Scott had asked me to lead a brief morning Bible study each day, which I was pleased to do. As the others sat on a rock slab facing the water, I shared comments on the critical characteristics of the sun, moon, and iron that make life possible. Then one of the group prayed, giving thanks for the fantastic wilderness, created by our great God.

In these meditations, I mentioned the stimulus for this book. Not too long before, I had read once again the words in Deut 4:9, where Moses, speaking about God's law, says, "Teach them to your children, *and to their children after them*." By instruction and example, Shirley and I had taught our children about the Lord, but since until just recently, we had lived far from our grandchildren, the opportunity to teach them had been limited. By highlighting some of these truths in a written account, I could attempt a more specific effort at the teaching commanded in this Bible text.

In Deuteronomy 6, the Israelite parents were commanded to teach God's words to their children, "when you sit at home and when you walk along the road, when you lie down and when you get up." The wilderness setting provided a great locale and extended time together to accomplish this task. The constant togetherness of canoeing, camp setup, meal preparation, fire building, etc., over a period of several days, provided a depth of interaction and intimacy which brief visits in more normal settings usually fail to allow.

For Shirley and me, the grandkids were, indeed, a crown of life. We treasured each one's individuality, especially in their growing adulthood. They were bright, well-behaved, funny, and interesting. Truly, they enriched our lives, making us feel like royalty, and through their parents, we bestowed them as valuable gifts to the world of their generation. What was of enormous satisfaction to me was their own appreciation of the wild places, and of its Creator.

This particular trip marked a milestone, in Brittney and Cameron paddling a canoe by themselves. I was a proud grandparent to observe the growth of their competence in the wilds, though that increasing mastery was challenged in our paddle back at the end of our journey. Setting out from our final portage in a sheltered bay, we were surprised by "big" water, pushed by strong westerly winds. Whitecaps were breaking and we could barely make headway. All of us were struggling to keep the wind from turning us sideways. I was especially concerned for Britt, paddling in the stern of her boat, since she had not paddled in severe weather and was probably unnerved by the waves. I slowed my paddling to let her move along side us, and showed her how to use a sweep stroke to exert more leverage in directing the canoe. She told me later it helped a lot.

Pulling into the lee of an island, we took a break and hoped the winds would subside. Fortunately, we were only a half mile from a protected shore that led nearly back to the landing. Soon we were battling again in the face of the gale, to a happy and successful conclusion. Now more than ever, I was proud of these two grandkids, paddling as well as the adults, on the fierce, wild water.

As it always is at the end of days in the bush, a hot shower, iced drinks, and a real bed, were highly treasured advances of civilization. A fine motel in Ely provided these amenities, along with a display of ancient cars. A group of antique car buffs was staying overnight before driving to their next destination. Our traditional feast at the local Pizza Hut was as satisfying as ever. Clean and well fed, we roamed the stores of Ely looking for this year's tee shirts and souvenirs, reminders of a golden time in our lives.

Driving home the next day, I had opportunity to wonder about the future. What would happen to these fine teenagers? What careers would they follow, who would they marry, would I live to see their children, would the wild country become for them a place to behold a glorious God? Hopefully so.

Jenna is now out in the working world, and finding significant pleasure riding horses in the western landscape of Theodore Roosevelt National Park in North Dakota. Jamie, too, is on his own. Brittney will soon be doing some college study in the natural worlds of Ecuador and the Galapagos Islands. The others are at various stages in their education. Will the outdoors continue to interest them as they enter mature years? Will any of them take a canoe trip on their own, or climb the hills, or roam the wild shores? Only the passage of time will answer, but I hope they will treasure His wilderness as I have, discovering in its splendors the great God who created them all.

A Sincere Thank You

To all the comrades on my wilderness jaunts, I express my genuine thanks. Your warm companionship, willing help with camp chores, uncomplaining labor in paddling and hiking, and cheerful smiles whatever the weather, have made my experience of the wilderness all the richer. Not only have I seen the splendor of God in the immediate surroundings, I have beheld it in each of your lives. I hope you have seen it in mine.

Mentioned in this book:

Chapter One: John Hall, Jim McCollum, Scott Larson.
Chapter Two: Sandy and Jim McCollum, Shirley and John Hall, Shirley Larson, Crandall Gustafson, George Wessman, Scott, Tami, Brittney, and Cameron Larson, Jenna Sitzer.
Chapter Three: Scott Larson, Karl Nordstrom, Crandall Gustafson.
Chapters Four and Five: Crandall Gustafson.
Chapter Six: Tom, Dennis, and Kenneth Larson, Ervin, Gary, and Phillip Torgerson, Scott Larson, Calvin Hopson, Shirley Larson, Phil and Roberta Torgerson, Dick and Judi Magnuson.
Chapter Seven: Scott Larson, Ervin and Phillip Torgerson.
Chapter Eight: Shirley Larson, Beverly Dean, Jules Gray, Amy Highsmith, Doug Beetner, Shane and Brent (whose last names I can no longer recall, Vince Rubino, Vickie Greiman.
Chapters Nine and Ten: Jules Gray, Bob Hamilton, Vince Rubino, Rosemary Hruska, Janet Taylor, Linda Beck, Vickie Greiman.

Chapter Eleven: Jim and Rosemary Hruska, Ron and Karol Flora, Janet Taylor.

Chapter Twelve: Tom Larson, Leonard Jacobson, Scott Larson, Lee Titus, Mark and Marc Wheeler, Craig and Chris Wood, Mel and Robin Winebrenner, Janet Taylor, Bob Hamilton, Jim and Rosemary Hruska, Laurie and Janice McLaughlin, Dick Grenell.

Chapter Thirteen: John, Barb, and Janette Hall, Forest and Steve Arnold, Dave and Judy Arnold, Roy, Paul, and, Karl Nordstrom, Jim, Sandy, and Mike McCollum, Ken, Steve, and Jeff Brown, Scott Larson, Bob Gossack, Rosemary Hruska.

Chapter Fourteen: Leigh Sitzer, Bev Dean, Mark Wheeler.

Chapter Fifteen: Alyssa Shilling.

Chapter Sixteen: Shirley Larson, Bill Morgan, Erwin and Katherine Parr, Ed, Joyce, and Shane DeHaan, Dave Magnuson, Bernie Goddard, George Hovan, Fred and Marion Steigleder, Brian and Mary Flaitz.

Chapter Eighteen: Glenn Sampson, Betty Heffernan, Glen Nelson, Carol Torgerson, Vince Rubino.

Chapter Nineteen: Crandall Gustafson, Fred Steigleder, Jeff and Teresa Clay.

Chapter Twenty: Shirley Larson, Roy and Margaret Cave, Richard Smee, Maurice and Jean Calvert, Floyd and Ila Granlund, Minnie Lang, Bob and Marie Curie, Scott, Leigh, and Karen Larson, Dick and Judi Magnuson.

Chapter Twenty One: Scott, Tami, Brittney, and Cameron Larson, Jenna Sitzer, Alyssa Shilling, Leigh and Christie Sitzer, Lynndon and Danielle Shilling, Jamison and Jordan Osborne.

Made in the USA
Charleston, SC
04 April 2012